Living the Science of Harmonious Union

Other English Books by Guru Nitya Chaitanya Yati

That Alone, the Core of Wisdom

Love and Blessings

The Bhagavad Gita

The Saundaryalaharī of Śankarācārya

The Bṛhadāraṇyaka Upaniṣad (3 Volumes)

The Psychology of Darśanamālā

Love and Devotion

Neither This Nor That But . . . AUM

Meditations on the Self

Experiencing the Īśāvāsya Upaniṣad

The Haunting Echoes of Spring

Living the Science of Harmonious Union

Principles and Practice of Patañjali's Yoga Śāstra

Guru Nitya Chaitanya Yati

D.K. Printworld (P) Ltd.
New Delhi

Cataloging in Publication Data — DK

[Courtesy: D.K. Agencies (P) Ltd. <docinfo@dkagencies.com>]

Nitya Chaitanya, ***Yati***, 1924-1999.

Living the science of harmonious union : principles and practice of Patañjali's Yoga śāstra/Nitya Chaitanya Yati.

p. cm.

Previously serialized in Gurukulam, a journal in 1986-1999.

Includes index.

ISBN 13: 9788124604946

ISBN 10: 8124604940

1. Patañjali Yogasūtra. 2. Yoga. I. Title.

DDC 181.452 22

Website: www.geocities.com/islandgurukula/

First Serialized in Gurukulam, English Language Edition, 1986-1999.
Now published in book format, 2009

ISBN 13: 978-81-246-0494-6 (HB) ISBN 10: 81-246-0494-0

Text design and layout by Nancy Yeilding
Illustrations by Andrew Larkin
Typeset in Taj

Published and printed by:
D.K. Printworld (P) Ltd.
Regd. office : *'Srikunj,'* F-52, Bali Nagar
Ramesh Nagar Metro Station
New Delhi – 110 015
Phones : (011) 2545 3975; 2546 6019; *Fax* : (011) 2546 5926
E-mail: dkprintworld@vsnl.net
Web: www.dkprintworld.com

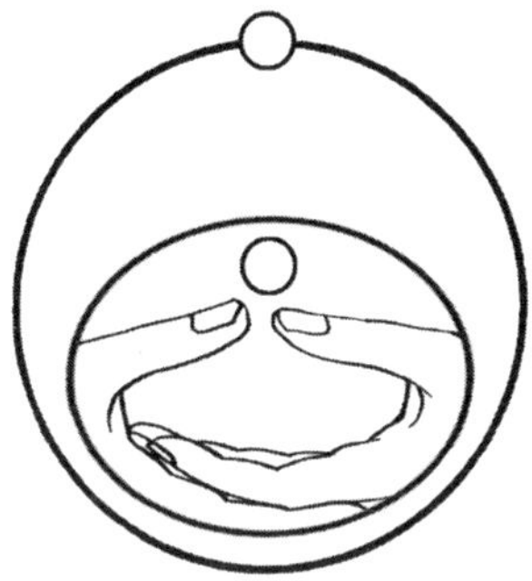

Contents

Key to Sanskrit Pronunciation

The sounds indicated in the examples are approximations of the original Sanskrit sounds. Only the consonants that are significantly different from English pronunciation have been included. Diacritics have not been used words commonly used in English or on most proper names.

a	like the a in rural
ā	like the a in palm
i	like the i in fill
ī	like the i in police
u	like the u in full
ū	like the u in rude
ṛ	like the ri in rig
e	like the e in prey
ai	like the ai in aisle
o	like the o in go
au	like the ou in loud
c	like the ch in chunk
ch	like the ch in much
gh	like the gh in loghouse
jh	like the geh in hedgehog
ṭ	like the t in true
ṭh	like the th in anthill
ḍ	like the d in dart
ḍh	like the dh in godhead
ṅ	like the n in sing
ñ	like the n in bunch
ṇ	like the n in under
bh	like the bh in abhor
ph	like the ph in uphill
ś	like the sh in shun
ṣ	like the sh in fish
ḥ	echoes the vowel that immediately precedes it

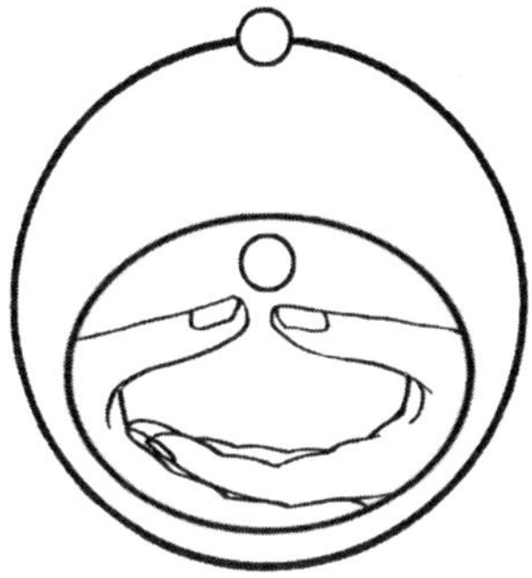

Introduction

At the turn of the twentieth century a wise teacher from South India described the culmination of Yoga in a very alluring manner: "When mind, the bumble bee, sips the honey-like sweetness of one's own bliss, fluttering ceases and is drawn into union."[1] This poetic description given by Narayana Guru echoes and elaborates the definition of Yoga given in one of the foundation texts of Yoga, the *Bhagavad Gita (VI:23):* "Yoga is disaffiliation from the context of suffering."

These definitions are not academic; they speak directly to our experience of life, which can range from being punctuated by suffering to being permeated by it. They also speak to our constant yearning and search for happiness. We are all acquainted with the fluttering, not to say, disturbed and agitated nature of our minds, as they respond to inner and outer provocations. Yet we have all tasted, sensed, or at least heard of the possibility of bliss. We want to make true lasting happiness our own, but don't know how.

The teachings of Yoga are a direct, compassionate response to human suffering. They are also very wise, offering a practical philosophy capable of guiding us from suffering to happiness. But we should note that the assurance given by the *Gita* is not that we can somehow escape or destroy the context of suffering but rather that we can disaffiliate ourselves from it. We suffer because we are afflicted with a case of mistaken identity. We see ourselves as physically and psychically separate, when, in fact, we are a part of one whole. Yet it is so easy to think we are nothing but the tiny bit of the universe that is bounded by our physical outline and defined by our experiences. From that mistaken identity, all forms of suffering follow, from the petty to the profound.

In the *Yoga Śāstra,* the science of harmonious union presented by Patañjali, the obstacles to happiness are expressed in compelling detail as: physical pain or distress, depression, doubt, exaggeration, laziness, hankering, insanity, having no firm ground for spiritual orientation, and instability. Although he wrote long ago, this list could just as easily have been compiled today. Whatever external causes of suffering we encounter, whether global, social, interpersonal, or intrapersonal, we as individuals experience them as our own pain, distress, confusion, instability, and so on. Even when the suffering of others evokes our compassion, we personally experience it within.

We suffer—and we seek happiness and freedom from suffering. Yoga originated as a natural response to this human condition. It is why it was developed, why its teachings have been followed, elaborated, and passed down from time immemorial to the present.

Yoga is as ancient as human history and reaches even beyond it to the past so distant that it is hidden by the shrouds of our unknowing. According to Alain Danielou, renowned scholar of Indian religion, history, and art, Yoga originated as long ago as the sixth millennium B.C.E. as an aspect of spiritual practices affiliated with the archetypal contemplative known as Śiva.[2] These extremely ancient beginnings are attested to by finds made in the sand-buried ruins of Indus Valley civilization, first discovered at the end of the nineteenth century. "These ruins, covering a considerable area of which only a tiny part has been explored, reveal the existence—between the third and second millennium B.C.E.—of one of the most developed and refined civilizations of the ancient world. . . . [I]t stretched as far as the Ganges valley and along the coast toward modern Mumbai. Mohenjo Daro—the best preserved of the towns of this civilization—is uniquely modern, with its grid of streets, its balconied houses, its bathrooms, jewels, engraved seals, system of writing, and so on. Such a city is the result of a very long-lived culture."[3]

Plentiful among the engraved seals of the Indus Valley were those bearing depictions of an archetypal yogi, sitting cross-legged under the spreading branches of a tree. According to Nataraja Guru, a penetrating mid-twentieth century philosopher who united Eastern and Western outlooks in his universal approach, "this figure of the man meditating under a tree has dominated the spiritual language of India persistently and continues to dominate it today as ever. Both literature and iconography are full of references to this archetypal emblem."[4]

Wherever we are in the world, we can readily call to mind examples that reveal how this potent image has spoken to people everywhere, most often as depictions of the meditating Buddha, but also of other wisdom teachers such as the Jain gurus, as well as iconographic representations of various saints and deities, both male and female. Regardless of our spiritual or religious affiliation, we are drawn to the serenity of the meditating figure, the gentle smile that indicates the happiness and peace we yearn for, sensing that it speaks of an inner foundation, a steadiness that can weather the storms of life.

As Nataraja Guru points out, this ancient spiritual

tradition also manifested in literature, in the histories, epics, and religious, philosophical, and mystical writings that preserved and developed India's indigenous spiritual heritage. The Dravidian Indus Valley civilization was highly developed long before the Aryan invasions. The roots of Yoga thus pre-dated Hinduism, which developed out of the initial clash (and subsequent synthesis) between the contemplative ways of the Dravidians and the aggressive sacrificial practices that marked the Aryan worship of gods who personified the forces of nature.

Both of the great ancient epics of India, the *Ramayana* and the *Mahabharata,* record this clash in symbolic form. Certain actual events related in these texts, both of which draw on even more ancient sources, are dated roughly to the third or second millennium B.C.E. Both epics make ample reference to Yoga as a discipline of senses and mind, practiced to gain spiritual insight and power. But more to the point is the section at the heart of the *Mahabharata* known as the *Bhagavad Gita*. It, along with Patañjali's *Yoga Śāstra,* is one of the primary and best-known sources of the teachings of Yoga.

In the middle of the first millennium B.C.E. the Buddha's early sermons gave expression to yogic ideas, particularly in the four *brahma-vihāras*—friendliness, compassion, joy, and equanimity—and the eightfold path, both of which are very similar to the tenets of *Yoga Śāstra*. Although its principles and practices are fundamental to the practices of the Hindu, Buddhist, and Jain religions, the science of Yoga is unrelated to any religion. The disciplines of Yoga are not predicated on any set of beliefs, and are not related to any forms of worship of God or gods.

But this scientific nature of Yoga does not mean it is divorced from our lives. It reveals intimate details of how memory and thought become cages in which we are trapped. Even more important, it offers us a clear approach and methodology to free ourselves. As the second chapter, the *Sādhana Pāda,* makes very clear, the disciplines of this science are not performed in a vacuum. In fact, they are predicated upon wholesome ethical behavior and the cultivation of values of universal and perennial significance. Although the practice of Yoga is an individual pursuit, it naturally results in greater harmony with others.

There is a lot of uncertainty, which has given rise to much speculation and dispute, about the date of composition of Patañjali's *Yoga Śāstra,* with estimates typically ranging from the third century B.C.E. to the third century C.E. Although the date cannot be fixed with certainly, "this brief text represents the earliest known systematic statement of the philosophical insights and practical psychology that define Yoga. Through the centuries since its composition, it has been reinterpreted to meet the needs of widely divergent schools of Indian Yoga, for which it remains an essential text."[5] Yogis and scholars agree that Patañjali was an able compiler and editor whose work helped to preserve and pass down the priceless wisdom of Yoga, the science of harmonious union.

The form Patañjali adopted, that of the sūtra, was often used in Indian philosophy. The word *sūtra,* which literally means "thread," refers both to the short statements or aphorisms of intense condensed meaning, of which the ancient philosophical textbooks were composed, as well as to the entire work consisting of such aphorisms strung together. Each of the six major systems of Indian philosophy have their "Sūtra" textbook, such as the *Brahma Sūtras* of Badarayana for Vedānta, the *Sāṅkhya Pravacana Sūtras* of Kapila for Sāṅkhya, and both Buddhism and Jainism have their Sūtra texts as well.

The condensed nature of the sūtra style—coupled with the intricate and subtle nature of Sanskrit, the language they were composed in—makes it imperative for us to have the aid of an able translator and commentator in order to understand the powerful teaching the *Yoga Sūtras* embody. Over the centuries, many wise and compassionate teachers in India took up the challenge of interpreting them. Some of the most well-known are Vyāsa in the fifth century, Vācaspati Miśra in the ninth, Bhoja Raja in the eleventh, and Vijñāna Bhikṣu in the sixteenth (who all wrote in Sanskrit).

In the nineteenth and twentieth centuries numerous scholars and teachers undertook the task of translation of both the original text and its commentaries into English. Sadly, the result was often a text in which Patañjali's intent of guiding us from suffering to freedom was obscured in the tangles of language and philosophical discursiveness. Still, several well-done translations and helpful commentaries were also shared with the world.

Another obscuration arose, paradoxically, through the manner in which Yoga became popular in the West. Instead of the comprehensive, holistic way of life expressed by Patañjali's *Yoga Śāstra,* Yoga was typically packaged—most often as a commercial product—as merely a form of exercise, a series of stretches, postures, and breath control, with an occasional nod toward meditation. All of this can be very beneficial of course, and it certainly must answer a need, as Yoga has not only become very popular, but also big business. A study done in early 2008 estimated that in the U.S. alone, almost 16 million people were practicing Yoga and that they were spending 5.7 billion dollars a year on Yoga classes and products.[6]

But the theory and practice of Yoga offer much more in the way of invaluable guidance, which this commentary reveals. Guru Nitya presented these insights and explanations as a series of classes for his students in the U.S., Singapore, and India, in response to their yearning for liberation from suffering. Published serially in the *Gurukulam* magazine[7] from 1986 to 1999, this commentary includes only the first two of the four chapters of Patañjali's work but, as Guru Nitya will make clear, it is a full exposition of the transforming path of Yoga.

Also included, as an appendix, are a series of "Letters to an Aspiring Yogi" that Guru Nitya wrote some years before commencing this commentary. Although they are placed after the exposition of the sūtras, they are a good place to begin, as they offer a basic orientation and initiation into the practice of Yoga. The text is necessarily rich with recurring technical Sanskrit terms, so a Sanskrit Glossary has been provided for ready reference.

With the compassionate wisdom of Guru Nitya as your guide, you are invited to enter into Yoga, and to benefit from its teachings and practices, leading you, like the bumble bee, to the heart of the sweet bliss of your own Self, which is the Self of All.

Nancy Yeilding

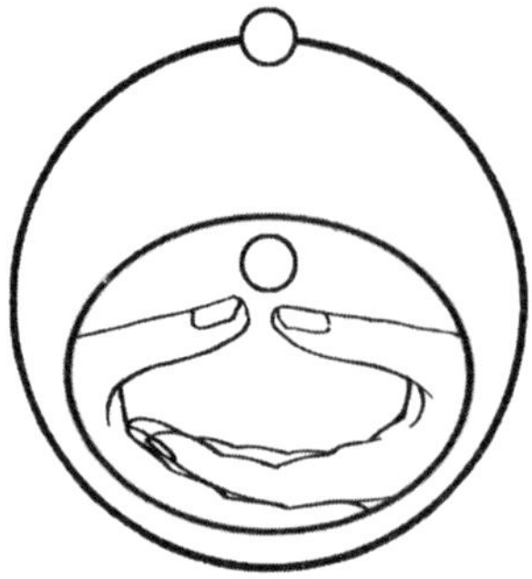

Preface

Yoga is the science of harmonious union with one's own self, the world, and the cosmic law that governs the entire universe, ranging from the cognizing of a sensation to the formation of a galaxy. From the title itself of the opening chapter, *Samādhi Pāda,* it is evident that the purpose of Yoga is to arrive at *samādhi,* the ultimate state of equipoise in which all problems of life are resolved. In the second sūtra, the methodology of arriving at samādhi is clearly stated as *cittavṛtti nirodha. Vṛtti* is "modulation or modification." The entire world can be seen as the expression of countless simultaneous modulations in and through a million devices of the stuff of the world. Here *vṛtti* is conjoined with *citta,* which means "the compulsive emergence of memories." *Rodha* is "preventing or obstructing any possible motion or movement." When *ni* is added to *rodha,* it means "total cessation." So *cittavṛtti nirodha* is "the restraint of mental modifications."

From the day of our birth, all through our life, what we experience is the continuous stream of consciousness. We see many people struggling to get at least a moment of rest from the streaming in of doubts, memories, thoughts, feelings, and disquiet caused by several apprehensions, fears, and imaginations that can all be classified under two heads: pain and pleasure. Most people are convinced that the modulation of consciousness can never be stopped. But when this universally accepted master of Yoga pronouncedly asks for its termination, we are encouraged to think it is possible.

The title of the second chapter, *Sādhana Pāda,* refers to the scope and possibilities of the study of Yoga. What we always experience is our confrontation with necessity. Every time we are confronted with a need, the question of how it can be fulfilled arises in our mind. We look for a potential to actualize. A possibility is suggested from inside. Then it is human nature to be hopeful and to look for probabilities. When we pass from a possibility to a probability, the possibility gains more clarity. When several possibilities are hypothesized, we find that certain postulations are more relevant to the given frame of reference than the others. A postulation can be actualized only by testing the validity of a chosen probability. This is a process by which we decide what cause can yield what result. When we see the result manifesting, we move from a postulation to its actuality. Thus we find out for ourselves that actualization of an envisioned result is the revelation of the solution to our problem.

The person who is bent on actualizing the realization of the potential envisaged in a certain probability is called a *sādhaka*. The postulation is called *sādhanam.* The actual performance or the exerting of energy in a methodical way to bring the actual from the potential is *sādhana.* One sound that is predominant in all these terms is *dha.* It has dynamic affinity with the sound *dhi,* which means "the discerning intelligence" in all experiences of certitude. In the case of the Yoga aspirant, the sādhanam being sought is samādhi. Three of the functions of consciousness—the interrogative (*manas*), recall and remembrance (*citta*), and the sense of agency known as ego (*ahamkāra*)—are all psychic forces that pull the faculty of judgment (*buddhi*) in different directions.

The discerning intellect should stand upright like a pillar *(ādhāna)* without being confused by disturbing thoughts, emotions, or a plethora of memories. When a steady state of consciousness is maintained by the intellect, the pull from all sides is met equally *(sama)*. That position is called *samādhāna* or equipoise. When intelligence maintains a continuous neutral position and does not yield to any emotionally tainted memory, the state that is stabilized is called samādhi. Thus both the *Samādhi Pāda* and the *Sādhana Pāda* point us toward the cessation of the modulation of consciousness.

Yoga is presented by Patañjali in the form of a series of aphorisms (sūtras), in which each aphorism is like a pearl strung on the necklace of the science of contemplative union and ultimate liberation. His *Yoga Śāstra* is usually looked upon as an eightfold ascending path *(Aṣṭāṅga Yoga)*, which is presented in detail in the *Sādhana Pāda*. The eight components, known as limbs, are grouped in four complementary pairs of discipline. The first pair is composed of *yama*, restraining from negativity, and *niyama*, carrying out positive programs of injunctions. When your mind is properly restrained and kept on positive programs, it gains a firm ground wherein you can restfully establish yourself for the advancement of your unitive vision. Remaining on such firm ground is called *āsana*, the third limb. When a steady state comes to the mind, *prāṇa* (vital energy) becomes regulated, the ascending and descending movement of the breath becomes harmonious, and energy becomes equally distributed. This is *prāṇāyāma*, the fourth limb.

The fifth limb occurs when the mind has been withdrawn from distractions *(pratyāhāra)*; this enables you to clearly see the beneficial norms of life. A normative notion comes in the form of a harmonized hierarchy of values. When all values of interest are structured around the peak or crowning value, life has a central principle to regulate thoughts, words, and actions. This inner principle is *dhāraṇā*. *Dhar* means "to support." Dhāraṇā, the sixth limb, is the supporting principle that keeps you always clear-headed and provides a stable basis for your programs of life. When the stream of consciousness flows evenly as desired and channeled by the individual, that harmonious flow is *dhyāna,* the seventh limb.

Just as all rivers flow to the ocean, when all thoughts and inner movements merge in a state of absorption, samādhi comes. Samādhi means "union." Most people think of the union referred to by Yoga as an act of conjunction of two disparate elements. This is incorrect. When a sleeping person wakes up, there is no conjunction. There is only the transformation of an innate nature, which is experienced as an empirical awareness. Similarly, in Yoga, what is happening is not a union with a second reality but a change from heterogeneity to homogeneity. In other words, you gain a unitive vision of life in your understanding, dedicated program of action, and progressive cultivation of happiness, which is identical with the happiness of the world.

The final two chapters, *Vibhūti Pāda* and *Kaivalya Pāda,* are not included in this volume, because—for people preferring to live the normal lifestyle of an individuated person—the instruction in the discipline of Yoga is completed in the first two chapters. A slight exception is that the first four verses of Vibhūti Pāda have been included because they flesh out the explication of the eight limbs.

The ultimate aim of Patañjali's *Yoga Śāstra* is to take a yogic aspirant to the state of being that is free of becoming, *kaivalya,* so the final chapter is *Kaivalya Pāda.* Kaivalya comes from *kevalam,* which means "pure" as well as "original." *Kevala* means "in itself" and "to be alone." In the process of going from the tumult of crowded worldliness to the state of aloneness the seeker passes through several kinds of affectivity and may develop certain hitherto unknown experiences. The term *vibhūti* is a technical name given in the science of harmonious union for any special affection generated in the consciousness of a person who consistently retains a certain impression in his or her awareness. Each type of affectivity—whether psychological, moral, or spiritual—is a distraction from the ultimate goal. So a yogic aspirant needs to know about the various affections that can arise and how they can be resolved. Patañjali places *Vibhūti Pāda* after the chapter on sādhana to guide the yogi to reach pure aloneness without being affected by many predictable distractions of allurement.

Many people have misunderstood the purpose of this chapter, seeing it as a study of supernatural powers to be actualized. Induced hallucinations have been called *vibhūtis* by pseudo-yogis, and the subject has been lost in crowd consciousness. Many aspirants have thus unfortunately experienced hazardous results. If you choose to explore further, we wish to caution you, dear reader, not to attempt *Vibhūti Pāda* by taking its sūtras or several of its prior commentaries literally. You need to keep your peace and patience to arrive at a precise and useful knowledge of *Vibhūti Pāda*.

Yoga is not meant to be the pursuit of any cult or creed anywhere in the world. It is a common path for all human beings, irrespective of their cultural, geographic, and religious affiliations. To understand Yoga in its finalized form, we can gain insights by looking into the science of contemplation preserved by the Śiva-lore of the prehistoric people, the gentle path of the Jainas or bodhisattvas, the sweet love-mysticism of the Vaisnavites, or the similar mysticism belonging to the Jewish, Christian, and Islamic visions of truth.

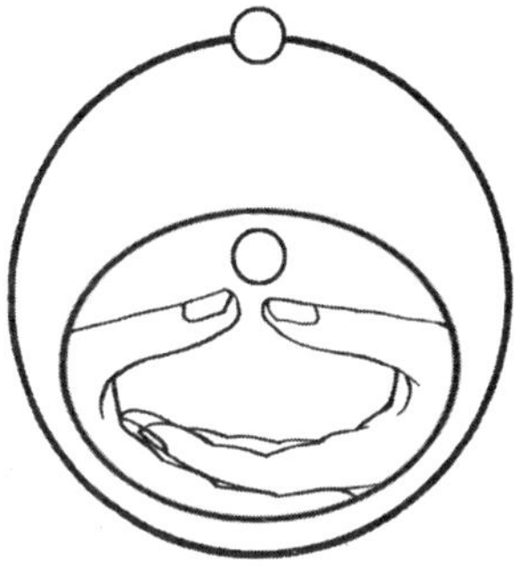

Chapter I: *Samādhi Pāda*

Patañjali's *Science of Harmonious Union (Yoga Śāstra)* is a textbook that is complementary to the *Science of Categorical Enumeration* (*Sāṅkhya Pravacana Sūtra*) of Kapila. The Sāṅkhyan epistemology is analogous to the evolutionary theory of an expanding universe. It commences with a paradoxical steady state in which the spirit of awareness *(puruṣa)* and the material of an inconscient nature *(prakṛti)* remain interlaced, suppressing the intrinsic quality of both. This is the state of the indiscernible (*avyakta*). Then the Sāṅkhyan theory proceeds to trace a progressive, centrifugal function in which categories after categories come into being and are elaborated. This continues until the self-propelling organism of one of the biologic species turns out to be a member of a social matrix in which he or she, as Rousseau puts it, is everywhere in chains and is laboring under the agonizing pain of his or her accountability for existence.

Patañjali commences his instructions from that point of evolutionary culmination, to guide a return to the aloneness of pure awareness that is attributed to the spirit as its pure and homogenous nature. Hence the aphorism, *atha yoga anuśāsanam*, is given as the opening statement of Patañjali.

Sūtra I:1

atha yogānuśāsanam

atha: now
yoga: contemplative union in harmony, *samādhi* (equipoise in consciousness)
anuśāsanam: the instruction, teaching, exposition [for]

Now, the instruction for contemplative union in harmony.

It is customary for a book that details a system of philosophy in India to begin with the reason for elucidating that particular philosophical vision. "Now" (*atha*) can have several meanings out of which we should highlight the most appropriate. Both in chronology and epistemological import, the Yoga philosophy of Patañjali is to be seen as sequential to Kapila's philosophic vision of cosmic projection. Considering this, "now" means: "After having heard Kapila's aphorisms of Sāṅkhya, *now* you will be benefited by familiarizing yourself with both the theory and practice of the science of Yoga."

The second and more important way to understand "now" is the state in which people exist at present, as individual psychosomatic systems with several aberrations, which are tending to become more and more pathological, and as members of a species that seems to be planning its own destruction with strife and hatred.

Vyāsa, the first commentator of Patañjali's Yoga (in the fifth century) thinks of the word *atha* in this sūtra as a pointer to specify the competency of the seeker who wishes to acquaint himself or herself with the science of Yoga. According to Vyāsa, Yoga is *samādhi,* "equipoise in consciousness." It is not the steady state of inert matter in its stagnation of evolution, but the continuous rebalancing of a poise that is kept up in and through the flux of a cosmic order of continuous transformation and transvaluation.

However great and wonderful the macro system of cosmic transformation, the seeker is an individual with his or her consciousness enmeshed in the biologic organism of a human body. The only equipment that is given to him or her is the organism's capacity for mentation. This functional core of individual consciousness is volatile in nature. It is described with the term *kṣipta,* which can mean a process of destructuring and consequently restructuring, thereby causing an internal change in the person's pattern of existence. This natural occurrence need not necessarily be equated with the conscious registration of the affective recognition of a specific value. But when the change happens from one manifested state to another, highlighted with the affectivity or afflictability of a value interest, it is called *vikṣipta.*

Flickering consciousness pauses for a split second, characterized by the veiling of consciousness in between one focus of consciousness and another. The shift of focus also implies the illumination of a new interest. A transient interest or attention can be momentary or persist for a period of time in which a highlighted interest becomes serial. At the terminus of one series there again arises a veiling, obscuration, or opacity that erases the identity of both the subject and the object. This most important function of the inertial quality of our psychosomatic system is generally underrated by most people because of the pathological condition that can be precipitated by the inertial factor, which is recognized both by Kapila and Patañjali as *tamas.* Vyāsa designates the recurring myopia between the focus of consciousness on separate value experiences as *mūḍha*, "forgetfulness."

Mūḍha does not operate alone. Consciousness is a flow. Unless there is a holding back, one interest is sequentially followed by another. There is no given rhyme or rhythm to the flow of consciousness. It is pressurized according to the bearing of an interest on the total persona of an individual. When several dynamic interests spring forth from the seedbed of interest, an inhibitory agent in the field of consciousness has to hold them in check until one interest is fully lived. This intercepting function is called *nirodha*. It is like an undetectable consciousness that polices around the field of focusing awareness, holding back any interest of a different nature.

When obscuration and inhibition play their proper role and a highlighted interest is allowed to prevail as an undisputed life interest, that gives a sense of satisfaction to the entire organism. Attention becomes concentered. This is the most powerful and useful role of consciousness. It is called *ekāgra*. Vyāsa, as a superior teacher with clear wisdom, extols the high value of the concentering of mind as the most conducive moment of harmonious union. In the light of ekāgra, or "concentration," the other functions of consciousness are looked upon as incidental and unimportant. When kṣipta, vikṣipta, mūḍha, nirodha, and ekāgra are taken as integral parts of the structure of the consciousness-generating principle in an individual, we cannot underrate the importance of any part. However, because of the possible association of vikṣipta, mūḍha, and nirodha with several psychopathological incidents in a person's life, they are looked upon with a certain suspicion if not abhorrence.

Vācaspati Miśra has written a further elucidation of Vyāsa's commentary on Patañjali's *Yoga Śāstra* called *Vicārādi Tīka*. According to him, Hiraṇyagarbha was the original teacher of Yoga. This is to be understood along similar lines as the statement in the *Bhagavad Gita* that the first principles of *brahmavidyā* (science of the Absolute) and *Yoga Śāstra* were taught by the Lord as the Sun-god Vivasvān, the father of Vaivasvata Manu. Here, "the Lord" is to be understood as the innate principle of control in everything and the source of all energy to function. The Sun in the firmament is looked upon as an overt symbol of the supreme light that is shining in all inconscient substances. To some extent, the solar Sun also physically rules over all forms of matter out of which the planets of the solar system have been created. In the *Bṛhadāraṇyaka Upaniṣad*, Hiraṇyagarbha and Prajāpati are the counterparts of a dialectical system of want and fulfillment, representing the dual principles of "the will to live" (*vaiśvānara)* and "the governing laws" *(virāṭ puruṣa)* by which life urges are to be fulfilled in the right manner so one becomes established in the realm of absolute satisfaction, characterized by the samādhi or absorption of the yogi.

A doubt can arise in the mind of the student as to why samādhi alone is considered to be Yoga, when there are other planes in which the mind can stabilize, such as in the case of those people who enjoy blissful states of ecstasy (*madhumati*), those who become dear to all as if they themselves have transformed into something similar to sweet honey (*madhupratīka),* and those who are rid of all sense of suffering (*viśoka*). The answer to this will become evident as we progress with our study and clearly understand the different kinds of samādhi that arise in a seeker's progress to the state of absolute aloneness, *kaivalya*, the ultimate goal of Yoga.

Patañjali gives his definition of Yoga in Sūtra I:2.

Sūtra I:2

yogaścitta vṛtti nirodhaḥ

yogaḥ: yoga
citta: mental, of the mind, mind-stuff, faculty of memory and recall
vṛtti: modifications, modulations, oscillations, functions
nirodhaḥ: [is the] restraint, inhibition

Yoga is the restraint of mental modifications.

Both Yoga and Vedānta allude to the inner organ *(antaḥkaraṇa)*, an inner mechanism with four distinct agencies of operation: the interrogative aspect (*manas)*; the faculty of memory and recall *(citta);* the faculty of judgment *(buddhi);* and the ego, the affective core that is intimately connected with the biological as well as psychological individuation of experiencing pain and pleasure and all such dualities of life *(ahamkāra).* The instrument of the registry of stimulation and recall of memory is a repository of all the colorations and conditionings that happen to a person during his or her lifetime. Hence all conditional reactions throughout life stem from this faculty (citta). Its modulation is called *citta vṛtti.*

Vṛtti, as the word suggests, has many implications. It is an operation in the time-space continuum that structures the several ensembles of the present. The sense of the present is generated by vṛtti. The "present" in Sanskrit is called *vartamānam. Vartanam* is existence; *mānam* is measuring. *Vartamānam* is the occasion provided for direct perception and evaluation. Vṛtti is also suggestive of repetitive function, *āvarti.* It is also the centripetal closing in from all sides that preserves an impression for future reference, *avṛtti.* It is also suggestive of a vortex that is formed in consciousness, a circular motion of repetitive thinking. In that sense it is *āvartini,* a whirlpool. In the formation of a vṛtti, a centrifugal reverberation that spreads out physically and emotionally occurs simultaneously with a centripetal containment of the experience within a certain limit. From all sides a closing in happens which, in physical terms, amounts to the consolidation of both the electrical and chemical energies involved in the reverberation.

Citta has a dual function. Sensations from the external world that are carried to the inner organ are registered in the citta in terms of the information that is sought after by the questioning, doubting, or emotionally activated mind. Then citta preserves the net outcome of the encounter between the sensory system and stimulus as data for future reference. As inquiry, judgment, and affectivity are all based on the registration, retention, and recall of memory, citta is considered to be the main body of consciousness. Hence yogis mainly concern themselves with the modification of this aspect that mimes the external world in every organism. It is very similar to a mirror reflecting the image of its surroundings, or the external world being mirrored in each bubble that clusters in a frothy mass of foam.

A simple pluck of the string of a vīṇā or any string instrument or a tap on a tuning fork is followed by countless frequencies of vibrations that can go on like encircling waves for a long time. Such an occurrence in memory is called kṣipta. After the repetitive process of maintaining its vibratory nature for a certain quantum of time, deflection comes. That is called vikṣipta, a specific occurrence. When this is happening to the consciousness that is latent in a living organism, the specific power of recognition of the internal transformation becomes dull. That state is called mūḍha, a stupor-like lack of clarity. It prevents a new focusing of attention on a third item; this is called nirodha. When nirodha prevents the admission of any new phenomenal attention, the spirit implied in the organism's biologic state brings in a clarity that can be one-pointed, ekāgra. This general mechanism of consciousness—motion (kṣipta), distraction (vikṣipta), stupor (mūḍha), restraint (nirodha), and one-pointedness (ekāgra)—functions autonomously and cyclically.

A question can arise regarding the admission of kṣipta, vikṣipta, mūḍha, and nirodha as constituents of mental modification, especially when we study consciousness with a view to directing it toward one-pointed attention in the intrinsic nature of pure consciousness. Most commentators cast aspersion on these four factors, interpreting kṣipta as the state of the distraught, mūḍha as the state of the stupefied, vikṣipta as the state of the restless, and nirodha as the state of the suppressed. When the smooth functioning of consciousness is negatively afflicted by any of these states it is only natural to categorize them as pathological dysfunctions or malfunctions. In our surroundings we can see people who are continuously in a state of being distraught such as in the case of infants and imbeciles. The state of the stupefied can be seen in those who are so pathologically withdrawn or infatuated that they behave like stupids. Vikṣipta becomes restlessness of a chronic nature in the case of a person afflicted with anxiety neurosis. Nirodha also becomes pathologic when, under pressure of paranoia or conditions of repression, one is afraid of admitting the occurrence of one's natural urges.

In spite of these four aspects of citta having a tendency in the long run to cause psychological dysfunctions, in the normal working of the mind, they all fall in their rightful place for consciousness to flow as a well-regulated stream. The five limbs of consciousness aid each other, especially arresting the flow of the stream meaningfully to make citta concenter in a specific value admission and appreciation. Patañjali wants us to know that this natural mechanism of consciousness is a rich phenomenon that can be employed to arrive at a supernatural glimpse of the noumenon.

Every mental modification that is invested with the performance of a *karma* (action) becomes a seed that carries the potential for future distress, infatuation, or stupefaction, restlessness, and suppression or repression. According to Vyāsa, this potential can be nullified by holding the mind in a state of absorption for a long time. When, in the modification of citta, concentration on its original pure nature happens again and again, that cleanses it of subsequent modifications, which come through actions performed unwittingly, unconsciously, or with deliberation caused by ignorance.

Such absorption normally happens when you feel an at-one-ment with the identity of an object of perception *(vitarka)*, the presenting of an idea *(vicāra)*, a sense of ecstasy *(ānanda)*, or the retrospective state of being absorbed in your ego consciousness *(asmitā)* without slipping into unwholesome states of ego cathexis. When natural absorption leads the modification of consciousness into a wholesale appreciation of any of these four aspects—perception, ideation, ecstasy, or ego identity—that is considered *samprajñāta* (cognitive or conditioned) *yoga* or *samprajñāta samādhi.* At a further level of absorption these fourfold movements of consciousness can be arrested by removing the incentive to perceive and the incentive to ideate, by the non-interest in pleasure-seeking, and by the absolute release of ego-consciousness. In such a state Yoga becomes more mature and aids the aspirant to the ultimate goal of aloneness, in which case it is called *asamprajñāta* (unconditioned or pure) *yoga* or *asamprajñāta samādhi*.

In yogis like the Buddha, samprajñāta samādhi amounts to total mindfulness and asamprajñāta samādhi relates to *śūnyatā* or the absolute void of phenomenality. In Vedānta samprajñāta samādhi relates to the consciousness of pure existence (*tanmātra anubhūti)* and asamprajñāta samādhi relates to the experiencing of unalloyed consciousness (*cinmātra anubhūti*). Of the fivefold components of citta vṛtti—ekāgra, kṣipta, mūḍha, vikṣipta, and nirodha—the latter needs special attention. When the citta is deliberating on any given topic of interest, nirodha naturally occurs to hold back irrelevant urges and interests. When nirodha becomes pathological, it causes various kinds of inhibitions and generates phobia and fear complexes. But the same nirodha becomes an instrument to discipline the entire range of citta for the persistent experiencing of concentration or absorption. In a subsequent sūtra, there will be a special reference to nirodha. Similarly, a special reference should be made to vikṣipta, which can occur in the form of an aberration of an established discipline. In fact, vikṣipta becomes one of the major impediments in the yogic disciplining of one's mind.

The world is a quintuplication of the five elements: grossness (earth), viscosity (water), thermodynamics (fire), gaseousness (air), and ethereality (space). In their horizontalized manifestation these give rise to smell, taste, form, touch, and sound. When there is no quintuplication and the elements are in their own state (*tanmātra*), they do not lend themselves to be experienced. Thus when the material basis of phenomenal manifestation is separated from pure consciousness, *puruṣa* (the Self) comes to its aloneness. The progressive step one makes from samprajñāta samādhi to asamprajñāta samādhi is that of going away from the quintuplicated phenomenal world to the pure state of one's Self.

In the definition of Yoga given in this sūtra there is no mention of the total restraint of consciousness. From that we deduce that cognitive consciousness continues to operate even when restraint is exercised. We can become more familiar with the principle of modification by taking into account both the source of the pure effulgence of awareness (puruṣa) and the aid to illumination arising out of nature (prakṛti). Their relationship is somewhat analogous to the illumination of an object by physical light such as sunlight. We do not see sunlight except as it is reflected from an illuminated object.

Similarly, puruṣa as such is not seen. When the pure light of puruṣa illuminates an object, that illumination is the person's cognizance. In that cognizance the person experiences not merely the self-effulgence of puruṣa but also the clear and pure mirroring quality of nature. That particular quality of nature is called *sattva* for the reason that it gives an identity of a cognition that is not falsified with any defect of the mirroring agent.

This is not always the case. The pure light of puruṣa can be intercepted by another aspect of prakṛti known as *rajas,* which has a disturbing quality. It acts like a colored glass that partially lends its own color to the cognition. Further, it has a power to distort both form and dimension, as well as to induce in the act of cognizance an altered pace of movement such as an urgency of apprehension.

The third aspect in the mirroring quality of nature has the capacity to arrest vision, freeze the cognized experience into a consolidated memory, and even conceal an object from being illuminated. If *rajas* has the dynamic to energize consciousness, this particular quality, called tamas, can deplete energy to an extent of inducing lethargy in the cognizing person and even hampering the clarity of comprehension.

Hereafter in our study of Yoga, these three qualities are to be remembered as integral parts of nature, which is always in a state of flux. No quality stands by itself. However, there can be a predominance of one quality over the other in different proportions. Even in the confused and vague comprehension where tamas dominates, there will necessarily be a certain amount of sattva to aid cognition because cognition never occurs without sattva providing the ground.

The immediate consequence of cognition is *prakhyā,* a comprehensive vision of an object or idea presented to the mind. Prakhyā is immediately followed by an excitement of psychic energy, which acts as a stimulant for the individual to react to knowledge presented to the mind. Consequent to the excitement, a certain action can follow. This is known as *pravṛtti*. Pravṛtti is a modification with a positive emphasis on action. The action may be an overt expression that pushes into service the organs of action—vocalization, creative function, motion, procreation, or excretion—which can occur in several ways, combined or separate.

However, even when these actions do not overtly manifest, there can be an internal function very much like an alchemic psychosomatic operation whereby a *samskāra* (a registration of the impression) is made. The registry of an impression is like etching a figure in metal or stone *(sthiti)*. It can remain until the total decomposition of physical constituents that serve as the physical, chemical, and biological basis of the mind.

During the wakeful hours the stream of consciousness winds its way through several objects, events, and assemblages of names and forms. In accordance with such encounters the inner bulk of consciousness (citta) is continuously sculpted into a permanent memory storage. Thus sattva, rajas, and tamas—along with their three counterparts, prakhyā, pravṛtti, and sthiti—fill our days and weave the biography of a person. In a feeble manner prakhyā, pravṛtti, and sthiti also occur in the subjective consciousness of dream where innumerable compositions of pre-established memories are reconstituted into many fictitious and exaggerated formations. We will come to that at a later stage.

When sattva is favorably aided by the energizing power of rajas, the disposition to act benevolently becomes enhanced. If the influence of rajas overbalances the dominance of sattva, affectability increases, attachment becomes very colored, and the desire to possess increases. In the place of the combination of sattva and rajas, when sattva and tamas combine, the disposition to act tends to stray more into negativity.

Deflections from ethical norms can bring in more and more corrupt practices. When a tamasic disposition becomes very strong, infatuation or blindness to reality brings total perversion. Effort is to be made from the side of the individual to steer past the corroding powers of rajas and tamas to regain the clarity of sattvic mirroring of the objects of perception and the conception of ideas. Only when the correct presentation of proper illumination is attained does the adherence to ethical norms enable one to build up a consistent character that can be called virtuous or spiritual. In all these functions the identification of the intellect and luminosity of puruṣa are so intensively intermingled that one does not see the intellect as different from the puruṣa.

When all the vestiges of rajas are removed from the sattvic mirroring of mind, spiritual virtue becomes dynamic and acts as an elevating catalyst called *dharmamegha*. When that happens, confused cognition (*vikalpa*) and creative cognition (*saṅkalpa*) cease to darken consciousness. Their place is taken by pure contemplation or *dhyāna*. The dhyāna that occurs in such a state is dharmamegha dhyāna. The expression, *dharmamegha,* is an allegoric way of saying that virtues (*dharma*) come like a rain cloud *(megha)* and favor the aspirant yogi. A cloud is taken to its destination by wind. Similarly, the physical and subjective effort of the yogi can take his or her discipline only to a certain extent. Thereafter—like a cloud being taken by wind—the disciplined mind of the yogi transverses in the spiritual realm without any ego-oriented effort.

Just as water is the flowing current of a river, psychic or spiritual energy (*citiśakti*) is the transforming medium of consciousness. However, like the constancy of the basic structure of water, citiśakti by itself never loses its nature at any time. Hence it is considered unchangeable and untransmittable. When and where intellect (buddhi) presents an occasion, citiśakti simply illuminates it. Buddhi is like the eye with which we look and citiśakti is the light that illuminates an object. Perception takes place only when the two occur together.

The discriminative function of mind that distinguishes puruṣa from buddhi should not be considered identical with the function of citiśakti because, even in the discriminative function called *viveka khyāti*, there is a touch of impurity. Momentary discriminations can happen in a mind even when it is cluttered with several latent impressions *(vāsanā)*. When the latent impressions persist in the form of concealed memories, the absorption you might get cannot be final. It is still a seeded condition from which any latent impression can sprout and present itself to fill your mind with all its accompanying urges for action and gratification.

A seeded state is called *sabīja*. When samādhi occurs to such a state of mind, it is a sabīja (seeded) samādhi or a samprajñāta, conditioned state. Only when all the latent impressions are systematically curbed and made impotent does the non-seeded *(nirbīja)* state come. In the non-seeded state pure absorption (asamprajñāta samādhi) can arise. Such absorption is pervaded with the homogenous pure consciousness that is identical with puruṣa. Thus Yoga can be either of those with conditioned states or of those who are freed of all conditioned impressions.

In Vedānta also there are similar classifications of the emancipated seers who retain a personal ego for moving about in this world with the intention of doing good to fellow beings, and those who are totally void of any ego and are consequently oblivious to their bodily needs and the claims of the phenomenal world on them.

The word *nirodha* that is referred to in the sūtra, when read with Vyāsa's commentary, offers two possibilities of interpretation. Vyāsa is known for his adherence to Vedānta.

According to Vedānta, realization is a total, in-depth experience that spells only one possibility: Self-knowledge is total. Either you know the Self or you do not. It cannot be known in parts. If Yoga is understood as total identity with the Absolute, that would automatically dispense with all creative cognitions (saṅkalpas) and confused cognitions (vikalpas). In that case, nirodha would not be an exercise on the part of the aspirant. If, on the other hand, graded perfection through practice (sādhana) is recognized, as in Patañjali's *Aṣṭāṅga Yoga,* one should look into four possible nirodhas in conditioned samprajñāta samādhi and also four nirodhas that alone can lead to unconditioned asamprajñāta samādhi.

The first exercise of nirodha deals with savitarka samādhi "absorption in a perception." The most natural experience of every person is a perception of an object: visual, auditory, tactual, cutative, or olfactory. Of these, the first three kinds are constantly experienced during the wakeful state. Although auditory experience is more intense than visual, the main distraction that comes to us is from the varieties of forms that are paraded before our eyes. Our attention shifts from one form to another. According to Vedāntins, the attention that goes to a form when we are looking at it has a back and forth movement of consciousness, now resting with the object of vision, and then centering in the subjective consciousness of the seer. This oscillation between seer and seen is called *bhāna vṛtti.*

Although for the purpose of orientation this can only be so, it is a common experience that a highly attractive visual form can rivet our attention to it for a long time, not letting the consciousness self-realize, even for a little while. In that case the perceiver and the percept enter into an intense identity. It is as if the vṛtti has become stabilized by the mode of the vision. Two nirodhas have already taken place in such an instance. One is the restraint or rather unconscious prohibition of any other form or interest from entering the established space of attention. This act of nirodha is a spontaneous and automatic function that the unconscious is capable of achieving. The second is as follows: the attention aroused by the subject presented to the puruṣa in an aesthetic appreciation of the intellect generates an ānanda which is akin to the very nature of puruṣa. Therefore puruṣa does not look for an alternative. This is a unity that is established between seer and seen and thus it satisfies the general requirement of Yoga, the union of the pairs of opposites.

The same may also be experienced through establishing a union between the hearer and what is heard. This can be achieved by isolating one sound, such as the *anāhata nādam* that you hear within yourself, and focusing consciousness upon it. The tactual experiencing of union quite often happens when your identification with the inner sensation of respiration cuts off your attention from your agency of respiration. Similarly, the restraint of the flow of consciousness can come through the focus on any single sensory experience. Nirodha can happen in many ways, and can always lead to a total identification of the experiencer with the experience (savitarka samādhi). However, this initial quieting of the mind only pacifies modifications temporarily and does not take away the potential for further agitation.

Savitarka samādhi can easily lead to savicāra samādhi, "absorption in an idea or a concept." Most people think that vicāra is a pure mental function. In reality, the conscious aspect of it is very physiological. We think with words and all words are ready to be articulated where the larynx is in conjunction with the tongue. Here the first restraint (nirodha) is that of not articulating the words of one's thoughts. A vicāra or idea comes like the formation of a wave from the depth of consciousness, climbs to a peak, and then submerges. But when the yogic aspirant enters into a serene envisioning of the significance of a single thought, the linear movement of vicāra is replaced by a contemplative appreciation of the *sphōṭa* (burst or flash of meaning) evoked by the word, which restricts the occurrence of another thought. Thus, the restraint that is caused by a fascinating thought itself prolongs the attention given to it. Savicāra sādhana, the practice of absorption in an idea, offers no external crutches to hold on to. Hence, it is not so easy as performing savitarka sādhana. Only in a mind where the seeded urges are less turbulent is savicāra union successfully effected.

Sānanda samādhi occurs as a result of an in-depth restraint in which the deep desire to be with yourself is united with the existentiality of your identity, generating a deep imperiential connection with the puruṣa's blissful nature (ānanda). This happens only when you promote yourself from savitarka to savicāra and savicāra culminates in a state of dhyāna, contemplation. Sasmitā samādhi presents itself when all wrong self-identifications—such as with the environment, the body, sensations, thoughts, and so on—drop off. It is as if you come to the center of your consciousness and do not recede with the ripples of centrifugal vibrations. The nirodha in this case is a centripetal adherence to the centering of yourself, such as in the case of having only one center for your psyche and the cosmos. Up to this point, the exercises in samprajñāta samādhi continue.

Citta is the most central piece of the psychosomatic mechanism. On one side it receives its animation from pure consciousness and, on the other, it has for its individuation a body endowed with the vital breath (or energy), sense organs, mind, and intellect. It can be swayed into different functional levels by the instability of the three modalities *(guṇas)* of nature: sattva (clear-pure, sublime), rajas (colored-passionate, kinetic), and tamas (dark-inertial). When the sattva modality becomes the dominant factor, citta becomes citta sattva. Only when the purity of sattva in its manifestation as citta is maintained can the yogi successfully carry out practices (sādhanas). Hence one has to take care of oneself with formidable nirodhas exercised on all sides such as in a reservoir where pure water is stored and is not allowed to be polluted by environmental factors. When the horizontality of rajas blows into citta sattva, its equipoise is disturbed and turbulence arises. Hence there has to be a constant vigil of the stabilization of sattva by practicing *vairāgya* (restraint). The equipoise of consciousness is to be established again and again through *abhyāsa* (repetitive practice).

Both in Vedānta and Yoga, *viveka* (discriminative knowledge) is given a high position. In Vedānta, *akhaṇḍa viveka anubhūti* (unitive discrimination of perception) is the tightrope on which the Vedāntin has to pace with unfaltering steps in absolute ease. In Yoga, viveka khyāti is the rope that leads an aspirant to dharmamegha, the cloud of showering virtue. Citiśakti (pure consciousness) is given high marks such as being infinite, immutable, untransmittable, and the illuminator of all. The finale of Yoga discipline is given in the next sūtra.

Sūtra I:3

tadā draṣṭuḥ svarūpe 'vasthānam

tadā: then
draṣṭuḥ: the seer, the witness
svarūpe: [in its] own essential nature or form
avasthānam: remaining, established, dwelling

Then the seer remains in its own essential nature.

This is the ultimate to which a yogi aspires. Just as light is used as an operational device to animate pictures in a cinematographic machine, the light of puruṣa is the controlling force that activates the stimulation of all five senses as well as the motor functions connected with sensations. In the normal course of life the intellect borrows light from puruṣa through citiśakti and assumes the reflected position of the seer. It relates with the empirical world through the sense organs and mentations, such as of a recalled memory or imagination, and transacts as if on behalf of the puruṣa.

But when the citiśakti is withdrawn and confined to the puruṣa, there is neither the buddhi animated by it nor the world of name and form illuminated by the light of the puruṣa. When there is no one to relate with, the only thing one can do is return to one's Self or remain as one's pure Being. Consequently the subject-object duality ceases and the individuated self, *jīva,* attains the aloneness of the pure effulgence of puruṣa. This is kaivalya. This is the only time the individuation of consciousness becomes bereft of conditioned states or the assumed colorations of the special significance of a given moment. Pure consciousness is self-luminous. It does not lose its power of knowledge simply because it is cut off from illuminated objects. When there is nothing to know, knowledge knows itself. This pure state of the Self is called puruṣa.

Sūtra I:4

vṛtti sārūpyam itaratra

vṛtti: [with the] modifications, activities, functionings, operations

sārūpyam: the identification [is] with the form or nature

itaratra: at other times, in other states, otherwise

At other times, the identification is with the modifications.

In the previous sūtra the seer is said to be established entirely in the Self. In such a state there is no conditional knowledge. In this sūtra, that state of the pure Self is compared to the state of a mind stimulated by the various inputs that come through sense organs.

This describes an imperiential state differentiated from the experiencing of mentation. According to behaviorists, the impact of the external world is received in the form of stimuli from objects of perception. The objects are experienced outside the central nervous system as the presentation of certain sensations that are easily associated with memories of the past and prospective imaginations in which the perceptions have some role to play.

A question of both epistemological and methodological import can be raised in this context. When a person experiences an object of perception, does the light of the puruṣa leave the boundaries of the body and go to the object for the purpose of illuminating it and becoming identified with the object illuminated by the Self? Or, as modern physical scientists believe, is the brain simply being conditioned by the electrical and chemical consolidation that happens in the central nervous system as a result of the incoming stimuli? According to Vedānta, the light that shines within is the only light by which the entire world and all living minds are illuminated. That is the one and only Self. There is no special cleavage anywhere in the universality of existence, knowledge, and the value of its beingness. The Vedāntin therefore thinks that the time and space where a thing is experienced is exactly where such experiencing is happening. This is quite contrary to what modern scientists postulate.

In Yoga, the fact of perceptual experience is looked upon as an indescribable phenomenality, which can be seen in the relationship between a magnet and iron filings. All that we need to know is that there is an irresistible interaction between them. Even so is the intrinsic relationship between the seer and the seen. Physical science deals with objects like persons, tables, chairs, hills, dales, and rocks. In principle they are all supposed to be manifestations of matter. However, nobody apprehends anything as matter in itself. Because the tangible properties of an object have a direct impact on the senses, the experiential confrontation is given a priority of recognition. Only through a secondary deductive inference does one surmise that all things are created out of matter.

In the discernment of the pure light of consciousness from the modified entities that bear name and form, there is a similar incomprehensibility of the Self. One of the four aspects of the inner organ—the judging and cognizing faculty known as intellect or buddhi—dominates the field of reasoning. It assumes the position of the Self by designating the central focus of reasoning consciousness as "I," and, for all practical purposes, effaces the distinction between the ego and the Self. Consequently, the Self hides behind its own light and projects its false identification with the ego.

The Sāṅkhya philosophy offers some helpful insights into the nature of the hidden Self. The original aphorisms of Kapila, known as the founder of the Sāṅkhya school of philosophy, are unknown. The present *Sāṅkhya Pravacana Sūtras* are said to have been composed by Pañcaśikha, the disciple of Asuri, who was a direct disciple of Kapila. According to Pañcaśikha, the nature of the pure Self is described by the word *darśana* (vision). Like Kant's thing-in-itself, darśana is pure knowledge knowing itself. Any shade of horizontalization that specifies knowledge is *khyāti.*

Prakhyā, derived from khyāti, is a clear or distinct cognition of the specific. It is a modification of buddhi.

In the explanation of the second sūtra, reference was made to the dynamics of prakhyā, pravṛtti, and sthiti: the horizontalization of knowledge whereby it stabilizes the agency of a crystallizing ego, which sets into motion a creative function in response to the initial horizontalization. It is the process by which the status of the knower changes into that of the doer. The instrumentality of the operational ability that is assumed by consciousness becomes an aid to individuated consciousness. The horizontalized cognizing power depends more and more on the instrumentality of mind for carrying out purposes that aid in increasing the pleasure items that are continuously annexed to the sphere of consciousness and in avoiding painful situations. Thus pravṛtti, or instrumental consciousness, becomes by and large a defense measure of consciousness. In this way a simple unit of puruṣa becomes a complex manifestation.

Vijñāna Bhikṣu, a sixteenth century Vedāntic commentator of Yoga, gives the following analogy for the instrumentality of consciousness that ensues from itself: "As a magnet, by drawing to it a piece of iron, does some service to its owner and thus becomes, as it were, a treasured possession of the owner, so does the mind serve its master, the puruṣa, by drawing to itself the objects around it and presenting them to puruṣa and thereby becomes, as it were, the very self of the puruṣa."

If cognitive consciousness is only one of the modifications of consciousness, who is the conscient being? In its role of discerning the validity of what is given, from where does the intellect obtain the norm to measure and for whose sake does the intellect discern? The biologic significance of these questions cannot be slighted. The life that has organized itself with many psychosomatic structurings of various energy forms and energy sources as the body/mind complex has to serve as an instrument to carry out a central purpose around which every bit of this organization clings.

What is normal in the course of life is to seek nourishment, help the organism to attain its full maturity, replicate one's kind, and establish a harmony that tends to become more and more satisfying as it attains a maximal degree of perfection. Everything happening in the organism has a rightful place in its scheme. Hence the question, "Who is the beneficiary of the organism's growth, maturity, replication, understanding, and satisfaction?" The most plausible answer is that there is an I-consciousness that plays the most central role, an "I" that is identical with the Self. Even unconsciously, all people say "I doubt, I know, I love, I am happy, I am unhappy," and so on. Does that "I" cause mental modifications or is the "I" a superfluous idea that is projected on each unit of modification for the purpose of orientation?

When we look upon the central piece as a seer, a cognizer, a witness, we distinctly see two aspects: the seer seeing and the seen unfurling like a series of pictures, or even as a continuous event that is being presented from an unknown entity; having been seen and appreciated, what has been presented never leaves the seer. In that process, the seer is provided with a world that is increasingly enlarging in the variety of its several dimensions. A continuous correlation is established between what is already known and what is newly apprehended. Also, an insatiable expectation arises, which is always looking for new experiences.

The seer and the seen are like an unending warp and woof that are continuously woven into certain accepted patterns intermingled with totally novel and unique impressions. What exactly is this modification? What is it a modification of? Like many criss-cross ripples making and unmaking patterns on the surface of water, modifications arise and subside as part of a flux, yet the depth of meaning of each passing moment is preserved forever. What masterminds this mystery? The whole thing is simply called vṛtti.

One of the most intriguing questions a yogi has to answer is how the puruṣa or pure Self lends itself to manifest as a personal ego in the individual. The personal ego or I-consciousness adopts many identifications that are contrary to the nature of puruṣa. In identifications such as "I am pleased, I am sad, I am frustrated," and so on, the phenomenality of certain modifications is owned by the ego. That, in turn, amounts to the puruṣa being held in bondage.

In Vācaspati's gloss on this sūtra, he offers two traditional analogies to explain this. When a transparent crystal, which has no color of its own, is placed adjacent to a red hibiscus flower, the crystal also looks red. The color looks as if it has been interjected into the crystal. Actually, no color has gone into it. It is an illusion caused by the proximity of two entirely different things. Similarly, pain/pleasure identifications of consciousness come as a result of the puruṣa's proximity with nature (prakṛti), where all dualities abound.

The other example given is that of a person looking into a soiled mirror, which makes the image look vague, blurred, and stained. Actually, the face that is reflected in the mirror is not the least affected by the stains on the mirror. Darkness is not a quality of light but light enables the identification of a object through the contrast of the illuminated part with the unilluminated. Similarly, the puruṣa also comes to distinguish phenomena through name and form.

One marked difference between Indian thought and Western thought is the absence of systematization in Indian thought and over-classification in Western thought. The *Yoga Śāstra* of Patañjali and its many explanatory elucidations can be treated as a text that is religious, philosophical, psychological, disciplinary, or a compendium of injunctions to be remembered. No one can say where metaphysical thinking stops and descriptive psychology begins. In Western thought, classical philosophers will not brook the inclusion of psychologizing in metaphysical reasoning, while the school of psychology insists on scientific precision and will not allow any introspective or subjective idea to be included as valid data along with factual events and figures that are considered respectable by scientists.

In an interdisciplinary study like the present one, these distinct approaches of the East and West make it very difficult to maintain an overall methodology that will do justice to the claims of both Western science and Indian mysticism. However, when there is a sameness between the subject that is approached and the goal that is aimed at, a scheme of correlation with functional clarity can be successfully employed.

The main process to be understood is the selection of one interest out of a plethora of possibilities on which attention is focused for a considerable time. In the Western outlook, an objective world of independent reality is assumed to be existing "out there" even though we do not know anything about it. So-called objectivity and demonstrative proof are derogatively spoken of by Sir Arthur Eddington as idols of the scientist who swears by them. The Indian pantheon of gods begins with Brahma the creator who creates world after world in the attempt to approximate aesthetic perfection. He creates out of nothing, by mere wish or word. This archetypal symbol can also be seen in the *Book of Genesis* in the Old Testament. In fact, both Eastern and Western mythologies accept the creative power of the word and the word materializing into matter. However crude this imagery is, it has a powerful message to give. From the very outset of human life the apperception of each situation is assessed by an individual as a context of need and fulfillment. That means individual consciousness is unfurling itself with a plan, a scheme, or protolinguistic vision.

The so-called external stimuli are the raw material out of which the creative artist—who is very active at the nucleus of consciousness—has to fashion a world of rich and varied forms, each symbolizing a deeply cherished value or fear of the individual. Only a fragment of a physical factor goes into the creation of an otherwise mythical elaboration of names, forms, relationships, values, and meanings. The creator emerges out of the act of creation; the knower emerges out of the act of knowing; the enjoyer emerges out of the constantly changing scenario that is continuously making demands on the person's sensory observation and faculty of judgment to evaluate the passing show. This is the problem that is presented in this sūtra. Even elements like water have to change to fit into the scheme of things, becoming vapor, droplets, or ice. This is also true of the psychosomatic system: an external environmental factor and an inner law of conformity have to come to a term of agreement through the mysterious function of a global homeostasis. We will have occasion to explain this as we go further.

Sūtra I:5

vṛttayaḥ pañactayyaḥ kliṣṭākliṣṭaḥ

vṛttayaḥ: the modifications [are]
pañcatayyaḥ: fivefold
kliṣṭa: [some] labored (painful), obstructed, afflicted
akliṣṭaḥ: [and others] spontaneous (not painful), unobstructed, not afflicted

The modifications are fivefold, some labored (painful) and others spontaneous (not painful).

The modifications of consciousness can be spontaneous or labored. We have already seen that consciousness is stream-like. Therefore, it is only natural for it to move from one form to another. The difference between the spontaneous and labored can be easily recognized by examining two states of mind, "seeing" and "looking." When the mind is passive and there is nothing engaging our attention, the panorama of the external world is presented to our senses. Without effort, we become aware of forms that are seen, sounds that are heard, and the tactual sensation of the warmth or cold of the air outside. On most occasions, these sensations are easily recognized without any discrepancy.

We get into a different frame of mind when we look for something such as in the attempt to isolate a special kind of bacteria in a sample of sputum or blood placed under a microscope. Then our attention has to be focused with effort so that the right object may be clearly seen. We cannot focus our attention on an object under study and go into a reverie at the same time. Many young students complain that when they study for an examination and want to master a piece, they feel sleepy and have to labor their brains to be attentive. If a person wants to present a controversial thesis before a learned audience, and if that person sees a rival who has disgraced him several times before, he may lose all confidence and be unable to present a formidable argument. These are occasions where the modifications of mind become labored.

The body is not to be understood as a mass of flesh and bones, and the mind as a vaporous epiphenomenon. The psychosomatic system is like a well-structured and fully organized device in which there are several ingenious faculties operating in liaison with several communications carried out by the influx of energies through the sensory system and the outward flow of energies through the motor system. The passage of a certain energy from the body limits to an interior faculty can be compared to a person finding his way through a jungle or a grassy meadow. When that person or several others walk on the same path many times, it becomes as clear as a well laid-out road. A similar kind of culturing process happens in the passage of energy through the neurons. The electrochemical consolidations that are made as a result of stimulation and the commands carried out by the motor system all register impressions. Many internal alignments are established.

The psychosomatic system is cultured through various kinds of programming. All programs are not received or performed consciously. To meet its biological needs, the body itself carries out several functions preliminary to the conscious performance of an act. Thus, half of the culturing process happens in the unconscious depth of the psychosomatic system. In most cases the terminus of these inner operations is marked by the illumination of an awareness where we become conscious of the result of a performance. This conscious process engraves several permanent features in our minds. Yogis call this the *karmāśaya* of the organism. When the process culminates in the conscious recognition of a perception or an action performance of the presentation of a value, it is called khyāti. Khyāti is a comprehension of the qualities of the object presented to the organism.

Even when a person is in utmost trouble such as being exposed to intense physical pain, social pressure, moral shame, guilt, restlessness, frustration, or depression, there is one spark of consciousness that is unaffected by any of these states. It simply reports: "I am now in this state." In that particular point of consciousness there is no pain, no fear, no anxiety, even though its counterpart may be in pain, fearful, sentimental, or hilarious. It is like a neutral witness faithfully reporting to the person concerned, "This is what is happening now." It is not a belabored finding. It is steady, consistent, and faithful. It has only the clarity of pure certitude, just like in mathematical logic.

A division can be made somewhat between the judging witness and the subject being considered by the judge. The witnessing consciousness is also the validating consciousness. It is as if the painful and the not painful streaks of consciousness are running parallel with an intermittent emphasis that is sometimes on validation and sometimes on affectivity.

Events are not registered on a clean slate. Each time a centrifugal reverberation is created in the psychosomatic apparatus, all the latent culturings of the past are stirred and the most relevant of the potencies that have been acquired surge into dynamic operation. This, in turn, creates new potencies to come to fruition in the future. If the painful *(kliṣṭa)* tendencies are slowly weaned off, the neutral witnessing consciousness *(akliṣṭa)* can shine forth in its full effulgence. Such is the view of Vyāsa about vṛtti, modifications.

Sūtra I:6

pramāṇa viparyaya vikalpa nidrā smṛtayaḥ

pramāṇa: [they are:] real cognition, right or valid knowledge

viparyaya: unreal or false cognition

vikalpa: confused cognition, imaginary cognition, verbal delusion

nidrā: deep sleep, dreamless sleep state

smṛtayaḥ: [and] memory

They are: real cognition, unreal cognition, imaginary cognition, deep sleep, and memory.

Sūtra I:7

pratyakṣānumānāgamāḥ pramāṇāni

pratyakṣa: direct perception
anumāna: inference
āgamāḥ: [and] authoritative verbal testimony, revelation
pramāṇāni: are the valid means of real cognition, right or valid knowledge

Direct perception, inference, and authoritative verbal testimony are the valid means of real cognition.

In sūtra five we were told that there are five modifications of consciousness, which include the painful (kliṣṭa) and the nonpainful (akliṣṭa). They are enumerated here as *pramāṇa* (real or valid cognition), *viparyaya* (unreal or false cognition), *vikalpa* (imaginary cognition or verbal delusion), *nidrā* (deep sleep), and *smṛti* (memory).

Prama means "certitude." The definition of *pramāṇa* is *pramakaraṇam kāraṇam pramāṇam:* "the cause by which one arrives at certitude is the right method, *pramāṇa*." Valid testimonials of methodology are called pramāṇa. Pramāṇa is a spontaneous function coming from the witnessing consciousness that provides certitude about the nature of the thing perceived or even the idea thought of. In the empirical world, certitude is more or less a conventional common consent that most members of a group give to the description of an object of knowledge that can be empirically experienced.

For instance, it is generally agreed that salt has a certain taste that is agreeable when moderately used in certain dishes.

When a pinch of common salt is shown to a person, it is usually recognized to be salt. It can even be distinguished from a spoon of sugar. In the empirical world, such knowledge is valid. When something is understood here and now, as others would also understand it, it is considered to be right perception. In Sanskrit, describing a thing as it is in the here and now is called *yathārtha*.

There can be a superior understanding of the same pinch of salt if you know the chemical constituents of its molecular structure, technically called sodium chloride. A scientist can push it even further to the extent of seeing the molecules in their primary atomic nature and seeing even the atoms as electrons flying around a nucleus. The electrons, protons, and neutrons can be further reduced to a mathematical entity, which can be called the ultimate truth of common salt. When we arrive at such knowledge, it no longer has any empirical value but it has a high scientific recognition as the ultimate knowledge, *paramārtha*.

Thus, between empirical validity and ultimate knowledge, there can be several shades of understanding. The static norms of the physical world cannot always give a precise understanding when they are applied in a changing world where all the finer elements of matter are in an eternal flux. To meet this challenge, geometry and algebra are put together and mathematicians have arrived at new instruments of normative measurement such as scalars, tensors, and so on. Whether it is mere empirical apprehension or mathematical and philosophical comprehension, the field where judgment takes place, the cognitive function, is not painful. It is akliṣṭa. For this reason, the modification of consciousness catalogued here as pramāṇa is considered non-painful.

A certain person claims he is God. Most people, on rational grounds, will immediately dismiss that claim as a hallucinative obsession. Do we know God so that we check with all aspects of the person concerned to verify the veracity of his claim? We do not. Two entities are involved that need to be observed and examined. The person before us has an objective, physical body that can be perceived. God is a philosophical notion that can be understood only in terms of subjective conceptualization. As we move from a percept to a concept, even when that concept is a direct counterpart of the perceived object, all the details of direct perception are dropped and a generalized idea is accepted, which has only the essential marks of the object already perceived. When the percept comes as a stimulation through the organs of perception, it activates the memory tags of corresponding concepts that otherwise remain dormant in causal consciousness.

In Western psychology, causal consciousness is identified with the unconscious. No perceptual identification is possible without the percept being instantaneously paired with its corresponding conceptual image. Neither the ancient sciences nor the modern sciences know where and how concepts are so conveniently stacked that their memory tags can be pulled. After developing the study of cybernetics we began to imagine that there should be something similar to memory cards held in the folds of the brain. So far, this claim has not been substantiated with proof of any biochemical substance that shows evidence of undergoing chemical changes in a one-to-one correspondence with everything perceived, registered in memory, and retained for recall.

In the most recent findings about the neurophysiology of the brain, researchers have come to the conclusion that there are no photographic mental images or tonal acoustic images configuring the brain that have any correspondence to the objects and sounds outside. New molecular theories have been put forward, based on the assumption that there are reverberations of certain hypothetical nets in the brain, which make some sort of a magical presentation of certain patterned designs that are experienced as the awareness of forms or sounds, or other sensory data. A detailed study of this phenomenon in terms of physiological psychology can be found in Warren McCulloch's *The Embodiment of Mind*, Richard Thompson's *Introduction to Physiological Psychology*, William R. Uttal's *The Psychobiology of Mind*, and *The Self and Its Brain* by Karl Popper and John Eccles. None of these studies are conclusive because the direct study of the human brain has been very meager.

Eastern schools have an entirely different way of approaching the study of the phenomenon of memory storage and recall. In the Indian approach, the individuated self is understood to have four alternating states, each with its distinct focus of consciousness. In a crude way their alternation is analogous to the changing of gears in an automobile. In Western physiological psychology, the closest we come to this idea is the shift from cortical to subcortical functions. The four alternating foci are: the world-generating consciousness (*viśvātma*), creative subjectivity (*taijasātma*), causally retentive de-structured consciousness (*kāraṇātma*), and all-witnessing omniscience (*turīya*). They proceed from the gross and physical to the transcendental.

Instead of tracing the occurrence of an experience from the provocation of a neuron of the physical body such as of the retina, eardrum, skin, and so on, the Indian always goes from the most transcendent to the causal, from the causal to the regenerative or re-creative, and from the regenerative to an actualization at the concrete level. This is a discipline never attempted in the West. Therefore, both its methodology and application should be studied minutely to gain a general understanding of the scheme we are speaking of here.

The difficulty involved was put in a poignant manner by Bertrand Russell when he said "You cannot make a clay model of Spirit." But from childhood we have always been presented with models to aid us in understanding ideas. We see, understand, and then believe. Now the order is to be reversed. Most people are not even familiar with the pure state of consciousness, which is said to be what we imperientially become in a state of total absorption, *nirvikalpa samādhi*.

The transcendental state has reference to pure, total absorption. The first stir in that is to be imagined as the nucleus of individuation whereby a vortex is formed in the otherwise calm and serene indivisible consciousness. In the continuation of individuation, the first major principle that comes into vogue is the time factor, the sequential movement that can be progressive or regressive. Ideas arise in a sequential manner, not with words as such, but as configurations in which the essence of all the five faculties of perception are blended in a holistic occurrence. This is the causal consciousness entering into the subjective realms of a self-created world of images. Pain/pleasure conditionings of these images act as incentives to look for the pleasurable and avoid the painful. From there on a more horizontalized actualization of consciousness arises to relate the subtle inner organs to their corresponding organs of physical perception. Now our psychophysical equipment is ready to select external stimuli to structure a world of interest with positive, negative, or indifferent value significance. The result is the registration of a perception at a physical level.

The certitude of what is experienced is not limited to the physical or physiochemical source of the energy that is highlighted in an act of perception. It always has reference to the total need of the person, which is a historical summation of all the evolutionary processes involved in the formation of each individual. That is why a return to the source, *pratiprasava*, is the most important theme to study in Yoga. The *viśva* (actualizing), the *taijasa* (imaginative), the *avyākṛta* (causal), and the *sākṣi* (witness) come in a graded manner. The most difficult part is to find in the neutral witnessing consciousness a negative streak that accounts for the furtherance of the causal, the imaginative, and the actualizing propensities of a living organism. In spite of the universal sharing of concepts and meanings, an individual's conceptualization is a highly specialized, unique phenomenon. It is that uniqueness that causes two people to come to variant conclusions. To remedy this variance in inferences, deductive or inductive, a second opinion is sought in the records of authentic wise people.

Every perception is a challenge. At most what comes from the external world is a quantum of energy that tickles a few receptors. The mind is required to interpret the source of that energy and formulate a meaningful picture.

There is a mysterious bond of polarization between the massive source of the radiation of light, the Sun, which exists millions of miles away from Earth, and the tiny little eye of a mango fly receiving that light, which triggers its program of the day. How big the Sun, and how minute the eye that sees it! From the eye's seeing comes the very significance of the universal functioning.

We can understand this better when we place ourselves in a particular situation. What is presented before us may be only a small object such as a book or a pen. The book or pen cannot hang in empty nothingness. They are to be placed in a spatial setting with several adjacent entities. There is always a total picture to serve as an appropriate background for any object we perceive. The luxury of such extensive observation—which the mind makes in full resonance with things existing outside—is only a fragment of our active perception. We remember and bring in a portion of the past history of the pen and book, which can sometimes be taken as far back as the hypothetical Big Bang with which the universe started. Similarly, the pen a person holds to write a prayer on world peace can bring to that person's mind the unpredictable and unexplored future of humanity.

Considering the vastness of the awareness that is appended to every tactual recognition, it is easy to see that we perceive little and infer a lot. There is nothing called pure perception. It is the quality of a concept with its inferential richness that gives meaning to every percept. Narayana Guru gives us an example to understand this very strange occurrence that is happening to all of us every day. A person enters a room for the first time and sees a pot. Instantaneously, he recognizes that the pot belongs to a very ancient age. It is easy to understand that a person can perceive the form and color of an object placed before him. In the present example, however, what impresses the viewer is the antiquity of the pot that he apprehends along with the perception of the pot. Guru gives another example. A person sees a tree in a dream and thinks that it is a very old tree. Here even the perception is only a subjective imagination. Even in imagination, a temporal assessment is inferentially carried out.

What exactly is happening in the faculty of perception when such enormous details of inferential reasoning are also included? Inference becomes even more complicated when we pass on from formal inference to dialectical reasoning where we are obliged to hold good to our own inference as well as inferentially, intuitively, or instinctively knowing what our mate or rival is seeing and inferring when placed in the identical situation. These are issues too complicated for an experimental psychologist. The theoretical physicist has an advantage over the practical physicist. Similarly, the experimental psychologist needs the collaboration of an intuitive philosopher at this level. It is for this reason that inference is complemented with the valid testimony of a master mind.

A mirror is a transparent glass piece with silver paint on one side. You can hold it facing any direction, up to any object, and see in it a true reflection of the objects before it. Although this is a very great miracle, we take for granted that a polished surface can reflect objects because of our familiarity with it. As we look through the five windows of sense perception, there is an invisible mirroring agent that synchronizes the pictures coming through the sense organs. This synchronized effect is what we call perception. For want of any clear comprehension of the event of synchronization, we postulate a mind and believe that it is functioning behind the senses. It is as good or bad as believing that there is a God who is managing the universe from behind. If we believe in our mind, there is no reason to disbelieve in God, because both hypotheses belong to the same order. As external organs can be clearly seen and verified, we know that the synchronicity of data, the selection made in structuring, the inflow of energy, and the ensemble that is configured are not attributable to any one sense organ. For the sake of convenience, we postulate an inner organ, the mind.

The cognizance of an object is not merely the passive witnessing of a figure, because it is accompanied by many bodily changes such as emotional upheavals, or the experience of anxiety, fear, or confidence in confronting a situation. The most important factor to reckon with in Indian psychology is the recognition of the primordial function of the Self as the perceiving and coordinating agent behind all perceptions. Take, for instance, a middle-aged person who has difficulty in reading or seeing when he holds a book at a normal distance. By holding the book far, or perhaps near, he can correct his vision. Nowadays, vision is corrected by glasses. Do the glasses have any power to read? The glasses do not see anything. If there is dirt, moisture, or grease on the glasses, the person cannot see clearly. It is also important to have a proper prescription. And yet glasses are only an accessory.

Similarly, what we call our external eyes are also accessories. Even the mind that is supposed to be gathering data from all the senses and putting them together into a meaningful configuration is not the seer. Its function can be tampered with by the use of alcohol or any stimulant of the brain such as mind-blowing drugs. The actual source of knowledge remains elusive.

To overcome this difficulty in explaining the function of the mind, the inner organ is further divided into four aspects on functional grounds: search, comparison with previous conditioning, decision-making, and value-affectivity. In the concept of the inner organ, the organic interrelatedness between physical, chemical, and biological operations and the elusive impact of members that congregate in the reception of the same stimuli are all to be taken together. In this joint venture, both helpful insight as well as defective functioning can occur. The next aphorism refers to the defective functioning that adversely affects the bona fide of perception.

Sūtra I:8

viparyayaḥ mithyājñām atad rūpa pratiṣṭham

viparyayaḥ: unreal or false cognition

mithyājñānam: misconception, erroneous or false knowledge

atad: not that

rūpa: essential nature or form

pratiṣṭham: established on, based on, occupying

Unreal cognition is misconception, not established on essential nature.

In empirical knowledge, the mark of truth comes from the irrefutability of a perception about which there is common consent. The idiom, "calling a spade a spade," is a classical example of the irrefutability of empirical facts. However, individual persons do not always see a physical thing as it is. It is even worse when the cognition involves psychologically or sociologically significant overtones. A mal-perception often arises from a misconception. Misconception is a phenomena that is to be studied in its origin, formation, and maintenance, which can all be emotionally tainted with circumstantial conditionings due to personality traits and sociological conventions.

In a snake-infested place, which fosters a hidden fear of getting into an encounter with a snake at any moment, a paranoid person who sees a small piece of rope lying in semi-darkness may forthwith take it for a snake. This is an instance of mal-perception generated by a conditioned fear of a snake form. Another person, hanging his naked feet down from his bed, when touched by a cat's nose, may shriek in fear thinking a snake is slithering by his leg. This is a similar mal-perception caused by a conditioned fear of touch. The coldness of the touch is taken by this frightened person for the touch of a snake. A child cries on seeing a stranger with unkempt hair and long beard, taking him for a weird character of whom the child heard in a fairy tale. In the first two instances, fear was roused because of memories of previous perceptions that had partial resemblance to what was being presented. In the third instance, fear was roused on the basis of an imagination that was put in the child's mind by verbal descriptions in a story.

In our own lives we can see that we are fed not with three but three million occasions of such conditionings. The human bio-computer can, in most cases, pull the wrong tag of memory and a vaguely presented complex can be easily complemented with an inappropriate concept. Sometimes the arousal of a strong emotion can be stimulated not by what we see, but by the absence of what we expect to see. A negative perception can have an even worse effect than a positive perception. If a person expects another to smile but sees a frown instead, a negative reaction can occur.

The crucifix above the altar of a Catholic church is a piece of metal or marble and there is no Christ in it. The Śivaliṅga of a Śiva temple or on the altar of worship in a home is only a fashioned piece of granite. There is no Śiva in it. Yet, the social convention of the Catholics makes it valid for all Jesus-worshippers to identify the metal or marble piece with Jesus. Similarly, the social convention of the Śiva-worshippers makes them reverentially look upon a piece of stone as Śiva. If a nonconformist treats the crucifix as a mundane thing or tramples on a Śivaliṅga, the public will even condemn him for acting in a sacrilegious manner. The physicality of what one perceives does not always correspond to the expected reality of an object.

In the quarrels of married couples or lovers, we can hear one of them lamenting that he or she is at a loss to show to the other the fire of love that is burning in his or her heart. In self-pity, many people lament that they are not understood by others. When a person thinks he is absolutely honest, it becomes unbearable for him to know that others treat him as a hypocrite. Thus, we can go on adding several varieties of examples in which the inferential perception of unreal cognition (viparyaya) abounds.

A two year old child asked for biscuits. Biscuits were not immediately available, so the mother said: "Wait for ten minutes until I send somebody to the shop for biscuits." But the child protested and said "I want biscuits that are not bought." Not knowing the tantrum of the child, the mother asked for time to buy them. But the child raised her voice and continued to shout, "I want biscuits that are not bought." Here is a case of viparyaya in which the child's mind is immediately tuned to a contradictory situation. The posture of the child is the same as that taken by opposition parties in parliaments, politicians who counter their rivals, and in the case of superpowers who hold out menacing threats to each other in a cold war situation. Not agreeing with the adversary is a defense tactic for self-existence. A hooded cobra can easily twist its neck to the right or left, to bite and discharge its venom. This natural ability of the defense mechanism to shift from one psychological set to another is not merely an incident of erroneous cognition but a wantonly-held bigoted position used to push away a threatening situation and aggressively support an indefensible stand.

In both the macrocosm and the microcosm, the two extreme limits are blinding darkness and blinding brilliance. Darkness is not merely the absence of light. It has the power to conceal. It shares with inertia the power of obstructing mobility. In his monadology, Leibnitz speaks of the gradation of monads that range from the darkest to the most brilliant, which can clearly reflect all other monads. In the West we come across concepts like the conscious and the unconscious. Nescience *(avidyā)* includes both the unconscious and the unknown. This is contrasted with knowledge *(vidyā)*, which is also sometimes identified with wisdom. What humanity always prays for is to be led from non-existence to existence, from darkness to light and from death to immortality. Thus darkness is identical with non-existence and death.

Vyāsa classifies the obstructing darkness into five states: *tamas, moha, mahāmoha, tamiśram, andha tamiśram.* Tamas is one of the three properties of nature and is a condition for delusion. Darkness and inertia make memory corrode and consequently partial or total forgetfulness (moha) can arise. When one forgets one's own true Self, false identification can easily follow. Thus moha is not mere forgetfulness. It can also indicate desires born out of forgetfulness. When forgetfulness is extreme, it is mahāmoha. Mahāmoha also indicates the generic forgetfulness with which all sentient beings are afflicted. In the power of cognition, people experience different degrees of confrontation with darkness. Beyond stepping up reason to a certain degree, many cannot move, and complain of incomprehension. Such a state is called tamiśram. When a person's vāsanās or samskāras are so very deeply conditioned, it is as if that person cannot raise himself or herself, even to imagine that there could be unconditioned states. Such absolute darkness to which individual minds are tied up forever is called andha tamiśram.

Sūtra I:9

śabda jñānānupātī vastu śūnyo vikalpaḥ

śabda: words, sound, verbal expression
jñāna: knowledge
anupātī: arising from, relying upon, following
vastu: objective reality, substance
śūnyaḥ: [and] devoid of, empty
vikalpaḥ: [is] imaginary cognition, confused cognition, verbal delusion

Knowledge arising from words and devoid of objective reality is imaginary cognition.

In the *Yoga Vasiṣṭha* a good example is given of vikalpa (imaginary cognition) in the form of a story retold to children. The story goes as follows: "Once there was a king and his queens were all barren. A hundred princes were born of the barren mothers. The princes mounted horses which had no legs and no heads and went galloping to the banks of a river which had no water. There they cooked food in pots which had no bottoms and fed a thousand brahmins who had neither mouths nor bellies."

A child's interest is only that of listening to a story. It need not make any sense. Even expressions like a "square circle" or "palaces in the clouds" produce some corresponding idea in the mind of the listener. It is a basic requirement of the consciousness associated with hearing to conjure up a form that can offer a basis for spoken words to be retained in the mind. These are like the ghosts of concepts. Like an artist making a collage, fragments of memories can be disassociated from their original context and a fresh composition can be made that has only a verbal basis and not any precise meaning as such. If someone says "In a forest I saw a chianchuchi which is a hybrid species of the praying mantis and a giraffe, with the spirit of a mosquito for its soul," the listener's mind will not altogether reject the possibility of such a composition. Further, the thought may even have a lyrical fascination and an artist may be tempted to paint it. Some of the most brilliant literary expositions that are considered classics fall into this category, such as Dante's *Divine Comedy*, the *Viśvarūpa Darśana* of the *Gita*, *Interior Castle* of St. Teresa of Avila and the famous vision of Ezekiel of the *Old Testament*.

We may ask, "Why should we study such phenomena?" In society, we do not live in empty psychic space. Like straw and waste paper that are abundantly used in packing cases to hold fragile things in position, people use a lot of meaningless word-garbage to ensure certain relationships and to accomplish deep interests of their own. When young lovers are together, they are so fond of listening to each other's voices that they speak what is commonly recognized as sweet nothings. Each one paints their future in glowing colors and offers a thousand promises as a mark of their love and dedication. Thus, a family unit is very often erected on a false foundation; disillusionment comes when the couple starts living together and facing the facts of life. Erotics stimulate illusory and hallucinative thinking, which can be exaggerated to such an extent of infatuation that the votaries can lose their grip with reality.

Similar situations arise when mass hysteria is whipped up by politicians who incite the imagination of the potential voters of a constituency with many false promises. Soon after the election is over, people sadly discover the emptiness of words. This can lead to political discontent, strife, and even civil war. Much more disastrous are the false imaginations that priests create in the minds of their congregates. Imaginary hells and heavens are painted in such vivid colors that even a man of science can be tempted to give the benefit of the doubt to the imagination-monger. Another terrible field of imagination is the advertising of consumer goods with fascinating media techniques such as of musical and colorful movies. Thus, the world of vikalpa can be considered our number one social as well as personal enemy. Like junk mail, from all sides we are bombarded with stimuli for indulging in false imaginations. They can adversely affect our creativity and the social reality of the situation in which we live and work.

There is a Tibetan story that illustrates the negative dynamics of vikalpa. It is customary in Tibet for a lama to give a present to his disciple when the disciple leaves the lamasery for good. A poverty-stricken lama had nothing with him to give as a gift to his departing disciple. He had an old donkey that was very sickly. The guru gladly gave away the donkey to his disciple. With much hesitation the disciple led the donkey down the steep terrain. When he reached the valley the donkey died. The disciple dug a pit and put the corpse of the donkey in it. While he was burying it a caravan came that way. The traders inquired what he was doing. He said he was burying his old guru. On hearing this, with great reverence the merchants made offerings of money and clothes at the burial site. Seeing the chance for a lucrative business, the disciple stayed there. Soon there arose a fabulous temple and all kinds of sickly people trudged their way to the new lamasery for spiritual healing. When the guru heard of his disciple's success, he also came to pay his obeisance to the sacred relic of the saint on whose mortal coil the lamasery was built. Then the disciple confessed to his guru that it was not a saint but only the donkey the guru had given him. On hearing this, the guru was very pleased. He said, "You are my most sensible disciple. The temple of my lamasery is built on the mortal coil of the mother of this donkey."

Such stories can be told about every religion of this world. Nothing is more handy for exploitation than colorful lies. So it is absolutely necessary that people should be spared from the evils of vikalpa.

Sūtra I:10

abhāva pratyaya ālambanā vṛttirnidrā

abhāva: [of] non-existence, absence, negation
pratyaya: [that has the] cognition, content, consciousness
ālambanā: [for its] substratum, basis
vṛttiḥ: [is the] modification, modulation, oscillation, function
nidrā: deep sleep, dreamless sleep state

Deep sleep is the modification that has the cognition of non-existence for its substratum.

To understand sleep one should know what modification is. We have already dealt with modification as coming into confrontation with sense objects or the recurrence of associated ideas in the form of thoughts or the recalling of memory. Thus there is always something to know, something to be confronted by. This we have already mentioned as prakhyā. The outgoing search is for objects, and turning in is to be with oneself. The awareness of either an object matter or a subject matter can lead to a reaction ensuing from the knowledge that is illuminated. This reaction is what we call pravṛtti. While prakhyā is an undisturbed state, pravṛtti is the generation of a lot of energy that circulates through the sensory and motor system. To remember each experience, the internal changes that happen electrically and chemically need to be held for some time so that they become consolidated into a deposit of an information bit for further recall. Thus there is a pause—an intermittent silence, a state of inertia—which comes naturally after every prakhyā and pravṛtti as an inevitable consequence. This is sthiti.

When sthiti overrules the situation, prakhyā and pravṛtti subside. As sthiti is a state of inertia, it is conceived of as an enveloping or veiling principle of nescience, the darkness of the tamasic property of nature. In such a case there can be only one prakhyā, the knowledge of nonexistence or tamas. But the cognizing consciousness does not become inoperative. It turns on itself. So after a spell of sleep, we can recall that our sleep was undisturbed. Thus, during sleep there is no cessation of modification but modification is not of the nature of external perception, nor of the nature of engaging in any action. Even when a person is sitting in jet black darkness, he can look around and see darkness. A person confined to absolute silence can certainly listen to silence. But silence has no specific mode to be copied. Sleep comes when we disengage our mind and sense organs from carrying out any mission: the senses are not particularly directed to any object; the motor system is not asked to carry out any errand; the peace to which we put ourselves helps us just to be. Where prakhyā and pravṛtti were dominant, sthiti now comes. The seer is cut off from all objects of perception. As modification is still going on, this state cannot be identified with samādhi or absorption.

Sūtra I:11

anubhūta viṣaya asampramoṣaḥ smṛtiḥ

anubhūta: [of] experienced
viṣaya: impressions, objects of sensory experience
asampramoṣaḥ: the not slipping away, not being lost
smṛtiḥ: memory [is]

Memory is the not slipping away of experienced impressions.

Memory is one of the most mysterious experiences that all of us have every day. What we presently experience disappears from our cognitive attention. Where does it go? Afterward, when we want to mentally reconstruct a situation that we have already lived, images that have approximate correspondence with what we have experienced reappear in our consciousness. Factually, what we see in such a recall is not physically presented to our senses. The recall is a purely subjective experience. Subjective means that it has no objective counterpart or corresponding data sitting outside. That means an experience that has gone out of awareness remains in some form within the cognizing system in a concealed manner. Freud and others in the West prefer to infer that experiences go out of consciousness into the unconscious and, on recall, present a corresponding image to our attention. This phenomenon presents many questions and cannot be easily explained.

What is basically implied in the study of memory is the human body and its constituent parts. We have memory of sight, hearing, touch, smell, taste. We have memory of time and space. We have memory in which all these factors are harmoniously blended to give meaningful situations. The senses and the mind contribute to the registration of experience. In that registration, some process takes place, which condenses the experience into a mysterious code or information bit. The most impressive fact about life is that there is a will to live. Even simple reflexes like the winking of an eye, the pulling of our feet from where they rest, sneezing, or coughing, are instantaneously programmed to aid the biologic continuance of the body with its sensitivity and manifesting states of consciousness. So, everything is happening within this body, and it is with thc definite purposes of self-preservation, self-continuation, and self-propagation. These being deeply ingrained biological principles that we share with all other living beings, most of the self-programmed actions and reactions of the psychosomatic system are not presented to the conscious mind. That is why we have to infer and make many shrewd guesses to understand the intricacy of the memorizing and recalling system.

We live in a world where the microcosm is poised to relate with the macrocosm and the macrocosm, without any conscious effort, aids the microcosm to be in alignment. Like the monads of Leibnitz, each one of us mirrors most of everything and everyone around us, with different degrees of clarity. The mirroring is happening with systematic selection and screening to suit the type to which each individual belongs and the motivations that are functionally operative in each individual. Mirroring also implies mimicking or imitating. The learning process is also a process of reflecting, imitating, and repeating what others are doing, saying, or experiencing. This is the general situation in which we are all placed.

We should also have a picture of this macro-micro setting to understand how the microcosm evolves to its maximal capacity to reflect and imitate the world around it. According to the Sāṅkhyan philosophy, which Yoga accepts, the self-conscious principle that is imprisoned in nature's device of the psychophysical system is puruṣa. It has its own stamp of existentiality. It exists by its own merit. It is *sat*. Or simply, it is. Secondly, it is self-radiant, *cit*. Its radiance is not light, but knowledge. That knowledge not only illuminates surrounding things, but also transforms itself into a conditional state of homogeneity by which it assumes the property of that which it reflects. All such reflected illuminations become meaningful to the perceiving consciousness of puruṣa. The meaning arises out of its own normative notion, which the yogis recognize as ānanda. This is a simplified picture of puruṣa.

Puruṣa can be conceived as a mathematical point having only location and no dimension whatsoever. In its elaboration in the spatio-temporal physicality of things, it can assume all geometrical forms and can be specific with the advantage of innumerable nomenclature. This elaborated system is known as prakṛti, or the somatic aspect of the psyche. Corresponding to the sat, cit, and ānanda of the puruṣa, the basis of the somatic elaboration (prakṛti) is composed of identifiable factuality (sattva), operational dynamics (rajas), and stabilizing fixations (tamas).

Although we cannot demonstrate the existence of any spirit as such, the anatomy of consciousness and its elaboration into the learning, remembering, and imitating mechanism can be seen in the morphologic structuring of the living body. At one end of the trunk is the head with sense organs for the input of various kinds of information. At the other end are the excretory organs of which the genitals are the most important faculty. In the mid-region of the trunk are the heart, the lungs, and belly, which are continuously replenishing the system with the physical energy that is required for the functioning of the organism. We have already mentioned the biologic requirement of the organism to grow to adulthood and propagate the species through its multiplication. The very word *prakṛti* means "that which replicates through its natural power of propagation." The existentiality of things is recognized with the cogitation that is taking place in the head. The pleasure of reproduction is experienced by the genital end of the body. All the emotional flurry that arises from the relating of existence with propagation is experienced in the mid-region, that is, the heart. The ear, the eye, and other sense perceptions automatically create in a person a subject-object duality of the perceiver and the perceived with which the perceiver is continuously relating through the acts of knowing and doing. If the sensory system declares the presence of a pleasurable object, messages pass from the head to the lower faculties and founts of energy are released from the lower region.

This reciprocation between the two extremes of the trunk is charted by the yogis who conceive of a parameter running vertically from the lower end of the body to the crown of the head. This parameter is marked with the channels through which vital energies traverse up and down. The ascending vital energy is recognized as *prāṇa* and the descending flow is called *apāna*. The slightest contact of the psychosomatic organism with a percept can alert the mechanism of vital energies.

Just as there is a physical source of light outside to illuminate physical objects, and the spiritual source of light within to receive the stimuli from outside, an individual also has two references in knowledge: one is the innate or genetic knowledge with which the individual has come into being; and the other is what is acquired from outside. Knowledge is a continuous process of modifying consciousness by relating innate knowledge with acquired knowledge. The matrix of consciousness is continuously changed by the unfolding of the innate and the comprehension of the external. Elaborations of this can be seen in the experimental and descriptive studies made by modern neurophysiologists. An organism is placed in the physical field of the mass that makes the body, the extension in which the body is placed with other bodies, and in a temporal scale of sequential and progressive change.

In correspondence with this physicality of the organism, it is also endowed with a consciousness in which every unit is labeled with appropriate names. Thus, two sets of functions are aligned from moment to moment: the perceiving of things and the recalling of their names. Perceiving is formal, with physical emphasis; recognition is conceptual and essential. For the factual brevity of the functional disposition of the living organism, it has a self-imposed delimitation of its value-horizon. A few themes are chosen as vital for its existence and many possibilities are allowed to slip away, mostly unconsciously, and sometimes with regret. Such is the composition of this organism in which memory plays its most important role to make life a purposive and meaningful reality.

Each cognition is pioneered with the presentation of a non-specific indication like the calling of attention. What occurs to our mind is the idea, "This is." The elaborated meaning is, "This is what is presented to me." "This" being non-specific, it is immediately followed by the question, "What is this?" That presents an occasion to look into previous experiences and assemble before our mind all relevant memories. Before the focusing of our attention on what is presented, an uncritical flash of judgment comes from the frozen past held together by tamas. Consequently, the first phase of cognition is bound to be prejudicial. Every occasion of cognition thus has a "this" and a "what" to look into. The "what" makes each cognition specific.

After the first flash of uncritical cognition, a need arises to connote the experience with more objective or critical confirmation. This is not a mere judgment of the data presented, but is also an evaluation of the worth of what is presented so that the right reaction can be made to it. Rating the value of anything leads to affectivity and, hence, three questions are before the mind of the cognizer: 1) Is it pleasurable and, in that case, can I possess it? 2) Is it painful and should I run away? 3) Is it passive and can I be indifferent to it? The answer has to come from our memory. Thus, memory is essentially conditioning with the colorations of pain, pleasure, and indifference.

In the Sanskrit language memory is called *smaraṇa* as well as *smṛti* and the Indian god of erotics is called Smara. This is an indication that the most remembered things are tied up with our libido or libidinal urges. Where the libidinal urges are pleasurably appeased, the sense of aesthetics is heightened. When Keats says, "A thing of beauty is a joy forever," he is equating beauty with aesthetic pleasure. Consequently, we develop attachment to the beautiful and pleasurable. In Indian mythology, Devi, the Creatress, is said to be harboring the god of erotics in her genital; she is described as "the beautifier of the three cities" of the past, present, and future, as well as the gross, the subtle, and the causal. She is polarized with transcendence, which is characteristic of Śiva, who is called "the burner of the three cities." Memory is the cause for bondage, and avoidance of relativistic memory brings freedom from the phenomenality of life. In short, the bulk of the content of mind is memory. And memory persuades a person to live obligatorily. The final goal of Yoga is transcendence, kaivalya, and hence smṛti or memory is considered a major obstacle or obstruction in the path of freedom.

Sūtra I:12

abhyāsa vairāgyābhyām tannirodhaḥ

abhyāsa: repetitive practice, application
vairāgyābhyām: by detachment, non-attachment, dispassion, desirelessness
tad: they [are]
nirodhaḥ: restraint, cessation

They are restrained by repetitive practice and detachment.

Every individual is subjected to two kinds of conditioning, genetic and environmental. Genetic conditioning is a conditioning in depth. This is viewed differently by Western schools and Indian schools.

The Western notion can be indicated by an example from Schrodinger. He calls our attention to a newborn calf. Just after the emergence of the calf from the cow's body, it lies helpless for only a couple of minutes. Then it gets up, walks straight to the udder of the cow, finds the teat of the mother without difficulty, and sucks milk. From where did the calf learn that this is how it should find its nourishment? After posing this question, Schrodinger says that in the calf there are the footprints of memories of ten thousand lives the calf has undergone. Schrodinger is a quantum physicist and not a theologian. He is not speaking of rebirth. His reference is to genetic reproduction and the accumulation of information bits as the stream of life passes from parent to child through countless millions of years. Thus the Western scientist sees the depth of memory as an evolutionary system responsible for the present biological world.

The Indian seers postulate the vertical perpetuation of an individuated personality that assumes new bodies after a pause called death. Thus the Indian seer sees a psychic depth whereas his Western counterpart sees a somatic depth. The Western notion is a horizontal view while the Indian one is vertical. Body and mind are not two separate entities. They are the polarized counterparts of a single system. The Western and Indian views can be profitably combined into a complementary whole. Whether taken genetically or as a psychic continuance, we come to the conclusion that every thought in us is deeply engrained. Our fear and hope are not surface manifestations. In that case, the problem of erasing a conditioning, changing a habit, and reorganizing our mind cannot be easily accomplished. The whole theory of conditioning and deconditioning is epitomized in a verse of the *Bhagavad Gita*. In chapter IV, verse 13, Krishna says: "The fourfold color grades *(varṇas)* were created by myself on the basis of innate disposition *(guṇa)* and vocation *(karma)* that accorded with each; know Me to be the maker of such, as also to be its non-doer, unexpended."[1]

The four colors spoken of here are analogically similar to Jung's classifications of extrovert and introvert. The two main dispositions are to be active by temperament or to be contemplative by temperament. Among the activists, there are those who are very obsessed with the necessities of life; they spend all their time tied up with action, especially of an obligatory kind. They slave under other people, seeking nothing but the physical sustenance of life. Such people's minds are colored with self-pity *(śoka)*. Because they are perishing in their state of despair as if they are dissolving in self-pity, they are called *śūdras*.

Then there are those who are obsessed with the need for security. They are always scheming and planning. With their cunning, they make reserves for themselves. They enjoy the freedom they buy with their earnings. They are the transactionists, *vaiśyas*. Then there are those who are romantic in their ideologies and are willing to sacrifice their body and leisure for upholding high human values. They take upon themselves the burden of facilitating an orderly, peaceful life for others in their community. They are *kṣatriyas*.

Then there are the pure contemplatives who value the freedom of their souls and sacrifice only a minimum of their freedom for the sustenance of their lives. Learning is their main pursuit. Wisdom is their reserve for security. They are *brāhmins*. These four classifications are natural colors that give specific characteristics to people's personalities through the laws that govern the biological, psychological, and sociological needs of the human species. Unfortunately, in India these have been looked upon as permanent classes and the system has degenerated into a rigid caste system.

In the *Gita* Krishna as a representative of the Absolute says, "As the abiding law in everyone and everything, I am the creator of psychic colorations." At the same time he graciously points out that each person can also be the undoer of the color that he or she has accumulated in the present life or through several lives. Where you are the undoer of the psychic coloration of your personality, the Divine does not interfere. Therefore, the Divine is said to be the non-doer of the transformation you effect upon yourself. In another of Krishna's teachings in the *Gita*, it is said that what can manifest in you can only be what is already latent in you. However, everything latent in you need not necessarily be actualized.

For your actualization, you require appropriate instruments, congenial environments, and the will to actualize. Thus it is up to you to live in an environment that is not conducive for drawing out the potentials of any evil disposition with which you are genetically endowed. Again it is up to you not to will an action that can strengthen an evil saṃskāra, a malignant disposition. It is again in your power to nullify the potentiality of a negative force by accentuating the positive thrust of a benevolent disposition. This freedom of the individual to change himself or herself, to reorganize the psyche, is given in the present sūtra as the cultivation of detachment and repeated exercise in the building up of benevolent dispositions as well as the eradication of malevolent dispositions. The cultivation of non-attachment is here termed *vairāgya* and the repetitive practice by which a desirable potency can be actualized is called *abhyāsa*. We will have occasion to go into these in detail in the chapter on discipline (sādhana).

The modifications of the mind ensue from its triple characteristics: knowing, doing, and experiencing. These correspond to the three terms we gave at the very outset: prakhyā, pravṛtti, and sthiti. Prakhyā is knowing. General awareness is the backdrop of the several roles we play in our drama of life. It is within this general knowledge that several modifications arise. Each modification comes from the special attention that is given to properties that affect our sense organs and the impact that a sense impression creates on the affectivity of our psychosomatic system. By affectivity we mean the dual principles of pain and pleasure, and consequent attraction and repulsion.

Pleasure, attraction, and the incentive to return to the same experience are motivated by self-preservation. Pain, repulsion, and the accompanying fear are the negative counterparts of the instinct of self-preservation, which is of the nature of defense. Thus prakhyā is a very large field of awareness that is tied up with all the major instincts of life. The natural interests of a living organism spontaneously accept the role of the farmer or the hunter, the role of the procreator, the role of the defender, and so on. In all these roles, the person has to become very active.

Humans are not merely physical animals. We have several other dimensions apart from the physical, chemical, and biological. The more subtle realms in which we live are the familial system in which we have to play definite roles, and the social matrix in which we have to represent ourselves as individual persons, as members of a family, and as those who carry out their civic responsibilities. This social dimension requires us to adhere to the mores of our society, to respect conventions, and to uphold the enacted law of the community to which we have to show our allegiance. As the past is overbearing in the form of the collective memory of the community and the recorded chronicles of the human story on Earth, the individual is a continuator of culture and tradition. Part of the culture is the aesthetic consideration of the community and the several trial and error adventures that people were undergoing during each age. It is like a tapestry that is woven through the ages; every person living in the present has to add or subtract a little in the interplay of aesthetic interest, which consequently becomes our personal contribution to that knowledge. Thus knowledge and action are always going hand in hand.

Every conscious appreciation of a situation is a new commitment to the world order. To uncoil our personal consciousness, which is interwoven with the collective unconscious, is not as easy as we might imagine. In certain cases there has to be an abrupt breaking or the burning of bridges. This process is called *tapas*. Tapas is the general name for the cultivation of detachment and the repetition of helpful practice.

However advanced in the execution of a throughgoing scientific technology and cool in the critical logical consideration of facts most Western scientists may be, their minds still seem to be haunted by some Semitic archetypes, such as an angry Jehovah and a cunning Satan. This is evident in Freud's concept of the super ego that is identical with the jealous and angry Jehovah. The satanic, rebellious hankering of the Devil is passed on to the id. The ego stands in between as the tormented sinner. The biographers of Charles Darwin are obsessed with his sins, which they see as extricating from God his power to create and having incest with Mother Nature by assigning her the ingenuity of instituting evolution. The Indian elite, on the other hand, could never pay more than lip service to their gods. An Indian god is never more serious than Shakespeare's Puck or Ariel. After all, Brahma, Viṣṇu, Śiva, and Devi are all only poetic fancies, metaphorically referring to deeper psychic realities.

We need to bear all this in mind when we think of the science of disciplining consciousness—Yoga—which is different from the religious pursuits instituted by theistic religions. Yogis refer to two tendencies of human nature: descending and ascending. One is to give oneself into the hands of nature's pranks and live like a pig in the filthy swamp of life, becoming uncouth and selfish like wild animals who ruthlessly kill their prey, or always living in fear like a deer chased by a pack of wolves. This is what they describe as the descending path of attachment (rāga) and delusion (moha).

It is to contradict these tendencies that tapas is prescribed. It is an ascending path like that of a fish swimming against the current, a boat going upstream, or climbing a mountain with a heavy load. To drop anything—including our own body or even mind—is always aided by the gravitational pull of Earth and the earthiness in our mental attitude. Only with resolute determination can we ascend the path. This ascending path of tapas includes several disciplines that are to be integrated into a single holistic attempt, which is at once a purification (vairāgya) and the actualization of a hierarchy of values (abhyāsa).

We are presented with a number of phenomenological illusions that are customarily recognized as the facts of life. A person with an uncritical mind deems them so until he or she becomes disillusioned. Theoretical knowledge of the truthful, the good, and the beautiful is to be obtained from a bonafide teacher or the source books of recorded wisdom.

As an aspirant yogi you have to take initiative with unflagging interest, to have a critical examination of your preformed habits, and then scrape or modify the behavioral pattern in such a manner that it is cleansed of ignorant adherence to evil or superficial modes. Instead of a static view of an effect or a cause, you are expected to develop a transparency of vision by which you can clearly see the manifested effect and the entire process through which, from the primeval cause to the present effect, the manifestation came. You should also have the sagacity to unhook all expectations of the future from the performances in which you are presently engaged.

Nature is said to have two inverse impacts on our minds. One is the concealing of truth and the other is the precipitating of imaginary pictures that are easily taken for true. The veiling principle is called *āvaraṇa* and the projecting principle is called *vikṣepa*. Eliminating the vikṣepa from our mind will automatically pull off the veil. Every moment is thus a moment of challenge to decipher the mystery of life presented in the form of enigmas, paradoxes, and conundrums. That is why it is said that there is no holiday in spirituality and no one can act as a proxy. In India, this straight and honest approach to life has been watered down to the level of puerile snobbishness in the name of devotion *(bhakti)*. Many spend hours chanting and singing and getting nowhere other than into hysteric frenzies and raising their blood pressure. In the second chapter of this book we will have ample opportunities to dwell on the details of the discipline and the methods of actualization of values.

Sūtra I:13

tatra sthitau yatno'bhyāsaḥ

tatra: of these
sthitau: [to] maintain steadiness, stilling
yatnaḥ: the effort, the endeavor
abhyāsaḥ: repetitive practice, application

Of these, repetitive practice is the effort to maintain steadiness.

It is our common experience that our mental alertness is not always the same. In the morning, our body and mind are fresh and it is easy to apply our mind to anything that needs close attention. After an intake of food, such as a heavy breakfast or lunch, the body metabolism is affected by the secretion and action of the digestive juices. The flow of energy into the motor system is reduced, attention becomes less, and there is even a tendency to doze off. As night advances the energy flow decreases further and it is hard to restrain sleep. No cogitation takes place in sleep and it is as if many faculties of the psychosomatic system are closed down temporarily.

It is with such a body and mind that we have to practice the very difficult equalization of the oscillating function of consciousness that moves between the knower and the known. Half of our attention is to be given to objects that are external to our physical person, and the other half has to remain with the cognizing consciousness. The fluctuating attention, which alternately gives the idea of "I am knowing" and "this is what is known," is a state where active modification is going on. In Yoga practice, this modification has to attain a state of serenity in which the vibratory function of consciousness becomes so very even that attention does not shift from the mental space it occupies to any new item of perception or cogitation.

The effort required is sometimes said to be equivalent to the attention applied by a person who is dealing with a lion or a tiger that is performing for the spectators at a circus. The slightest slackening in the ringmaster's attention can result in a wholesale tragedy. Another example is given of a man balancing on the blade of a sharp sword. The same principle is nowadays spoken of as biofeedback. We can take an example of biofeedback to show how the yogi manages to successfully keep up the effort to occupy the neutral zero of consciousness and remain in that state, first for a long time and then perhaps forever.

One of the devices used in biofeedback training to establish the alpha wave of the brain is as follows: the trainee sits upright in a comfortable position. Three colored bulbs—red, yellow, and green—are placed at eye level. Cathodes are fixed on her temples and forehead and connected to a polygraph device. A person's brain waves are usually active between beta and delta waves. If they are delta, the red bulb will be the indication. When they oscillate between beta and delta, there will be alternate flickering of the yellow and red lights. If the trainee can compose her mind and make it as serene as possible, the red light will go off and the oscillation will be seen between the green light of alpha and the yellow light of beta. Finally, when the alpha is well established, the green light will show itself steadily. Then the trainee knows that her alpha is established; the green light she sees acts as a biofeedback. She puts all her efforts into being effortless and retaining the green light. It is a circulation of energy between the perceiving eye of the trainee and the motor system with which she restrains energy from flowing into any channel of distraction. In the beginning it seems very difficult, but after four or five trials she automatically becomes familiar with biofeedback and the neutrality of attention comes to stay. This mechanical conditioning, or rather electrical conditioning, requires her to look at an object outside. To that extent, she is confronted by perception.

In advanced yogic training, the yogi does not lean on any such crutches. The exercise is kept going by simply not feeding any memory with another associated memory. As a result, cognizing consciousness turns on itself to cognize cognition. Even that can be tiring because attention is also associated with an activation of the mind supported by rajas. Rajas can corrode into the serenity of sattva and the yogi can consequently become exhausted. Where there is a depletion of mental energy caused by the over-activation of rajas, tamas sets in with its benumbing inertia, and the attention lapses into fatigue and sleep. Thus rajas and tamas are two cardinal enemies of meditation.

Consciousness is not static. It is like a flowing stream. There are several conveyors of flow within us. The bloodstream flows through arteries and veins. The vitality of our breath is carried to all parts of the body through conveyors of prāṇa. There are channels where lymph flows. The nervous system is a matrix of conveyors carrying sensory and motor energies. The yogis add one more conveyor, *praśānta vāhita,* that which carries peace to every cell of our being.

Because of the many stimuli that bombard various receptors in our sensory system, the agitation that is brought in through our sense organs is different from that which comes from any other organ. Although the world is attractive in its colors and varied in its forms, by simply dropping the eyelids we can hold back the stimulation arising from sight in a fraction of a second. We cannot shut out the sounds that enter our ears in the same manner. Smell is another villainous stimulus that can attack us when we do not desire it in the least. With some will power we can refuse to taste what we do not like. Nowadays there are devices to regulate the heat and cold that come through the faculty of touch.

To gain tranquility, we have to secure our consciousness from exposure to the five sensory stimuli. There are a number of devices very ingeniously invented and practiced by yogis to tackle each sense organ. Most people close their eyes. This is not always an effective method because, to most people, closing the eyelids is a preparation for sleep. Of course, sleep can stop the agitation that comes from external stimuli, but it also brings the inertia of tamas and may encourage indulgence in daydreams. On the other hand, those who want to keep their eyes open need to have disciplines that can stop the wandering habit of the eyes and stabilize their interest in one single form. At this stage we do not want to enter into the very many methods devised by Yoga practitioners, but we'll offer a few general suggestions.

Advanced yogis isolate the agent of illumination from the object that is illuminated. In other words, they focus their attention on the light that falls on an object rather than being carried away by the effect of light and shade that suggests phenomenological forms. When a person acquires the ability to see only the light and not the illuminated object, nothing separates the light of consciousness from the external light that consciousness illuminates through the act of reciprocation. Thus the seer sees the seer in a union in which the seer, the act of seeing, and the seen do not have separate identifications.

Similarly, on hearing sound, an advanced aspirant can discard the suggested meaning of the sounds as a conditioning of the faculty of audition. Instead, the yogi goes into the homogenous vibratory function of all sounds and listens to the unbroken sound that is beyond all patterned sound formations. This is what is called merging into the voiceless voice of *nāda brahman* (absolute sound).

The most difficult stimulus to pacify is that coming through touch, especially where the touch has an erotic purport. Two persons are erotically aroused when they touch in a certain manner. It is not by cultivating an external numbness in the skin that we pacify the impact of touch on our system. When we extend the sphere of love from the individual and specific object of touch to the all-embracing, we experience the touch of the Absolute called *brahma samsparśa*.

Even when these modes of pacifying our consciousness from being stimulated by external entities are all successful, there are other sources of agitation that come from our own physiologic malfunctioning. What makes life so easy is our respiratory system. Even the slightest malfunction of the prāṇa that interferes with evenly breathing in and breathing out can be an obstruction to peaceful consciousness. Prāṇa is a handle not only to tackle the body but also to pacify the tormenting mind. Equalizing prāṇa and apāna, the ascending vital breath and the descending vital breath, can have great effect in harmonizing the functioning of the body and, consequently, in securing inner peace. So yogis watch their breath, cultivate intimacy with its natural rhythm, and correct it if the breath is too short or very hard. If breathing is incorrect, and the lung air is not respired fully, that can create a cumulative effect of carbon dioxide or carbon monoxide that is not fully flushed out. The varieties of breathing exercises (prāṇāyāma) and the literature explaining the process and discipline are many and we do not intend to make any reference to any particular form of prāṇāyāma here.

Even when the body remains still and the prāṇa is harmonized, the mind can be frequented by chains of thoughts and other forms of mentations. To get rid of these inner irritations, we have to tune to our higher understanding of consciousness and apply that knowledge to devalue the entertaining of thoughts, ideas, and memories that are unwholesome. Here knowledge is used with advantage.

When even thoughts are controlled there are blockages that stop us from going beyond the pale of consciousness; these blocks are constituted of thoughts that are made up of words. A breakthrough at this level is bound to be mystical and non-verbal. After going deep into such states of consciousness, we come to a state of waiting in peace and receiving light or guidance from within. Thus the field of pacifying consciousness and remaining in serenity is enormously vast. In one lifetime it is not possible to explore all the paths and employ all the methods. What is most appropriate for a person to know and practice will be given in chapter two.

Sūtra I:14

sa tu dīrghakāla nairantarya satkārāsevito dṛḍha bhūmiḥ

saḥ: that, this [is]
tu: and
dīrghakāla: for a long time
nairantarya: without interruption
satkāra: [and] with devotion
āsevitaḥ: being well attended to
dṛḍha bhūmiḥ: firmly grounded, established

And this is firmly grounded, being well-attended to for a long time without interruption and with devotion.

Even simple habits—such as smoking or drinking tea or coffee—cannot be easily erased. The conditioning that arises from nicotine, caffeine, narcotics, and so on can only have a short history. But the conditioning of our psychosomatic systems through genetic transference from one bodily state to another has a continuous history of several million years. It is from such an unbroken, consistent repetition of behaving in a particular manner or arousing certain urges through the long force of genetic habit that we behave in a certain way in our present bodily form. Correction can be carried out only by consistently engaging, for long periods of time, in practices that amount to the devaluation and decoloration of the conditionings that have gone into the system. From our personal experience we can easily understand that our bodies are such that they can acquire a habit of repetition. This vulnerability of the body and mind can be fully taken advantage of in teaching it to obey. If a person starts a new routine of rising regularly at four o'clock to study, after about a month he or she will automatically wake up at four. This discipline can be broken by forcefully keeping oneself in bed after four o'clock in preparation to sleep. Then the habit of waking up early can be replaced with another habit such as sleeping until eight o'clock in the morning.

Our superficial conditionings that have been consciously acquired can be changed at a surface mind level. But in order to change the deeper conditionings that are controlled by generic principles of biology and atavistic imprinting in the psyche—and establish in their place a special attitude, a disciplined way of life—we have to change even the contents of our dreams and dislodge certain memories that are religiously adhered to by the community to which we belong.

Our social behavior is not rationally grounded. It has been instituted with the aid of irrational fears generated by a community over several centuries. For example, the Muslims and Christians consider it a great virtue to live in fear of God and to believe in the accountability of each person on a supposed day of final judgment. Guilt feelings and various kinds of neurotic repressions arise out of the pressure of collective consciousness or even the collective unconscious. Most of the normative notions of ethical life go against natural urges, especially those related to sexual behavior.

We have already mentioned that practicing discipline is like climbing a mountain with a heavy load on your back. An aspirant should have a lot of energy resources to tap; in the pursuit of perfection a lot of energy is consumed. To facilitate this you have to economically portion out as little energy as possible for carrying out the daily vocation of life. The remainder of your energy is to be entirely used for advancing toward your goal. In youthful folly, much energy is wasted on programs that are specially conceived for the vain display of the ego and for the temporary gratification of sensuous craving and sexual infatuation. People who are preoccupied with autoeroticism and other unnatural forms of gratification disturb their sex rhythms. They not only impoverish the perennial energy supply of their bodies, but also endanger the tranquility of their minds by indulging in activities that they consider shameful.

The purification of the mind needs careful planning and the execution of it takes long periods of time. Sri Ramakrishna says that if you mix creamy milk and water, they blend easily. But if milk is left to curdle for a sufficiently long time and its cream is churned out, then the cream (butter) can even be kept in water and the two will not mix. Similarly, you have to isolate yourself from the mad rush of competitive life to give your mind a sense of stability. After a long period of sublimating your crude urges, you come to the gathering of the cream of your spiritual life. You can then return to society and assume the position of a therapist or an educator. All such self-training needs time and devotion.

Sūtra I:15

dṛṣṭānuśravika viṣaya vitṛṣṇasya vaśīkāra sañjñā vairāgyam

dṛṣṭa: seen, perceived
ānuśravika: heard of, promised
viṣaya: sensory objects, enjoyments
vitṛṣṇasya: in one who is free from thirst
vaśīkāra: mastery, power
sañjñā: consciousness, full knowledge
vairāgyam: detachment, non-attachment, desirelessness

Detachment is the consciousness of mastery in one who is free from thirst for seen and heard of enjoyments.

The thoughts and deeds of most people are in the form of reactions to the encounters to which the body and its sense organs are exposed. They strongly identify with their bodies. Like a musician who tunes her instrument to sing an appropriate song in a given situation, people who have deep body consciousness think that they are always called upon to look and appreciate, to listen and admire, to touch and feel elated or excited, to taste and enjoy, to smell and appreciate the shade of fragrance presented to the nose. After long years of discipline and through proper understanding, some people, like Janaka, become oblivious of the ego-body relationship. The yogi in such an instance is called a *videhi*.

A videhi may breathe, eat, drink, and function like a

normal person, but he is always oblivious of his physical state. It is not pain and pleasure that decide his behavioral pattern. In heat and cold he behaves as if he is not aware of the heat and the cold. The body may have sensations but the sensations do not connect with his value-cognizing field where he prefers one over the other. In the matter of hunger and thirst, he does not go in search of food or water. He partakes of food and drink only as a routine course and does so only when his attention is called to it by someone else. He experiences no strong attraction or avoidance. It is not that he suffers or tolerates whatever is happening around him. Instead, the witnessing consciousness becomes more strongly established than the reacting consciousness.

A videhi does not shun community or his natural station in life. He doesn't do anything peculiar. While being very normal in his disposition to everything around him, he sets a model for others of not exaggerating one's physical body ownership. For such a person, there is no entertaining of pleasurable situations. Buddha considers the root cause of all human sufferings as the unavoidable thirst to satisfy one's desires. When a person is not hungry and not thirsty, he is perfectly poised and is not assailed by a sense of need. This lack of lust or any sort of thirst is the main mark of a videhi.

There is a sect in northern India known as the *udāsins*. Their discipline mainly centers on the ideal of videha. The novices of the udāsin school are called sannyasis. They are people who have discarded environments that can strongly remind them of their bodily existence. That is the first step. Thereafter they become indifferent. They transcend social obligations and feel free to behave as they automatically feel in situations where they are not subjected to any enticing encounters. Then they mature into the state of being *virakta*, unattached on all sides. They look upon values that are considered most important in social circles as meaningless or, rather, they don't look upon any values at all. They are naturally very withdrawn people. Their example doesn't really square with the model which Janaka, a legendary videhi, set for the people of his time. His ideal was to be absolutely normal in transactions and never to exaggerate anything on the basis of physical obsession or inhibition.

The example of the udāsins actually comes closer to the ideals of the *prakṛtilayas,* those who have merged into nature. They treat their bodies as part of this world. The Sun, Moon, stars, mountains, and rivers all exist in the world and they think of their bodily selves as part of the same phenomena. They behave somewhat like lower animals that have no norms of ethical behavior, but act upon the pressing needs of the body. However, instead of becoming indulgent as animals are, they drift away from the externality of their nature (prakṛti) to the witnessing consciousness within (puruṣa). You may find a prakṛtilaya person sleeping under a tree or dwelling on a riverside, walking naked or eating raw food. They don't mind if other animals also come and share their food and they are not bothered by what others think of their nudity or seemingly uncouth behavior. In spite of such external crudity, their minds dwell always in the serenity of the pure consciousness of puruṣa.

These two examples can throw some light on the transcendence of desire and obligatory conformity. Freedom from desire and the transcendence of obligation remove all sense of fear from the mind. The two possible forms of fear that can afflict a person are the fear of physical cessation and the fear of ceasing to be of any importance or value in the estimation of contemporary society. A videhi or prakṛtilaya has no desire to live or die. Physical death can come any time. That does not disturb them. Apart from the pure light of puruṣa and the constantly changing mechanics of nature, there is no separate person to which separate merits and demerits can be attributed in the eyes of others. These are some of the ideas that can be developed in the context of a person who has no thirst for pleasure or recognition.

Those who are in resonance with the self-luminous light of pure consciousness become aware of the bondage to which a person is subjected in the world of phenomenality. The best example of this can be seen in Plato's cave allegory. When people are attuned to their identity with the shadow-world, they are instinctively led by nature's urges and live like pigs or brutes of the jungle. Once they know that their nature is of light and not darkness, the love for freedom emerges. In the cave allegory, Plato describes the utter discomfort experienced by a person who realizes that he or she is bound to phenomenality. In *Vivekachūḍāmaṇi*, Śankara compares the discomfort of a person who is turning to spirituality to the desperation of a deer that finds itself surrounded by a brush fire. Another analogy is of a fish in a pond in summertime when the water is fast evaporating. Sri Ramakrishna describes it as the struggle of a person who is forcefully kept immersed in water. How such a person struggles to breathe is like a person who realizes that he or she is in bondage.

In the world of transaction, linear thinking and logical reasoning are helpful. But true spiritual insight comes from intuitive flashes, which Henri Bergson speaks of in his *Introduction to Metaphysics*. The intelligence that does not depend on previous conditioning is *nirvikalpa buddhi*, unconditioned intelligence. As an aspirant, you know how the incarnate (flesh and blood) aspect functions at a lower level of biologic evolution. From that, you longingly look toward your pre-incarnate reality, which is of pure light, not imprisoned in the cage of a body. When you can discriminate between the pure aspect of the disincarnate and the morbid aspect of the incarnate, a new discriminative power is developed. It is called *viveka khyāti* or *prasaṅkhyāna*. In the state of the incarnate, experiencing pain and pleasure through sensations is considered very important by embodied beings. Śankara discredits experience *(anubhava)* as not pertaining to the Self (ātman). The English word *ex-perience* clearly indicates its own limitation: it is knowing something outside the Self, that is, the non-Self. Śankara substitutes anubhava, experience, with *anubhūti,* imperience: an identification that comes through the establishment of an inner unity aided by intuition. It can only be imperientially comprehended.

Where viveka khyāti, the discriminative light, is well established, you gain the power of *vaṣīkāra* (mastery). Vaṣīkāra, the most mature aspect of detachment, comes in three stages. The first stage is called *yatamāna*. A *yati* is a person of inner control. With consistent restraint, holding before yourself the normative notion of nirvikalpa buddhi, you establish yourself in the yatamāna state. It is followed by *vyatireka*. When two values are before you, a discriminative judgment should be applied to see which is conducive to your liberation and which leads to bondage. In life, you have to turn away from many things that are likely to have miserable consequences. Stripping yourself away from the wrong value is vyatireka.

The third aspect is establishing yourself in the *ekendriya* (single sensory stimulus) aspect. When the five sense organs are receiving their separate sensations, the mind becomes a blend of the data received from all five. Mind is dampened with the cumulative effect of heterogeneous sensations. When a yogi separates out the data received through one sense organ and detaches from it all the previous associations with which the sensation from that particular organ is conditioned, his or her reaction will be decidedly different. Only by practicing the detachment of the associated ideas of all senses other than that with which you are concerned can you understand what exactly is meant by ekendriya concentration, that is, giving your full attention to the exact stimulus that comes through the ear as a sound, or the eye as a flash of light, or another sensory item. All this will be further studied in the chapter on practice.

Sūtra I:16

tat param puruṣa khyāter guṇavaitṛṣṇyam

tat: that
param: highest, ultimate, supreme, transcendent [*vairagya*]
puruṣa: the Self
khyāteḥ: through awareness or vision of the
guṇa: the three qualities, triple modalities, or primary constituents of nature *(sattva, rajas, tamas)*
vaitṛṣṇyam: there is freedom from the least desire for

That is the highest *vairāgya*: through awareness of the Self, there is freedom from the least desire for the three qualities of nature.

The common tendency of people is to look around and see what is impressive, to listen to the testimonials given by a number of people in high-sounding hyperbole. This is not only for meeting the daily needs of life and receiving therapy for physical illnesses, but also to tide over social repressions, familial obligations, mental imbalance, and the choice of disciplines in the search to attain the highest goal of life.

Scriptures of most religions treat their votaries as if they are immature people with animal instincts and a discrimination that is no better than that of children. Moral norms are taught with the help of anecdotes and parables, which forcefully describe how wickedness is drastically punished and good is always rewarded. Believers' minds are fed with the lures of an enchanting heaven, a place where the most exaggerated hedonistic pleasures are lavished on those who are selected to enter paradise. In the same manner, hell is described as a terrible place of torture. Both the preachers and their congregations forget that when they die their brains and sensory systems transform into dead matter and thereafter the dead have no bodies to experience pain or pleasure. When the faithful are told that they might go to hell and be cast in the burning flames of brimstone, the fear of being scorched comes to them. Such outright stupidity is enshrined in the most adorable scriptures of all religions. Most people remain ethical in their outward life, fearing such punishments, and do good to others, coveting an honored place in heaven. Henri Bergson, in his *Two Sources of Morality and Religion,* exposed the dubiousness of static religion and closed morality. The alternatives are dynamic religion and open morality.

When people fall sick, they look for hospitals that have the largest number of beds, the biggest building complex, where doctors come and go in the most costly cars. Boasting of the amount of money that is spent on medical bills becomes more important than having a safe recovery. For education, children are sent to schools where admission is difficult to get, where the fees are the highest, and where children of the wealthiest section of the community attend. Little consideration is given to the quality of the teachers, the worthwhileness of the syllabus that is adhered to, or the quality of life imparted to children during their school days.

This is the tendency against which Patañjali warns. Your choices should be based on right knowledge, which you can find manifesting in your own innermost soul. The knowledge spoken of here is *puruṣa khyāti* or *ātma vidyā*. It is a recognition that the brightest light you can have to guide a harmonious life that blossoms with higher values is already your heritage. You can find it just like a great work of art is brought to light from a granite or marble piece, by chipping off whatever conceals that form in the block of marble or stone.

All forms of Yoga arise from a conviction that nobody is lost, totally and forever. There is hope of reaching the highest perfection that is possible for each to attain. This is the Third of the Four Noble Truths enunciated by Lord Buddha. The First Noble Truth is that life is miserable on five counts: birth is painful, ignorance is painful, disease is painful, separation from those whom one loves is painful, and death is painful. The Second Noble Truth says that misery ensues from desires. The Third Noble Truth says that it is possible to get over all the pains of life. The Fourth Noble Truth is described as the renunciation of all desires.

Hope in life should not be the false hope of a fool. True conviction of deliverance comes from the knowledge that your innate reality is the Supreme Self, which is indestructible, pure, and not tainted with any confusion that arises from the phenomenality of life. What was previously described as the discrimination of the Self from the non-Self (prasaṅkhyāna) is the right reason to rejoice. Having a proper perspective on the horizontal principles of the phenomenal world and the vertical unfoldment of the spirit helps a person to pursue the path of righteousness with all earnestness and to eschew the path of evil with determination. Such a seeker is not in any state of frenzy. Earnestness keeps the enthusiasm unflagging and consistently steady. When your needs are few and you don't exaggerate your social placement, life becomes so very simple that it can be handled with great ease. The *Bhagavad Gita* says that the lust for pleasures may be weakened by starving yourself of them, but if you see the Absolute, you will become totally free of all craving. What is important is to gain viveka khyāti, the knowledge that you are already a manifestation of the highest spirit that is most pure in its essence.

The ideal of a yogi is to establish a voluntary governorship over the autonomous functioning of his or her psychosomatic system whereby conditionings and colorations of the operational system are always attuned to an approximate perfection of normalcy so that the innate balance can be consistently maintained. Life of an organism can be described as a rhythmic alternation in the release and control of energy. The two kinds of energy that are constantly released for the growth, maintenance, and continuance of the system are physical and chemical. The physical can also be termed as electrical. The conveyor of electrical energy is the nervous system. Chemical energy is endocrinal, also known as hormonal.

The physical or electrical aspect belongs very much to its parent cosmologic system and chemical or endocrinal energy stems from the purposive intentionality of the individuated living organism. Although chemical energy is produced in the glands that belong to the somatic counterpart of the psyche, the engineering of its potent chemistry is governed by the purpose at hand from moment to moment, as well as by what is designed for the long-term efficiency of the system. In relation to the electrical energy that is released and controlled, neuronal devices are meticulously controlled by synapses. This is a self-educating system in which all the stored up information of the individual, the conscious planning of one's reaction to the environment, and the biologic and genetic scheme of unfoldment operate as a tri-basic function of the prāṇa, mind, and physical instrumentality of life. The role of this aspect is very much that of a designing engineer whose needs are looked into and supplied by the endocrinal system.

It is significant that the endocrinal glands are named *granthi* in Sanskrit. A *grantha* is an authoritative book. A granthi is one conversant with authentic injunctions and commandments. The reciprocal relationship between the nervous system and intra-glandular reactions includes a very peculiar device through which the rational is guided, governed, and controlled by the irrational. The irrational is not, however, chaotic. It responds to the slightest suggestion from your conscious mind about the ultimate purpose or goal to which your life is attuned.

The chemicals involved in the hormones are so rare and unique in their composition and function that they can hardly be synthetically produced by any human device. Yet they can be plentifully manufactured in your own body by arranging your thoughts in a certain manner and directing your vital breath (prāṇa) in a significant way. It is not by resorting to artificial means that this rare feat is accomplished, but by merging yourself closer and closer to the inner texture of nature's ingenuity. When you can forget the carrying out of your private and vested interests and be in full attunement or rather at-one-ment with the higher intentions of nature, you automatically come to a state of oneness or aloneness (kaivalya). Thus, for the prakṛtilaya, one who is merged in nature, kaivalya comes as a logical conclusion.

This beautiful function can be seen by studying the marvelous control system of the endocrinal glands. When the gland receives a message to release hormonal energy, the first thrust that comes is a little more than what is needed. The overseer of psychophysical welfare, which belongs to what the yogis call prajñā, is described in the *Māṇḍūkya Upaniṣad* as the overseeing principle of control *(sarveśvara)*. It neutralizes the excess energy that is released with what physiologists call a negative hormone. This is very similar to what physicists call negentropy, which counters the Second Law of Thermodynamics. Thus the physicochemical interaction in the biologic set up makes a person alternate between non-knowledge *(kincitjñattva)* and all-knowledge *(sarvajñattava)*. This is the grand scheme of attaining kaivalya by regulating values.

Sūtra I:17

vitarka vicāra ānanda asmitā rūpa anugamāt samprajñātaḥ

vitarka: [of] perceptual confrontation or configuration, object of perception

vicāra: presentation of an idea or concept; ideation

ānanda: [experience of] value or normative notion

asmitā: identification with the center of one's consciousness, ego identity, sense of individuality

rūpa: the appearance, form, nature

anugamāt: is accompanied by

samprajñātaḥ: cognitive or conditioned [absorption]

Cognitive absorption is accompanied by the appearance of perceptual confrontation, presentation of an idea, experience of value, or identification with the center of one's consciousness.

A living organism has a vertical continuance of its life (will to live) and a horizontal placement in an environment that is mostly conducive to the meaningful prolongation of that particular life form. In infra-nature where lower forms of life thrive, adverse environments are avoided through natural means such as the extinction of the species or a process of evolution by which special features of adaptation are accepted in a marked manner through varying degrees of mutation. Higher animals and even some lower forms like birds and fish are capable of migrating from one place to another, which gives them the ability to choose suitable environments for habitation.

In modern psychology, for the purpose of scientific brevity, only observable and measurable physiologic changes are given primacy in the study of sensory perception and consequent physical and mental reactions to environmental demands. This limitation has considerably affected the validity of the results. The sense organs are like the doors of perception and they are not to be considered as the real percipient in a living organism. There is a constantly reverberating inner core where the individual being identifies its central consciousness, asmitā. Although it is somewhat vulgarly designated as the ego, asmitā is a demarcation of consciousness within the bounds of which the intensity of a particular value significance is vividly experienced from moment to moment. There is nothing good or bad about the pooling of consciousness with a personal identification. It is a natural event that occurs as the nucleic core from which consciousness is outwardly spreading centrifugally and inwardly converging centripetally. The purpose and meaning of one's life is felt most strongly within the bounds of this consciousness, which is kept ever alive, vigilant, scheming, planning, and operative for all the general and specific purposes for which the individual lives. The consciousness of that area presides over a treasure chest of memory bits that have been accumulated through several life forms in the passage of the genes or the persona from body to body.

According to modern physiology, stimuli come in the form of energy such as sound vibrations, light beams, tactual pressures felt in the form of heat or cold, gravitational pulls, and so on. They spatially affect the receptor ends of a number of neurons; the spatial summation decides the intensity of the stimulation to focus the cognizing power of attention. Another dimension given to physical stimulus is the temporal duration of the bombardment of the sensory receptor. With the pooling of spatial and temporal summation, the organism reacts.

To the yogis this approach is very superficial. The depth aspect of the individual's life history and the consequent priorities of the person are not given any attention at all by the physiologists. As we have mentioned earlier, according to the yogi, attention is directed as a selective function in terms of the priorities of the individual's preservation, growth, reproduction, and continuance, and the efficient coordination of the organism's psychic and somatic organic functioning.

This is mainly established on the basis of conditioning, which is called samskāra when it is still in the process of consolidation, and vāsanā when it has become an established inner conviction, a memory consolidated in depth, which is not in need of fresh modification. A rat instinctively recognizes the presence of a cat and vice versa, even before these two creatures see each other. Similarly, when a person has the intense inner need for a certain environmental factor, that need gives priority to the reception of certain stimuli that are sure to be found in the vicinity where the organism experiences urgency. The spatial and temporal summation of stimuli that would normally be expected in a given circumstance are overridden by an intense inner need. Thus the perceptual confrontation that an individual experiences is not always a static witnessing but involves many topological factors of high emotional or intuitive significance. In any case, out of the millions of stimuli that come to the organs of perception, only those which contribute to the gestaltation of one particular value configuration are given attention at a time. This is what is called vitarka.

Vicāra is a logical confrontation. Whatever is cognized is to be reconstituted in the mind with language and logic. Even a person who is well-versed in different languages has to choose, at any given time, the particular language form in which perceptions are to be assessed, and reactions and thoughts spelled out. This immediately makes one adhere to the semantic requirements of that particular language. Subject, predicate, and object are interrelated with proper syntactical consideration and the logistics of each word formation are looked into. When this is done with satisfaction, it can also lead to relating the situation to previous experiences with the recall of memory. Thus one enters vicāra from vitarka. The value assessment (ānanda) that ensues can be pleasurably elevating or painfully agonizing, or it can prepare the mind to give up further consideration and slip back into the volatile functional core state (kṣipta), so that consciousness can step into another realm of interest.

A perceptual experience has a circular motion. From I-consciousness, attention flings itself into the awareness of a new theme indicated by "this." Then—after vitarka, vicāra, and ānanda—it comes back to the I-consciousness, asmitā. When the consciousness that undergoes modification at every stage of this circular movement is stabilized at the vitarka aspect, it becomes *samprajñāta savitarka*. If it stabilizes at vicāra it becomes *samprajñāta savicāra*. If at ānanda, it becomes *samprajñāta sānanda*, and if at asmitā, *samprajñāta sasmitā*.

This sūtra also implies the scheme of the *praṇava, AUM*. The first three aspects—savitarka, savicāra, and sānanda—are to be understood in the light of the wakeful transactional consciousness, the conceptual world of dreams, and the causal consciousness of conditioning marked by deep sleep where pain and pleasure are both negated. The final aspect, sasmitā, has a dual nature, microscopic and macrocosmic. The central focus of personal consciousness where one experiences the pulsation of "I am" is a timeless and spaceless notion. The same can be extended to its utmost infinitude. The combination of these two aspects of the Self is presented in the great dictum, *aham brahma asmi*, "I am the Absolute," in which *aham*, the personal self, and *brahman*, the transcendental totality of being, are interchangeable.

Sūtra I:18

virāma pratyayābhyāsa pūrvaḥ saṁskāra śeṣaḥ anyaḥ

virāma: [the] cessation
pratyaya: [of] cognition, content, consciousness
abhyāsa: repetitive practice, application
pūrvaḥ: preceded by
saṁskāra: registered and preserved impressions, formation of incipient memories
śeṣaḥ: the residue of [remains]
anyaḥ: [is] the other *(asamprajñāta samādhi)* [in which]

The cessation of cognition preceded by repetitive practice is the other *(asamprajñāta samādhi)* in which the residue of registered and preserved impressions remains.

The discipline of Yoga is based on a descriptive psychology of the functions of the faculties. The four inner instruments of cognition are the interrogating mind, the recalling memory, the evaluating intelligence, and the affective self-consciousness. In all persons these four work normally with short spells or quanta of energy. Consequently, the interest that is held in each item of cognition is of short duration.

For instance, when a thing is presented before the organs of perception, the question arises, "What is this?" The attitude of interrogation ceases as soon as the intellect is programmed to evaluate the given subject based on the recall of previous experiences. Once the subject is predicated with its mark of distinction and identification is established, the intellect ceases to work on that program. Then, unconsciously and spontaneously, the recorded identification is stacked away in the unconscious and the memorizing faculty goes into silence.

The affection that has been caused by cognitive consciousness in the form of questioning, evaluating, and registering may bring a surge of pain or pleasure. Then that also abates so that the stream of consciousness can go to a fresh item of experience. Thus all perceptual confrontation has a natural beginning and a natural termination.

As a self-discipline, the yogi can take any such experience and prolong the duration of the modification of the inner organs in an identical state by precipitating a reverberation of the same order continually and contiguously so that consciousness is held in the same location for an extended time. When that is attained, one is not a mere enjoyer *(bhogi)* but becomes a disciplined perceiver who is oblivious of time. In such a state one is a yogi who is experiencing concentration, ekāgra. This is when the neophyte yogi is using a positive experience as a plank for yogic discipline and consequent achievement of contemplative balance.

In the same manner the yogi can use the negative counterpart, the cessation of an experience, for another discipline. Where a cognition disappears into a state of oblivion, the entire stream of consciousness can also vanish. Perception, recall of conception, and affectivity are all transcended and the yogi remains in a state of absorption. For such absorption there can be four leads: absorption into the vanishing point of a perceptual encounter, absorption into the vanishing point of a conceptual or intuitive insight, absorption into the vanishing point of the cessation of pleasure or affectivity, and finally, absorption into the vanishing point of the conscious self merging into the cosmic or universal Self. While such absorptions hold fresh conditionings at bay, they do not terminate any experience that has already been registered. Registered experiences still remain as potentials for future life. They are technically called samskāras, processed and conditioned experiences.

Sūtra I:19

bhava pratyayaḥ videha prakṛtilayānām

bhava: [of] being, existence
pratyayaḥ:[the] cognition, content, consciousness
videha: [for those who are] bereft of body identification
prakṛtilayānām: [and those who are] merged with nature

The cognition of being for those who are bereft of body identification and those who are merged with nature.

When the physicality of the human body is inactive, most of the functions of the living organism come to a silence and the person dwelling in the body experiences rest or even goes to sleep. In such a state, our consciousness can technically be called videha, freed from the body or bereft of body identification. Even when the person who has gone into such a restful state returns to wakeful activities, the witnessing consciousness remains unaffected by pain or pleasure. This central consciousness can detach itself from all the agitations and pain/pleasure dualities that we may experience with sensations, as well as from thoughts that are stained by moral or intellectual conflicts. This detached inner awareness that is never stopped by the eventualities of life—remaining the same in times of rest and of feverish action—is often recognized as the shining one within us.

The eye that sees is afflicted with the stimuli that bombard the chemistry of the physical eye. But the faculty of vision remains unaffected. The same is true of all the senses of perception. The mind is considered to be a sixth sense, also animated by an unmodulated consciousness which, in substance, is none other than the same witnessing self that is lending its light to the sense organs and its dynamics to the organs of action. Although this entity is in the body, it continues its course as if it does not belong to the body. A yogi who continuously remains in that detached state is called a videhi, even when he or she lives as part and parcel of the mainstream of transactional life.

There is another aspect that is not the least worried about what is happening to the physical world. That is the matter that goes into the transformation of things and the laws that govern the structuring and de-structuring of bodies. Those who have total identification with the perpetuation of the magic show of the phenomenal world are not vexed by birth, growth, change, decay, and cessation. This pure state of total identification with nature can be seen in the fetus. This state—which, in essence, is hardly distinguishable from a child's ignorance of the socio-physical order—can also be seen in those who are absolutely in tune with nature. Most animals who are controlled entirely by instinct have this quality of detachment. A yogi who is similarly in perfect resonance with nature and nature's laws is called a prakṛtilaya.

To those who are in these categories, there is no special discipline to undergo. They are real in themselves and there is nothing new to realize. For those of us who alternate between conscious appreciation of physical-sociological-biological and other changes, a long term discipline is required to take us to the four above-mentioned points of absorption: objective identification, subjective identification, value identification, and identification with the Self.

Sūtra I:20

śraddhā vīrya smṛti samādhi prajñā pūrvaka itareṣām

śraddha: faith

vīrya: energy, vigor
smṛti: memory, mindfulness
samādhi: absorption, equipoise in consciousness
prajñā: discernment
pūrvaka: preceded by, having before
itareṣām: for others

For others absorption is preceded by faith, energy, memory, and discernment.

A body is healthy when it is structurally sound and functionally well-coordinated, with all the relevant faculties. Corresponding to the inner cohesion and harmony of the body, the mind can have a well-settled inner cohesion based on a sense of security. From that sense arises both hope for the future and stabilization of the present. This inner stabilization is induced by a deep faith in your basic stand and understanding. Such a stabilizing disposition is called *śraddha*, faith.

When you have faith and a will to achieve, all the dormant sources of physical and mental energy are unlocked. They are automatically channeled into your best effort for the achievement of whatever is programmed. One of the greatest mysteries of the human psychosomatic system is the flow of energy from certain hidden sources within the neuromuscular system. The conversion of dormant energy into momentum that can give tenacity to your will and muscular power to your body in response to the demand made by a scheduled program has not been fully investigated and understood. Dr. Jung and psychologists like him have made a division between physical energy, mental energy, and psychic energy. However, they have not succeeded in giving an acceptable explanation of these varying terms. In Yoga this energy is simply called *vīrya*. The replenishing energy of vīrya is always coming from the food that one eats. For this reason, the Upaniṣadic philosophers thought of food as the most primary phase of the Absolute.

Even when you have inner nourishment and a lot of energy to spend, you can sink into an inertial or lethargic state if your mind has no promise of the future to look into. It is like the chemical components of the nerves which, on interaction, produce an electrical impulse. Interest has to stimulate the fount of energy to make vīrya leap into action. The catalyst to rouse vīrya is always a preconditioned state that comes in the form of a recall of memory. Memories never come as singular gestalts. It is like pulling a string from a thread ball: several associations come one after another, presenting pictures of hope or disgust. Vīrya is utilized either to get into an aggressive action of acquisition or for the purpose of fleeing from fearsome situations. Memory need not necessarily always be your personal acquisition. A master's mind can infuse into a closely related, intimate mind a picture of his or her own memory, which in turn acts like a postulation that guides the neophyte to imitate the master.

In the discipline of Yoga, the finality of perfection is marked by the total absorption into which you can go in the performance of each sādhana. After the completion of each item of disciplinary performance, there comes a degree of clarity, or, in other words, you gain greater wisdom.

Sūtra I:21

tīvra saṁvegānām āsannaḥ

tīvra: intense, keen, strong
saṁvegānām: [for those with] ardor, enthusiasm
āsannaḥ: [samādhi is] near, impending, immanent

Samādhi is near for those with intense ardor.

Sūtra I:22

mṛdu madhyādhimātratvāt tato'pi viśeṣaḥ

mṛdu: mild
madhya: moderate, medium
ādhimātratvāt: and intense
tataḥ: [a] further
api: also
viśeṣaḥ: differentiation [is made]

Also, a further differentiation is made of mild, moderate, and intense.

What is important in this context is to have as clear an idea as possible of the psychobiological nature of desire. In the West, the innate concepts of drive, propensity, emotion, and desire are explained in terms of the will to live, élan vital. The only energizing force that is known to modern physiology is the release of certain chemical substances such as adrenalin. But how exactly that becomes an energizing force with corollaries of glycogen and other chemicals has not been fully investigated.

In the Indian context the operation of a desire is considered to have two opposing monitoring forces. One comes from the nature modalities of prakṛti, in which rajas is considered a volatile force that can either lend its support to sattva or dominate as a passionate, goal-oriented energy expenditure. All the major instincts of a biological organism, such as those to seek nourishment, propagation of the species, and self-preservation, are taken care of by the nature-oriented propensity, *prakṛti vīrya*. The other basis of desire is to reassume the pure state of the Self (puruṣa), which is opposed to the demands made by natural longing.

In most people, these opposing energy channelings cancel each other out and very little energy is left with which to conduct the daily chores of life. Three major driving forces that can easily become exaggerated into pathological energy expenditure are the erotic passion to possess and dominate your love object; the insatiable greed to possess the means to dominate others; and a hankering after future security that is goaded by anxiety and paired with the hoarding of exchange-value tokens such as cash. To transcend the physically impressive needs of the body and mind, you should have a clear envisioning of the spiritual worthwhileness of seeking union with the Absolute or realizing the supreme nature of your Self. If the former kind of demand is like driving down a hill, the latter, your spiritual pursuit, is of an ascending order. A lot of stamina has to be put into the disciplining of your body and mind, even to bring it to a stabilized position from which to commence your ultimate search.

Vyāsa points out that—to warm yourself to the task—there are nine kinds of gradations of evoking energy from its hidden sources and spending it ingeniously for the actualization of the highest values you conceive. The first division that Vyāsa makes is between seekers with mild energy, medium energy, and intense energy. The second series relates to the orientation that each group has in terms of persisting consciousness or spiritual awareness. Some have only a faint idea of their spiritual awareness and some have a middling consciousness of the call of the spirit. There are others who are supremely conscious of the spiritual foundation on which phenomenality rests. Then there are those who are capable of drawing energy to support spiritual consciousness. In that also, variations can come according to a person's ability to tap the dormant energies that can be experienced physically, mentally, and psychically.

Love and hatred are catalysts that evoke the flow of energy. Hatred can cause a sudden surge of energy that adversely affects the entire physical system of a person. This is short lived, like the bursting flames of ignited gasoline. Love, on the other hand, is a steady flow that produces more and more energy in the long run. The purer the love, the greater is the chance of furthering the continuous flow of energy. Hatred has within it an intermittent operation of ambivalence in which obsession and inhibition operate side by side. In the case of love, inhibition soon wears out and both receiving and giving become obsessive.

In the spiritual pursuit, the idea is to give up totally and the receiving acts like a fountain where what is given in the form of love is received back in the form of grace. Even when a person is physically weak and confronted by adverse situations, the love to give increases. This is evident in the case of Indian saints like Tukaram and Mirabai and Christian mystics like St. Francis of Assisi and St. John of the Cross. Their physical debilities did not stop them from channeling large founts of energy to the accomplishment of their spiritual goals.

Sūtra I:23

īśvara praṇidhānāt vā

īśvara: spirit par excellence, supreme spirit, noumenon, higher Self, designated by *praṇava, AUM*

praṇidhānāt: by continuous contemplation on

vā: or

Or, by continuous contemplation on *īśvara*.

Innumerable are the people who are seriously pondering over the meaning and significance of this world in which we find ourselves to be placed. For each person, innumerable are the objects to be discerned. Thus, there is a plurality on the subjective side and a plurality on the objective side. However, at the time of contemplative observation, study, evaluation, and judgment, you think only of your inner light. Several questions can be put, but all questions can be reduced to the singular faculty of interrogation. Several judgments may be made, but all judgments can be given the status of verified truth, the certitude of the Self. There is no end to the items of memory that are recalled, but they can all be looked upon as relevant recall. Whatever the meaning of an experience, it is basically affective; affection is the feeling content of the experience in terms of pain or pleasure. Thus, on the subjective side, systematic reduction is made in all contexts to unify all plurality to the imperiential state of a unitive knower.

A corresponding methodology of reduction is accepted on the objective side. All experiences can be considered as items of a gross world of transactional verity, a subjective world of conceptual composition, and the residual existence of a consciousness that turns upon itself. Finally, all these are accepted as the phenomenal variegations arising out of the immanence of a transcendent supreme being.

The methodology of reduction is a universally accepted formula for the systematization of philosophy. The Sāṅkhya philosophy is basically dual in its epistemology. It accepts a plurality of souls (puruṣas) and a homogenous principle of nature (prakṛti) as the counterpart of puruṣa. Thus in Sāṅkhya there already exists a neatly worked out reduction on the side of prakṛti. There is not anything unbecoming in attempting a similar unification of puruṣas by marking out one puruṣa that is distinct from all individual souls and yet has a place in the animating principle of all individuated beings. The yogic practice (sādhana) concerning prakṛti is that of handling the operations of sattva, rajas, and tamas with discernment. This can be well balanced with advantage by holding īśvara (or the spirit par excellence) as a model for directing the subjective consciousness to relate in an appropriate manner with the changing experiences that alternate between the wakeful, the dream, and deep sleep.

This ingenious device of bringing in īśvara as the twenty-fifth category in Yoga epistemology marks its distinction from the Sāṅkhyan epistemology, which has only twenty-four categories. Instead of diversifying the epistemological cohesion of the system, the twenty-fifth category unifies it in a remarkable manner. We will begin to appreciate the significance of admitting īśvara in the philosophy of Yoga as we move further to the ensuing aphorisms. Usually īśvara is glibly translated into English as "God." Īśvara is not God, at least not God in the Christian or Islamic sense of that term. In the following aphorisms we get a clear definition of īśvara.

Sūtra I:24

kleśa karma vipākāśayair aparāmṛṣṭaḥ puruṣa viśeṣa īśvaraḥ

kleśa: affliction, obstacles
karma: action
vipāka: [and] fruition
āśayaiḥ: [by the] propensities
aparāmṛṣṭaḥ: unaffected, untouched
puruṣa viśeṣaḥ: [is] a distinct puruṣa
īśvaraḥ: spirit par excellence, supreme spirit, noumenon, higher Self, designated by *praṇava, AUM*

Īśvara is a distinct puruṣa unaffected by the propensities of affliction, action, and fruition.

As we have seen, in Yoga the dual factors into which the reality of this world is divided are the procreative energy (prakṛti), and the monitoring consciousness (puruṣa) that is involved in the transformation of that energy such as in the projection, existence, and dissolution of each individual person. In that concept, three factors are involved: affliction, action, and fruition.

The world that is manifesting in and around us is always in a state of flux. Change is a categorical imperative for a being to come into existence and work out its course. When one billiard ball hits another, both the balls deflect and move in accordance with the momentum that is created with the randomness of the hit. The direction a ball is about to move is unknown to the balls, even though the player has in his mind the approximation of a guess, which is the main factor in the continuous maneuvering of the game. Similarly, there is an overall uncertainty presiding in the moment-to-moment envisioning of the life process in an individual who comes into existence. This irremediable ignorance with which a person commences his or her life course is the affliction that is spoken of here.

Avidyā or ignorance is the main characteristic of affliction. A randomness that assumes a course of purposiveness, and a purposive maneuvering that is mounted on a horse of uncertainty work hand in hand. With innumerable such occurrences of randomness all around, the course of action is determined within the field of uncertainty. That is called *karma*.

Karma begins, as it were, as a nameless drive. Then, through the sequences of the channeling of energy, in the relations that are established, and in the values that are reckoned, karma can ultimately be seen as moving from an incentive to act to a goal that is actualized. This process is called the fruitioning of action, *karma vipāka*.

Such is the routine course of every individuated person or consciousness that presides in a unit of procreative energy that functions as a living being. The binary principles of procreative energy and presiding consciousness are both transcended by a third factor named in the previous aphorism as īśvara. Īśvara is free of affliction (kleśa), action (karma), and fruition (karma vipāka). Here, from the pluralistic concept of several puruṣas subjected to the affliction of ignorance and engaging in a multitude of activities, we come to a noumenon that is not affected by the phenomenon.

Sūtra I:25

tatra niratiśayam sarvajñatva bījam

tatra: in that [īśvara]
niratiśayam: is not exceeded, unsurpassed
sarvajñatva: of the omniscient
bījam: the seed

In that īśvara the seed of the omniscient is not exceeded.

The īśvara of the Yoga system is identified with praṇava, AUM. To understand the marks of that identification, one should know the structural relationship of the fourfold aspects of praṇava: the wakeful, the dream, the deep sleep, and "the fourth." These can also be respectively termed as the responsive, the imaginative, the causal, and absorption.

The responsive, designated by "A" in AUM, is limited to the sphere of the perceptual. In the world of interaction between individuals, and between individuals and things, the most important thing is the relation between seemingly independent factors. In the gross world, each thing has its own special mark of identification and there are common characteristics by which individual factors can be classified. The knowledge of the laws that regulate the harmonious coexistence of things, both in their static state and dynamic interaction, has determined them to be unvarying. That is why humanity has succeeded in evolving sciences relating to different fields such as chemistry, botany, biology, psychology, and sociology.

Both the laws and the knowledge of the laws have frontiers beyond which they cannot be pushed. At best, every knowledge concerning relative factors will necessarily be relativistic also. In plane geometry the sum of the three angles of any triangle will be one hundred and eighty degrees. Similarly, in simple arithmetic, two and two will always be four. Even if wisdom becomes crystal clear, the knowledge of the relativistic sphere, of wakeful consciousness, will always conform to certain norms that can never be improved upon. This limitation is referred to here with the word *niratiśayam*. A common person may have only a limited notion in this field. So, naturally, effort can be made to expand that knowledge till it reaches the natural frontier of relativistic comprehension. When the final limit is touched, that is described as omniscience, so far as the transactional field is concerned.

As we move on to the world of projective imagination, limitation does not arise out of the qualities of one object confronting the qualities of another. Rather, it depends on the creative energy of structuring conceptual elements of gestaltation so that even when one goes into extreme elaboration, the structural interrelationship between ideas is not violated logically, aesthetically, and ethically. In this particular function of consciousness also, there is a natural limitation beyond which imagination cannot go. Nobody can imagine that the shortest distance between two points could be a curved line. The mind refuses to accept that possibility. We cannot conceive that A and not-A can be at the same time, in the same place, in the same sense.

Within the field of imagination, which is technically called *svapna*, there is another kind of determining factor where we do not have to limit ourselves to the physical requirements of the familiar world of gross objects. As in Picasso's creative art, there can be the transposition of parts. Still, that can be valid. Within the second field of praṇava, which is indicated with the letter "U" in AUM, those who arrive at the frontiers of the world of imagination are recognized as master poets, master artists, master playwrights, and so on. In this case also, omniscience is marked by the unfoldment of a person's creative power so that it can be taken to its ultimate possibility.

The third aspect is confined to the world of cause and effect. What is not present as a potential in the cause cannot manifest in the effect. Conversely, anything manifested as an effect is indicative of a latent cause, a hidden seed. Here, the limitation arises from a pulsation within manifestation, expanding from a cause to an enlarged field of effect and, in the same manner, centripetally turning inward to epitomize the entire effect into a causal factor. This process, which is going on interminably, is happening in the unknown and unconscious. Therefore, the entire perspective of it is not available either to perceptual observation or to conceptual comprehension. The limitation here has for its frame of reference the time-space continuum and the intrinsic laws that govern the origin, expansion, reduction, and dissolution of mass.

Omniscience in this case is when the process in the unconscious has been maximally interpreted to the conscious mind. When a person cannot go farther into the niche of the unconscious, the omniscience of causal consciousness reaches its insurmountable frontier.

Ultimately, everything that has gone into the perceptual, conceptual, and causal is to be seen as the horizontalizing phenomenality that is happening within a determined possibility within the noumenon. The omniscience in this respect becomes modified with the canceling out of the knower and the known. In īśvara omniscience is to be understood in the sense in which we have understood knowledge finding its norm within the four limbs of praṇava, AUM.

Sūtra I:26

sa pūrveṣām api guruḥ kālenānavacchedāt

saḥ: that [is]
purveṣām: of the ancients
api: also
guruḥ: the teacher
kālena: by time
ānavacchedāt: not being limited

That is the teacher of the ancients also, not being limited by time.

One of the most popular invocations of the guru principle with which most Indian people begin their study or work is the praise given to the guru as creator (Brahma), sustainer (Viṣṇu), and dissolver (Maheśvara), with a final assertion that the guru, in reality, is none other than the Absolute:

aum gurur brahmā gurur viṣṇur
gurur devo maheśvaraḥ
guruh sākṣāt param brahma
tasmai śri gurave namaḥ
aum śāntiḥ śāntiḥ śāntiḥ

The first three references—Brahmā, Viṣṇu, and Maheśvara—are indicative of the time segments of beginning, middle, and end. These three segments are transcended by pure duration—absolute time—which is beginningless and endless. The phenomenality of creation is a cyclic process like the spurting of water in a fountain: it remains visible in the process of rising and falling, then it becomes one with the water of the reservoir, only to be thrown up again in the next moment.

Life on Earth is also cyclic. The process of obtaining a body, using it for carrying out whatever action is appropriate, and finally having it disintegrate, to be transformed again into the instrument of another living being, is just like the water circulating through a fountain or the same metal being cast again and again into new bodies by a smith. In such processes, the water or the metal are not enriched by the specific transformations they have undergone. But life is not like that. Each embodiment enriches it with the registry of various experiences.

The cumulative effect of undergoing such experiences becomes embedded in the genetic stream, the selective mold through which evolution sustains the biologic principle of Earth, which thus has in it a record of ceaseless learning. At each phase, wisdom is obtained from a teacher provided by the benevolence of time to make a crucial step. Such are the teachers whom we reverence as Buddha or Jesus, Vasistha or Visvamitra, Sankara or Ramanuja.

Apart from such teachers who appear at specific periods

in the history of humankind, there also exists—in and through all such teachers and in our own personal understanding—the eternal teacher who has been guiding the destiny of all through the millennia of the evolution of life on Earth. That supreme teacher is venerated here as the ever-burning light of wisdom that is enshrined in the heart of all.

Sūtra I:27

tasya vācakaḥ praṇavaḥ

tasya: its [īśvara's]
vācakaḥ: signifier, word
praṇavaḥ: [is] praṇava (AUM)

Īśvara's signifier is praṇava (AUM).

While in the philosophy of Vedānta there is only one īśvara, which is the same as the universal Self, this is not the teaching of Yoga. In Yoga, īśvara is *a* puruṣa, not *the* puruṣa. The difference between them is that the puruṣas in you and me are subject to the five kleśas—ignorance (avidyā), attachment (rāga), aversion (dveṣa), egoism (asmitā), and excessive love of life (abhiniveśa)—as well as to the impact of karma and the maturation of the causal potency of karma (karma vipāka). We are subjected to these but īśvara as a puruṣa is not affected.

We have to think of a model puruṣa as being like the monad of monads of Leibnitz. Leibnitz speaks of the monad of an unpolished stone, the monad of a polished stone, the monad of a dew drop, the monad of a child's mind, the monad of an adult's mind, the monad of an educated person's mind, and the monad of monads. All these monads reflect in each other. Light reflects from each in varying degrees. There is less darkness in the polished stone than in the unpolished stone, in a dewdrop than a stone, and so on.

The monad of monads reflects everything without darkness. Similarly, the puruṣa that is īśvara is not afflicted; it is perfect. Yoga suggests that we should make our minds conform to this īśvara. This is a philosophy not only of duality but of plurality. Empirical science can go with this very well because Yoga epistemology has been adopted from Sāṅkhyan epistemology, which admits of a duality and a plurality at once. In the functional evolutionary outlook presented by the Sāṅkhya of Kapila, there is an interrelation that is holistic.

Patañjali describes īśvara as: perfect, omniscient, the revealer of everything, and the teacher of all from time immemorial. How does īśvara teach? With sound. Suppose you hear the sound "flower." You may remember how a particular kind of flower looks, then another and another. Many perceptual forms can be elaborated in response to one conceptual sound. From the beginning of the world, by offering a name that stands for a whole group of things, many possibilities arise. *Flower* is only one name. The Oxford, Webster's, or Random House dictionaries have thousands of such names, and they represent only one language. There are dictionaries for the French, German, Dutch, Japanese, Chinese, Dravidian, Arabic, Persian, and African languages.

Think of this one teacher who has been giving all these names that stand for thousands of objects, different in shape, color, and qualities. There are not only sounds of names, there are also sounds of verbs. You can say: "The train is running, the child is running, time is running." A single concept can have very wide variations. It is with such elaboration given to the revelation of sound that we should understand īśvara as the revealer of both the experiential and imperiential factors from which the perceiver and the perceived manifest.

If you take geometrical figures such as three points, they lend the possibility for lines. Lines make angles possible, angles make triangles possible, and triangles put together can become squares and parallelograms. In fact, the entire world is a geometrical elaboration. Īśvara is omniscient in the sense of being the enunciator of the laws of all geometrical figures. Even figures as variant as squares, circles, and triangles can stem from the same law. The radii that go from the center of a circle can touch every point on the circumference. In fact, that is one of the laws implied in the radiation of light and the propagation of sound.

There is no end, if one tries to list the omniscience of īśvara. Even when termites are making a nest, the law that decides exactly how two columns are to be finished, and how the termites should build from the columns to make an arch, is an archetype of architecture. Īśvara is not only a revealer to humans but a revealer to termites also. When a larva in water matures and comes to the surface and unfolds its wings, īśvara reveals to the larva that it can fly.

Thus, even a piecemeal meditation on the omniscience of īśvara can fill us with wonder. This Yoga concept that is added on to the Sāṅkhyan epistemology as the twenty-fifth factor, when elaborated into the four modulations of sound in AUM, not only inspires our appreciation for the mysterious and inexhaustible attributes of īśvara, but also initiates us into the yogic discipline of contemplation.

Sūtra I:28

tajjapas tad artha bhāvanam
tad japaḥ: [by] its constant repetition
tad artha: its meaning

bhāvanam: [and] dwelling upon in the mind

By its constant repetition and dwelling upon its meaning in the mind.

The word *mantra* has two meanings. In scriptures like the Ṛg Veda, mantra means "praise." A more technical meaning given in *Yoga Śāstra* is "that which saves a person by meditating on it." Most people think mantra is some sort of a magic syllable that can be taken from a book and then repeatedly articulated. That is like learning to drive a car or to play an instrument like the vīṇā or to swim in the ocean by reading instructions in a book. There has to be an experienced person giving his or her attention as an instructor to teach anything that is to be accomplished with practice. In the case of instruction in *mantra yoga*, the teacher should be a fully experienced person, a *mantra dṛṣṭa*.

Suppose somebody hears that by discovering *gavayam* in the forest, one can be benefited. A person who goes to the forest, not knowing gavayam, will not know what to look for. Is gavayam a stone, a tree, an herb, an animal, a bird, or an insect? Someone who goes to the forest without knowing how to identify gavayam will be at a loss. It is the same if one does *mantra japa* (mantra repetition), not knowing what to perform or what to expect. Only a person who has contemplated on a mantra and gotten the illumination of the energy ensuing from it can be a mantra dṛṣṭa.

The mantra we articulate is *vaikhari*. Mantras like AUM, HRĪM, ŚRĪM, and so on are structured with specific notes or sounds. Each mode of sound is a vibration with a certain quality according to its amplitude, frequency, and tenor. These are all measurable as aspects of physical vibration. A sound heard by the ear or articulated by the tongue can burst into meaning in consciousness *(sphoṭa)*. When it bursts into meaning, a mental picture is created. The same can happen with a vague image seen by the eye. If you see a fruit tree such as a mango or apple tree on the wayside or in another's garden, the impression it causes in your mind is only of a tree. But when you have a tree in your own garden that you have planted, tended, fertilized, and watered, the future benefit of the tree is considered as a significant factor. You look upon your own tree as a promise of the future and will be quite concerned about any harm that might befall it. In the same way, a mantra is planted in the student's mind by the guru or instructor. Like a gardener, the instructor is always watching how the energy of the mantra is released over time and how it is reciprocated by the aspirant.

A mantra is structured with letters that in Sanskrit are called *akṣara,* meaning "the imperishable." The person who articulates may perish but what is articulated remains as an imperishable word for all posterity. In the previous mantra we have seen that the praṇava, AUM, is the designator of Īśvara. When a seer like Vyāsa gives to the world the mantra *AUM kṛṣṇāyanamaḥ,* he is looked upon as the mantra dṛṣṭa, the expounder of that mantra. As the mantra is a designator of Krishna, Krishna should be treated as the deity or spiritual dynamics behind that mantra. We can go deeper into the meaning of the mantra *(bhāvana)* by relating ourselves to the mantra dṛṣṭa and pursuing the significance of the mantra with the intention of gaining the insight of the seer who is filled with love and devotion to the deity Krishna.

In the same manner, when we meditate on AUM, the mantra given to us by Patañjali, Patañjali becomes the rishi or the mantra dṛṣṭa and Īśvara is the spiritual dynamics of the mantra. As we sit to repeat AUM in our minds, it is not to be done mechanically but by visualizing Patañjali passing on his revelation to us. Planting a mantra in our consciousness is like preparing the ground *(mūla)* and sowing in it a seed *(bīja)* that will sprout in the course of time *(kilaka)* and ultimately flower forth into the wisdom ensuing from the mantra, culminating in the utmost satisfaction that we seek *(phala).*

The initiation into a mantra is given ritualistically. When a person plants a sapling, he builds a fence around it so that a straying animal may not bite off its leaves or careless people may not tread on it. Similarly, if you are entering into the discipline of mantra japa, you should choose a convenient place where you will not be easily distracted by others. When a tree has grown into its mature size, it does not need any fence. Similarly, when you are established in the full significance of the mantra with which you are disciplined, all rituals drop away.

Japa is "continuous repetition" of the mantra, in the present case, AUM. Japa is intended to include the burning away of the dross of the mind (tapas), becoming intimate with the true nature of oneself *(svādhyāya),* mentally suggesting the general direction in which the revelation of the Absolute can be expected (bhāvana), and establishing coordination between the conscious mind and the unconscious from where an archetypal revelation is believed to be arising (abhyāsa).

When you repeatedly say the same word, it may produce monotony, which can induce a hypnotic slumber. When the mind turns into a tangent, if it is again and again brought back with deliberation to the attentiveness with which the mantra japa was started, this will help to dispel lethargy and inattentiveness. This is how tapas or the burning of the dross of the mind happens.

The nature of the Self and the nature of the Absolute are not different. When you try to get into intimate relation with the nature of the Absolute, that automatically gives insight into your own nature. Thus, self-study (svādhyāya) manifests.

Bhāvana is taking aid from imagination. When the teacher reveals the nature of the Self, he or she is likely to use the dialectical approach of defining its characteristics from both a positive angle *(svarūpalakṣaṇa)* and negative angle *(tadastalakṣaṇa)*. However, because of your social and cultural exposure, there is always the danger of your mind being led astray to anthropomorphic versions of the Absolute. You may think of the Absolute as a blue-bodied person with curly hair decorated with a peacock feather or as the grotesque figure of a man hanging on a cross. This kind of imagination only brings distraction. Even so, there has to be some direction in the mind that symbolically suggests what you are looking for. Thus bhāvana is both helpful and not helpful. Obsessive imagination can only bring a caricature-like notion of the Absolute to the mind. Instead, your imagination needs to be supported by the substantiality of a perennial truth. Having the right bhāvana or imagination is essential in the experiencing of praṇava.

Repetition (abhyāsa) is recommended so that conceptual correction can be effected by going deeper and deeper into your experiencing of truth. The establishment of coordination between the cogitating mind and the so-called mindless state of samādhi is achieved by repeating the experience.

Exercise

Breathe as gently as possible, silently chanting AU *with each in breath and* M *with each out breath. After breathing in, hold the breath inside for a short while, without straining. After breathing out, gently hold the breath outside for a short while. As you do so, note the functioning of three kinds of energy: your will (iccha śakti), your action (karma śakti), and your knowledge (jñāna śakti).*

Continue breathing gently, silently chanting AU *with each in breath and* M *with each out breath, holding the breath inside after each in breath and outside after each out breath.*

Sūtra I:29

tataḥ pratyak cetanādhigamo'pyantarāyā bhāvaś ca

tataḥ: from it [the repetition of the praṇava mantra]
pratyak: the turning inward, the centripetal
cetana: [of] consciousness
adhigamaḥ: [the] attainment
api: also
antarāya: [of] obstacles, impediments
abhāva: [of the] non-existence, absence, negation, disappearance
ca: and

Also, from the repetition of the praṇava mantra, the attainment of the disappearance of obstacles and the turning inward of consciousness.

Consciousness is like light that oscillates. The two-way movement of light can be described as centripetal convergence and centrifugal divergence. In ordinary people who are exposed to the fivefold stimuli coming from the objects of interest of all five senses, two locations are again and again established, one in the object and a corresponding one in the subject. The outer stimulus haunts the individuated consciousness and sensory knowledge oscillates between the object of interest and the I-consciousness of the agent of perception. Even though the inward-moving consciousness *(pratyak cetana)* can ultimately reach the core of one's being and find its identity with the Self, this is thwarted by the oscillating consciousness. After establishing an inner picture that corresponds to what is experienced outside, the oscillating consciousness returns to the external object to establish its relationship with the source of the new interest.

The outward-going consciousness (*parāṅga cetana)* that is luring consciousness to the object outside is called vikṣepa. *Kṣepanam* is "depositing;" vikṣepa is "depositing the interest of the individual in an external object." But when praṇava is meditated upon, the unitiveness of the threefold consciousness becomes merged in the fourth and, as a result, parāṅga cetana is inhibited by the wholesomeness of unmodulating consciousness. Only pratyak cetana is allowed which, in its ultimate convergence, goes to the very core (pratyak) of the Self. By repeatedly thwarting the outward-flowing consciousness, the hindrances to imperiential empathy with the core aspect of the Self become weaker and weaker. Because of the salutary effect of continuously repeating praṇava, the outward-going tendency of consciousness is arrested. This enables the twofold benefit of dissipating all obstacles in the path of Yoga and making the aspirant yogi spirit-oriented.

Sūtra I:30

vyādhi styāna samśaya pramādālasya avirati bhrānti
darśanālabdhabhūmikatva anavasthitatvāni
cittaviksepāste'ntarāyāḥ

vyādhi: physical pain or distress, disease
styāna: mental depression
samśaya: doubt, paranoia
pramāda: exaggeration
ālasya: laziness
avirati: hankering after objects, sensuality
bhrānti: insanity, delusion
darśana alabdhabhūmikatva: having no firm ground for spiritual orientation
anavasthitatvāni: instability

cittavikṣepāḥ: [cause] distraction of the mind, misplaced memory

te: these

antarāyāḥ: obstacles, hindrances

Physical pain or distress, mental depression, doubt, exaggeration, laziness, hankering after objects, insanity, having no firm ground for spiritual orientation, instability—these obstacles cause the distraction of the mind.

This sūtra is a listing of nine causes of major disturbances that can be seen manifesting in most people. The first one is *vyādhi*. The word *vyādhi* comes from *vedha,* which means "pain or distress." The psychosomatic system is structured so carefully that it functions harmoniously when all the interlaced parts are in good form and each is contributing its function correctly. The mind and body are like two bulls dragging a cart or two wings with which a bird flies. A machine that functions twenty-four hours a day, seven days a week, all year round, all through life, will necessarily have wear and tear. Even a single nut missing from a mammoth machine can cause a disaster in its whole functioning. Similarly, in the binary body/mind relationship, the dysfunction of either the mind or the body makes the other also useless. When the body fails, it is called vyādhi, literally, the "distress-giving entity."

To arrive at a certain goal, even if you have the best mode of transportation, if you have no mind to get up and drive your vehicle, you will be sitting lost in boredom. As years go by we see more and more people who are exposed to mental depression. They know they have to get up and act, but they cannot even make up their mind to hold a pen. This is the dysfunction that comes from the mental side called *styāna*.

The body and mind can each get in each other's way. The

mind is willing to go, but the body sits there like a heavy load; the body is ready to move but the mind is apprehensive about allowing the body to function. The result is like a driver of a car who puts his feet firmly on the accelerator and the brake at the same time—a lot of commotion goes on inside but nothing happens. Such a person is aware of the dreadful waste of time and that itself causes the drainage of energy. Consequently, energy cannot be channeled in any direction. One of the greatest tragedies in human life is that many hours are wasted each day because of this kind of inability to take a decision. That is *saṁśaya*.

When a machine is operating only at a throbbing level and not put into gear, it gets overheated. It is the same with our body/mind machine also. Sitting in one room and endlessly ruminating causes grievous distress to the nervous system and this causes many people to exaggerate. They become nervous, irritable, and unable to cope with anyone or anything. Such a delirious state is *pramāda*.

An exaggerating mind spends too much energy in a short time and the body and mind feel exhausted. Nature's prevention of further deterioration is to take away further incentives to act, making the body and mind lazy. This is *ālasya*. The will to live is such that fresh quantums of energy are released that give incentives to the mind to look into new avenues of interest. Consequently, the previous decorum of life is given up and the person may function in a weird manner, perhaps even becoming antisocial, a nuisance to self and others. This is the state of *avirati*.

When a person's desire to enjoy becomes uncontrolled, he or she is only aware of the enjoyment of the desired object and unaware of the appropriateness of the situation. A person who is infatuated with desire tends to speak aggressive and disrespectful words and may even behave like a brute. Hysteric exultations and manic-depressive behavior may manifest in such a person. This is *bhrānti*.

A person who is very devoid of will power and concentration will always be searching for a new path, while failing to pursue any discipline to the extent of it yielding any result. Sri Ramakrishna compares such a person to one who digs a hole a couple of feet deep for a well and then abandons it because it has not yielded water, then digs another hole two feet deep and abandons it, and so on. Such a person is always at the beginning of a path and never accomplishes anything, having no clear idea of what exactly he is looking for. The state of such a visionless person is called *darśana alabdhabhūmikatva*.

Like the unimaginative person who cannot direct himself consistently to an achievable goal, there is the restless, unsteady person who is always full of plans but who does not know how to execute any of her programs. She is endlessly waiting, like an angler who is sitting on the bank of a river that has no fish in it, with neither a hook nor any bait at the end of her line. This is the state of *anavasthitatva*.

Each of these nine obstacles causes a lack of clarity in a person's cogitating intelligence. Then memory, instead of being structured, is amorphous. This causes distraction of the mind and obstructs the path of Yoga.

Sūtra I:31

duḥkha daurmanasyāṅgamejayatva śvāsapraśvāsā vikṣepa sahabhuvaḥ

duḥkha: pain, misery, distress, sorrow, suffering

daurmanasya: despair, depression

aṅgamejayatva: shakiness, uncontrolled movement of the body

śvāsapraśvāsā: [and] hard breathing, inhalation and

exhalation

vikṣepa: [of] distraction

sahabhuvaḥ:[are the] companions, accompaniments

Pain, despair, shakiness, and hard breathing are the companions of distraction.

Kham is space. If we live in a space full of sunlight, flowers, and beautiful things that make us happy *(su),* then we say we are living in a good space *(sukham).* But if our living space is cluttered with darkness, obstruction, misery *(duḥ),* then it is a negative space *(duḥkham).* The experience of time comes from motion happening in your living space. Each motion-producing state is called *kāla.* In the living space of most people, the fluctuations of time bring happiness and unhappiness alternatively. Only when these alternations cease can you say you have transcended time and space.

When sukham is not there and your living space is darkened, your mind refuses to function and a state of depression *(daurmanasya)* comes. The result is *aṅgamejayatva,* which means you feel acute physical weakness such as shivering and unsteadiness. You no longer feel you can function efficiently. Your inner agitation and mental anxiety cause your breathing to become hard. When a person is afflicted with pain, all the symptoms enumerated here come together.

Here, Patañjali is not cataloguing the eternal pains of life. He is calling our attention to a common occurrence in which a person is assailed with negative energy. When such negativity comes and torments the mind, reflected pain comes in the body as well and the body shows signs of malfunction. The interference caused by painful manifestations in the yogi's living space needs immediate therapeutic correction.

Sūtra I:32

tat pratiṣedhārtham ekatattvābhyāsaḥ
tat: these, that [obstacles]
pratiṣedha: removing, preventing, counteracting
artham: for the purpose of, in order to
eka: [of] one
tattva: truth or principle
abhyāsaḥ: repetitive practice, application

For removing these obstacles: repetitive practice of one truth or principle.

The arresting of obstacles occurs when concentration on a single principle is practiced. For example, if a person smokes, the smoke of the tobacco pollutes his lungs and brain. If he decides to stop smoking, even after taking this resolve, he will continue to desire to smoke. This makes the issue a more serious one for him. It also gives him an opportunity to begin to look deeply into his mind and find many peculiarities that he had never noticed before. Not to smoke becomes a challenge and his resolve not to yield builds up will power. His mind returns to that resolve again and again and his decision gains the status of a meditation.

Sūtra I:33

maitrī karuṇā muditopekṣāṇām sukha duḥkha puṇyāpuṇya viṣayāṇām bhāvanātaś citta prasādanam

maitrī: friendliness
karuṇā: compassion
muditā: gladness, delight

upekṣānām: equanimity, indifference
sukha: happiness, comfort, pleasure-giving, pleasurable
duḥkha: pain, misery, distress, sorrow, suffering
puṇya: virtue, goodness
apuṇya: vice, without virtue
viṣayāṇām: toward the spheres
bhāvanāt: cultivating
citta: mental, mind, mind-stuff, faculty of memory and recall, main body of consciousness
prasādanam: [is] clarified, purified

The mind is clarified by cultivating friendliness toward happiness, compassion toward misery, gladness toward virtue, and equanimity toward vice.

In the previous sūtra we were told that by continuously practicing any one discipline we can get over the obstacles (kleśas) in the path of Yoga. Here Patañjali is enumerating four situations of life. They are: 1) when you see that your environment is conducive to happiness; 2) when there are painful occasions in your environment; 3) when you are witnessing a virtuous action; 4) when you are exposed to vice. As your environment changes, it is better to resort to that particular discipline that is most appropriate for each situation.

Let us take, for example, the state of happiness that comes most naturally in an environment where you are not provoked by anyone or disturbed by anything. Even when you are fortunate to be placed in a situation where nobody is being offensive, you are often not induced to be friendly with that situation. Most people become lazy when there is no challenge in life and start losing interest in everyone and everything around them. You are always surrounded by fellow human beings, animals, birds, plants, and a changing panorama. When these are all obliviated by your self-indulgence, human beings look like mere shadows. Even family members and co-workers are looked upon as people of no consequence. Thus your attitude becomes unfriendly, devoid of any enthusiasm in your caring and sharing. Thus most people miss a great opportunity to discover in the person who is sitting next to them or working as a comrade one of the finest friends to make. It is to avoid such a tremendous loss that you are asked to cultivate positive friendship with whomever you are exposed to or are relating with.

The person who is bracketed with you in social life may seem uncouth or overbearing. If you cultivate your identity with that person, then it becomes your duty to transform him or her into a very likeable person. You can accomplish this not by aggressively intruding into the lives of others but by helping them to understand themselves and making common programs with them so that no one need feel that he or she is alone in this world without a comrade to assist.

Even if her child pulls away and becomes hysteric when she tries to give it a bath or some such help, a mother does not become hostile to the child. Her only concern is what is good for her child. When you adopt such an attitude of active interest in sharing all your good moments of friendliness with another person, they gain a more and more sympathetic understanding. You are not only making a friend but helping him or her to be an adorable friend.

In the practice of any discipline, consistency and continuity are absolutely necessary. So, your friendship with another should not be a short-term experiment. Your sincerity has to prove itself by its continuous prevalence between you and the other person. When you share your happiness with another in the same situation and by the same cause, you multiply your happiness. No joy is a true joy unless you can share it with another.

In ordinary friendships the element of attachment and

passion tends to become predominant, but in maitri this aspect is absent. Instead, maitri is a bipolarity that leads the mind to a sense of calm serenity. This is opposed to the kind of friendship that causes the arousal of disturbing emotions. The attitude of maitri is practiced by continuously applying it in your relationships.

The other three disciplines of cultivating compassion toward misery, gladness toward virtue, and equanimity toward vice can also become your continuous meditation.

Sūtra I:34

pracchardana vidhāraṇābhyām vā prāṇasya

pracchardana: [by the] expiration, ejection, expulsion
vidhāraṇābhyām: [and] retention
vā: or, also
prāṇasya: [of] breath

Or, by the expiration and retention of breath.

This sūtra is to be read along with the sūtras preceding and following it. In sūtra thirty-three Patañjali gave us a method by which the mind can be stabilized in a higher state. Then alternative methods are described in sūtras thirty-four through thirty-nine, as is indicated by the use of *vā* (or, also) in each sūtra. Throughout the epistemology of Sāṅkhya and Yoga we can see alternatives being brought together in this way to establish a discipline for the search for higher truth or values.

As we will see in Sūtra II:29, Patañjali describes the science of Yoga as having eight limbs: restraints *(yama)*, observances *(niyama)*, posture *(āsana)*, regulation of vital forces *(prāṇāyāma),* withdrawal from distraction *(pratyāhāra),* holding the focus of the mind *(dhāraṇā),* contemplation *(dhyāna),* and absorption *(samādhi).* People who are impressed by the activities of hatha yogis have done two disservices to the study of Yoga. First, they have interpreted posture (āsana) as the practice of several physical exercises, when Patañjali simply said that one's posture should be comfortable and steady. Similarly, the regularization or equalization of the vital energies (prāṇāyāma) has also been misinterpreted as a kind of breathing exercises taught by the hatha yogis. However, Patañjali's own usage of "or" (vā) in this sūtra clearly indicates that prāṇāyāma is permissible and not mandatory. The only aim of the practices *(kriyā yoga)* outlined in sūtras thirty-three through thirty-nine is explicitly stated in sūtra thirty-three: to clarify the mind. All that is aspired for is a steady and cheerful state of mind.

Continuous contemplation on friendliness, compassion, cheerfulness, and equanimity is recommended as a practice for those who are naturally disposed to a contemplative attitude. When a person wants to exemplify personal values like friendship or compassion, he may find that he cannot easily forgive someone who has been consistently unjust and aggressive toward him, or show compassion to a person who has tortured him on a previous occasion. The negative conditioning already built in his system through previous experiences gets in the way of the actualization of his ideals of friendship and compassion. Knowing this limitation of the human mind, Patañjali offers an alternative that can be definitely carried out because it is in an area over which the aspirant has control: the outgoing and incoming breath.

Some of the vital functions in the body/mind complex are voluntary, while most are autonomous. Breathing is one function that can be done voluntarily or left to the autonomous system. Autonomous functions happen without our conscious direction, while voluntary functions are deliberated. Here, an exercise is given whereby an autonomous function is temporarily transferred to a voluntary deliberation. Usually we breathe without any knowledge of it unless we have some disease like asthma or tuberculosis.

Breathing is an internal function in which an external organ is involved. Fresh air enters the system through the nostrils by the autonomous expansion and contraction of the lungs. The vital breath (prāṇa) that goes into the lungs mixes itself with blood, which carries oxygen to every cell of the body. Thus breathing is a holistic function that is alternating with a coordinated operation of lungs and heart. Oxygen is supplied to the cells, then carbon dioxide and other pollutions are seweraged from the cells to the lungs and exhaled. Of this complex process, we can voluntarily interfere with the preliminary stage, inhalation, and the final stage, exhalation. Conscious and unconscious operations are so interlaced in respiration that, through it, we can observe the complementary nature of psychosomatic functioning.

It is a great device of Patañjali to assign to prāṇa such an important role in pacifying both the body and mind as the aspirant observes how the gross air that enters the nostrils helps the digestive system to oxidize the ingredients of the food that goes into the stomach and intestines, then how that nourishment supplies energy to the central nervous system to become not only sensations and feelings, but also to develop a stream of consciousness by which the entire life is governed. At one level prāṇa is only gross air and at another level it is the subtlest thoughts with which we envision the supreme truth. There is nothing more important than prāṇa to help us to have an all-embracing discipline that can affect both the body and mind. Unfortunately, some people, not knowing the intention of Patañjali, do all kinds of breathing exercises. Seeing the grotesqueness of such exercises, Ramana Maharshi described them as the torturing of prāṇa *(prāṇa pīḍanam).*

There is one area of uncertainty in the sūtra. The first word is *pracchardana* which means "expiration" or "ejection." It is followed by *vidhāraṇābhyām,* which means "retention." Different yogis take this in different ways. Some think that, after emptying all the breath from the lungs and then breathing in, air should be retained for some time inside. This is called *kumbhaka,* potting the air (*kumbha* means "pot"). Breathing in is not actually mentioned, so another group of yogis say that it means *not* breathing in immediately after the expiration of breath. Holding the breath outside after exhaling has two virtues. One is a complete purging of the polluted air from the system. The other is cultivating a consciousness that you are breathing voluntarily, by which a discipline can be established of transferring the agency of breathing to your voluntary system.

But this should not preclude again filling the lungs with air. The objection against holding the breath for a long time could have some reference to the cumulative effect of carbon dioxide, which can not only affect the lungs but also can raise the threshold of the preconscious mind and generate enzymes that are directly responsible for hallucinative disturbances. This subject will be discussed further when we come sūtras forty-nine through fifty-three of the second chapter.

Sūtra I:35

viṣayavatī vā pravṛttir utpannā manasaḥ sthiti nibandhanī

viṣayavatī: [when absolute] interest is shown to a sensory experience

vā: or, also

pravṛtti: activity

utpannā: that will bring
manasaḥ: the mind
sthiti nibhandhanī: to a steady state

When absolute interest is shown to a sensory experience or activity, that will bring the mind to a steady state.

The function of the mind is divided between the sensory system and the motor system. In a crude way we can relate the function of the mind to the maneuvering of a machine by its operator such as the driver of an automobile. The driver of the vehicle trains himself to be in full cognizance of several matters that need to be coordinated for the safe driving of the car. When the individuated person is functioning in the body/mind system he or she also has to treat the body as a vehicle.

There can be stumbling blocks in the path of the vehicle so the driver has to be cautious not to hit them. The path may ascend or descend. The fuel supply is to be limited on the descent and increased on the ascent. The brake is to be applied whenever appropriate. If the engine is overheated or the water has evaporated, the driver needs to check the condition of the engine and give immediate care to rectify the defect.

In the driving of a car, two things take place simultaneously: the continuous cognizance of the path, the vehicle, and the driver's intention, and the details of the manipulation that are to be carefully attended to. In our daily life we are either very much in an action program or in a contemplative situation. When we listen to music, for instance, we don't have to manipulate anything but only attune ourselves to the melody and rhythm of the music.

In this sūtra we are told how the natural function of the mind on the sensory or motor side can conveniently be converted into a discipline (sādhana) to bring the mind to a high degree of efficiency and harmony. Irrespective of the sensory experience or kind of activity in which we are engaged, by giving our full attention to it we can attain Yoga, which is defined in the *Gita* as "dexterity in action."

Sūtra I:36

viśokā vā jyotiṣmatī

viśokā: [by meditating on the] sorrowless state of inner joy
vā: also, or
jyotiṣmatī: [one can attain] luminosity of intelligence

Also by meditating on the sorrowless state of inner joy one can attain luminosity of intelligence.

The human mind is very often compared to the Moon. Mental diseases are often described as lunatic conditions. The phases of the Moon are lunatic. From the new Moon up to the full Moon there is a steady waxing of the Moon's brightness and dimension. The full Moon looks like a perfect sphere and it has a very pleasing effulgence. Then it begins to wane until it becomes perfectly lost in the shadow of Earth. These two phases are shared by the human mind. People become exuberant in their joy on full Moon nights and many people go into states of depression when the new Moon comes.

The Moon cannot escape the tragedy of alternatingly becoming bright and dark because it is a satellite that has to orbit around Earth. As Earth and the Moon are spinning and rotating with different speeds, the bright phase and the dark phase are bound to alternate in fixed periods. In the case of a person, there is no permanent casting of shadow or flash of light, yet the human psyche, in some strange way, shares the cosmic phenomena. Even the happiest person is sometimes seen in an unpleasant mood. Certain schizophrenics who are usually catatonic sometimes find themselves lifted out of the dark for a few days to behave normally or even become euphoric.

The altering states coming from external circumstances can correspond to a person's altering psychic states of consciousness. As human nature is not so fixed as the cyclic changes of the heavenly bodies, it is possible for a person to take therapeutic measures to redress psychic malfunctions. Of the four inner organs, intellect is the brightest and can be used as a handle to rectify inner discordance.

Humans are very fickle. If for some days you are exposed to a congenial environment and if, on a certain day, the expected symbol of love and acceptance is not there, you can suddenly feel perturbed and subject yourself to a lousy state of mind. Someone in the vicinity can be thought of as the cause for your disturbance and a whole range of paranoia can be kicked up. When this happens, your hilarious laughter is gone and the muscles of your throat, face, and lips go heavy with a strange atrophy so that you cannot even smile on seeing a friend.

You are being tortured from within through no one's fault, yet you feel so helpless to wriggle out of that state. Depression crushes your entire psyche in its steel claws. If you take care to look at one bright spot such as a beautiful poem, a melodious music, a wonderful episode in your own life or another's, and keep attuned to it with the intention of purging away the blues and increasing the inner state of joy, the spark can turn into a glow, the glow into a flame, and the flame can ultimately become a conflagration of joy.

Sūtra I:37

vītarāga viṣayam vā cittam

vītarāga: fixed on freedom from attachment
viṣayam: to sensory experience
vā: also, or
cittam: the mind, mental, faculty of memory and recall, main body of consciousness [acquires steadiness]

Also the mind fixed on freedom from attachment to sense experience acquires steadiness.

The term *vītarāga* in this sūtra can be taken either as the ideal of transcending attachment or as a person who has transcended human passions such as attachment. An impersonal way of contemplating on an ideal is difficult for the beginner. Hence most interpreters put a positive stress on the example of a person who has transcended passions. In verse seven of his *Atmopadeśa Śatakam,* Narayana Guru describes the superior way of idealizing the state of transcendence as going beyond all relativistic clichés. Then, as second best, he recommends to those who cannot establish themselves in such an ideal that they engage themselves in the service of a contemplative who has understood the fourfold secrets of AUM and has thus transcended all relativistic affinities. In either case, the stress is on the ideal of transcending emotional attachment.

When we look at the lives of great people of mature wisdom we see that compassion wells up in them for matters that look insignificant to others, while they look unconcerned in matters of personal loss and on occasions when others would be agitated. In the personal life of Lord Buddha, Jesus Christ, Mohammed the Prophet, and many others, we can see that they are in a solid state with regard to their personal integrity. All the same they are receptive of the pains and agitations of the people around them. As they are moved to compassion, they dedicate all their time in the service of all sentient beings. At the same time, they remain unmoved in witnessing the transient ways of the world.

We cannot straight away discipline our minds. However, we have control over our physical bodies and the functions of our faculties of action. So it is easier to handle those areas. After controlling external behavior, we can go into the formations of our will, the nature of our desires, and the source of our urges, and bring discipline there also. When we see the example in a living person we are encouraged to follow suit and achieve the same results in ourselves also.

A person who lives constantly in transcendence, such as one's guru, is also a human being. We are encouraged to watch how such a person overcomes situations that should cause agitation. Although in the beginning it may look as if we are only imitating our model, in the course of time our choices become habitual. Then it is no longer imitation but a spontaneous adherence to higher ideals and we also become established in the tranquility of a yogi.

Sūtra I:38

svapna nidrā jñānālambanam vā

svapna: dream state
nidrā: deep sleep, dreamless sleep state
jñāna: knowledge
ālambanam: [by] contemplating on
vā: also, or

Also by contemplating on the knowledge derived from

the dream state and the dreamless sleep state.

The nature of the Self is pure consciousness. The fourfold inner organs of the individuated mind manifest within the ambit of this pure consciousness. The inquiring faculty, memory, intellect, and the affective ego all derive their light from the pure light of the Self in order to function as the faculties of the individuated self (jīva). Just as the one light of consciousness, when received by the different organs, manifests as different functions such as doubting, remembering, judging, and becoming affected by pain and pleasure, the five senses are differently stimulated by external energy. Consequently, the ear hears, the skin feels, the eye sees, the tongue tastes, and the nose smells. When the four inner organs (mind, memory, intellect, and ego), in conjunction with the five sense organs, become stimulated by external objects, perception takes place.

The wakeful experience is the most gross and specific experience of the individual. The perceptual experiences derived through the senses are all reduced to their characteristic qualities and stored in the faculty of memory so they can be reproduced at any time. In wakeful consciousness the individual is relating himself or herself with the universe. The nature of that relationship is one of measuring and judging the qualities of the individual items that constitute the universe. Hence the wakeful state is said to belong to the physical perceiver of the universe *(viśvābhimāni)*.

When we withdraw our senses from external objects and no longer depend on stimulation from outside, we are still conscious we exist. We can still bring in the ego to function as the central locus of consciousness. All impressions gathered from perception can be recalled with form, name, color, and other perceptual qualities. These impressions, along with conceptual images, can be restructured and put into compositions of dreams, which can be as impressive as external perception. We are not completely in the dark when we are dreaming; there is a light within us *(tejas)*. Therefore the consciousness prevailing during dream hours is called the perceiver of the inner light *(taijasābhimāni)*.

When we enter into deep sleep the flickering I-consciousness also vanishes. However, when we come out of that state, we do not experience any break or discontinuity with the past. Instead of thinking, "I did not exist for some time," we recognize that we had a very peaceful experience of an undisturbed state. As that state can be remembered, it is one of consciousness that does not undergo any specific modulation (prajñā).

These are the three cyclic transformations of consciousness, all happening on the ground of pure consciousness which is the fourth (turīya). Most people think of their wakeful life as the only important factor. But here Patañjali says that just as you can meditate in the wakeful state on an object of consciousness, you can also meditate on the inner light that makes compositions of dreams, the shining aspect of consciousness. He also says you can meditate on the unmodulated consciousness of deep sleep for the eradication of the haunting impressions that are continuously created through a process of culturing psycho-physical experiences.

Sūtra I:39

yathābhimata dhyānād vā

yathā: as
abhimata: desired [by oneself]
dhyānāt:[by] contemplation, even and harmonious flow of consciousness

vā: or, also

Or by contemplation as desired by oneself.

Yoga is not to be imparted like a collective drill that is given to squadrons or battalions of soldiers. Each person has his or her own biological, sociological, and cultural history, background, and heritage, which makes Peter different from Paul. What is absolutely necessary to Peter can be quite superfluous to Paul. Recognizing the uniqueness of each individual, Patañjali states that the most suitable discipline for each person is that which he or she can wholeheartedly accept.

In the *Bhagavad Gita,* Lord Krishna gives Arjuna thorough instruction in the science of the Absolute and the unitive way of actualizing the essence of supreme wisdom. Every aspect of Yoga is graphically described. In the eighteenth chapter, when Arjuna becomes mature enough even to be initiated into *mokṣa sannyāsa yoga* (unitive way of ultimate liberation), he rededicates himself at the feet of the Lord and requests him to command what he should perform. In response to this request, Krishna says, "After critically examining all my instructions, you choose to act exactly as you desire." Krishna does not hold his beloved disciple at the leash of any obligation. The disciple is fully free to choose what is most appropriate to him. Here Patañjali also emphasizes this supreme teaching in Yoga, which offers absolute freedom to its votary, making it clear that, ultimately, everyone has to help himself or herself. Thus this sūtra is very significant.

Sūtra I:40

paramāṇu parama mahattvānto'sya vaśīkāraḥ

paramāṇu: [from] the finest (minutest) atom
parama: [to the] greatest
mahattva: infinity
antaḥ: extends
asya: the yogi's
vaśīkāraḥ: mastery

The yogi's mastery extends from the finest atom to the greatest infinity.

Yoga is the canceling out of the pairs of opposites whereby the dualities in principles and the multiplicity in manifestation can all be reduced to one single unitive principle. No science is possible unless the scientist has a methodology of reduction by which the multitudinous factors implied in the study can all be reduced to a single primeval substance or entity. In the same manner, the scientist should have a method by which the unified principle can be re-elaborated systematically into the manifoldness of manifestation. The Yoga of Patañjali claims to have such a binary method, which implies both the unifying reduction and the power of methodic elaboration.

In one sense we are all sharing one physical universe with one set of physical, chemical, biological, and psychological laws. Yet when we individually look at that world of experience, my world is entirely mine and your world is entirely yours. Brick by brick and moment by moment we each build up our own world of experience. When we retire from our conscious life into the unconscious we have to fold the world of time and space and bury it in the oblivion of our unconscious. In one sense the world is created in this moment, then gives way to be modified, regenerated, and lived in the next moment.

Our conscious creation is negligible compared to the

multitudinous causes and effects that go into the making of the unified experience of each moment, which are coming from the unknown and unconscious as a tremendous mystery. When something is being manipulated in you by the unconscious, you experience it only as an autonomous presentation. It is as if you are a baby, not taken into confidence by the supreme owner of your life.

Here, the expositor of the science of Yoga is calling our attention to two separate entities. The first is the individuated consciousness that has a glow of awareness. Whatever is happening there is understood as the mentation of the individual. The other is the psychobiologic organism to which the person belongs, which in its turn is part of a universal matrix, of which most areas are hidden from the purview of the individual. This is recognized as the great principle, *mahatattvā*.

A third factor is not elaborated or spoken of here. It is the unifying principle of the conscious and the unconscious elements. They are interlaced in such a manner that what is presently experienced only as individuated consciousness can be brought to bear upon the entirety of the supreme principle, so that the individual can become a receptacle all through. Then no part is unfit to articulate what is otherwise monopolized only by the unconscious manipulator of life. This aspect has been elaborated by Sri Aurobindo in his *Synthesis of Yoga*.

Sūtra I:41

kṣīṇa vṛtter abhijātasyeva maṇer grahītṛ grahaṇa grāhyeṣu tatstha tadañjanatā samāpattiḥ

kṣīṇa vṛtteḥ: in one whose mental modifications have been attenuated

abhijātasya: transparent

iva: like
maṇeḥ: a crystal
grahītṛ: the cognizer, the knower
grahaṇa: the act of cognition, the knowing
grāhyeṣu: [or] the cognized, the known,
tatstha: remains in
tadañjanatā: taking the form or color of that
samāpatti: stabilization of consciousness

In one whose mental modulations have been attenuated, consciousness remains stabilized in the cognizer, the act of cognition, or the cognized, taking the form or color of that, like a transparent crystal.

We have an outward-going consciousness. Its windows are our five organs of perception. Through the five senses we do not come into contact with five objects or five thousand objects but countless objects of interest. The stimuli coming from external objects through the sense organs are continuously causing disturbances in the inner organs. Those disturbances are mentioned in this sūtra as vṛtti. The main discipline of a yogi is that of withdrawing the inner organs from the multitudinous impacts of the senses and turning them to the very source of one's own inner illumination, which is attuned to pure existence, pure subsistence, and pure value.

During your whole lifetime you have been continuously conditioned with the impact of various energies coming from the outside world. For most people—who have only gained the training to know gross objects with name and form—it is not easy to extricate the conditioned power of cognition from the impact of the external world. A discipline is needed so that turning in can be practiced and made a reality. For that, you can do certain exercises such as abstracting a value that is seen as manifesting in the outer world. Importance is given to the value that makes something attractive rather than to the physical place, object, or event in which the value manifests. This is a process of turning in from the world of concrete objects to a pure form of knowledge. This turning in from the exterior to the interior is *pratyāhāra*. When this exercise is done several times, your identity with the inner reality becomes more stable and more easily recognized.

Let us take for example the discipline of cultivating friendship. Even when the mind is provoked by external circumstances that go against maintaining friendship, the will to be disciplined by friendship is strengthened by the desire to be unitive. This helps you to belittle the importance of provocation and hold onto friendship. That retention is dhāraṇā. Maintaining that retention by reliving friendship again and again trains your mind to have a new habit that is opposed to old habits. Previous conditioning is weakened by the new conditioning. Ultimately, there shouldn't be any conditioning, but you cannot arrive at that state immediately, so you apply a method of deconditioning.

When all conditionings are scraped off, recall and association become less frequent and stability is established. The inner organs undergo a drastic change. The ego is no longer paranoid about the countless messages brought in by the sense organs. For instance, even if a person is shouting scandalous words at you, if you treat it only as noise, then you put up with some noise and you are not provoked. In this way the external world is nullified to the yogi. When the ego, the questioning mind, and memory recall are all pacified, the intellect, like a transparent crystal, reflects only the pure light of the Self. That prepares you for emancipation from the bondage of the world.

Sūtra I:42

tatra śabdārtha jñāna vikalpaiḥ saṅkīrṇā savitarkā samāpattiḥ

tatra: in the
śabda: word, sound
artha: meaning
jñāna: [and] idea, knowledge
vikalpaiḥ: [in] confused cognition, imaginary cognition, verbal delusion
saṅkīrṇā: commingled, blended, mixed up
savitarka: in an object of perception, perceptual configuration or confrontation
samāpatti: stabilization of consciousness

In the stabilization of consciousness in an object of perception, word, meaning, and idea are commingled in confused cognition.

This sūtra will yield its full meaning only when we have undergone the disciplines given in the second chapter of the aphorisms. Here we are only introduced to certain procedural aspects of the discipline.

From the very early days of our childhood, the free flowing energy of our consciousness was interrupted naturally with the presentation of objects to the senses. This was supplemented by elders drawing our attention to specific objects with conscious deliberation to link percepts with names and names with concepts. As a result, when sensory confrontations come, we automatically shift our consciousness from the arresting object to its name and to the meaning that both the name and the object have for us. When such a confrontation comes, the first occurrence is an oscillation of consciousness between the perceiver and the perceived. On the side of the perceived, we note its form and name. On the side of the perceiver, we observe the impact in terms of pain and pleasure, attraction and repulsion. As every experience is to be processed and retained as part of our culturing, the substance of the name-form content and the accompanying psychic state are blended and kept in memory. Thus the mind has three areas of interest: the object, the subjective reaction to the object, and the idea of the object that can be recalled to the mind as a mental object or word image.

In our attempt to attain concentration, we try to inhibit the continuous fluctuation of the changing modes of consciousness by stabilizing consciousness in one of the three areas. However, the force of habit cannot be immediately restrained. The mind will compulsively go again and again from the object of perception to the ego that tries to reckon with the ongoing consciousness, to the unconscious formation of the impression, through the process of reducing the entire experience to its essential quality and preserving it like a seed. It takes quite a while for consciousness to stabilize, to come to samāpatti. Until then, there will be a mixing up of all three aspects of the perceptual mode *(saṅkīrṇā savitarka).* The intermediate stage is a confused state with a stable image arising out of the confusion.

When we try to contemplate, we do not get full concentration or stabilization immediately. The mind will be fluctuating. But after a while we experience occasional lapses in the frequent flowing in of stimuli where non-perception manifests and thought becomes arrested. If, after some struggle, a full identification with one of the three areas, such as the object of perception, is established, that is savitarka samādhi.

Sūtra I:43

smṛti pariśuddhau svarūpa śūnyeva artha mātra nirbhāsā nirvitarkā

smṛti: the memory
pariśuddhau: is purified, clarified
svarūpa: its own (or essential) form
śūnya: devoid of
iva: as if
artha: [and the] object
mātra: alone
nirbhāsā: [is] illuminated
nirvitarka: [in] unobstructed or unmodified consciousness, without perceptual confrontation

In unobstructed consciousness, the memory is purified, as if devoid of its own form, and the object alone is illuminated.

Before we can understand *nirvitarka,* we need to know the meaning of *tarka* and *vitarka.* The five senses in the body are like five look-outs. Each gives a different kind of experience such as sound from the ear or sense of hearing, touch from the skin or sense of touch, and so on. When our individuated consciousness is flowing out through any or all of the organs of perception, it is again and again confronted by the indication that something is being presented to it. The indication of a presented object is first recognized with the idea of "this." It is immediately followed by the question, "What is this?" This places an obstruction in the free flow of consciousness.

Let us take an example. A person enters her room for contemplation. When she sits and looks at an object of worship, her mind is first confronted by the idol. Then she explains it to herself saying, "This is a śivaliṅga, an idol of Lord Śiva." The initial specification of the object is tarka. Considering the object by naming it is vitarka. When she begins to contemplate on the object of confrontation, her consciousness becomes split. While she is looking at the idol śivaliṅga, she also remembers how that word is written in a language familiar to her. The written word is only a verbal symbol. When it is pronounced, it produces quite a different sound image. Neither the written nor spoken word, *śivaliṅga,* bears any resemblance to the idol. The word belongs to the world of verbal function.

From that, her mind shifts back to the particular form of śivaliṅga that she perceives with her eyes. Then many associated ideas come rushing into her mind as a historical narration of the evolution of the concept of Śiva from the prehistoric days of Mohenjo Daro to the present, and the presentation of the story of Śiva in the *Śivapurāṇa* and many other Hindu books. Other presentations of Śiva such as the dancing Śiva or the androgynous Śiva come to her attention. There is a confused commingling of the verbal, the visual, and the symbolic aspects, all caricatured by her own memory. As this presentation in memory is opposed to concentration, it is called vitarka.

The yogi adopts the discipline of letting go of all irrelevant aspects such as any personal relationship with that idea and with things that are unrelated to the particular gestalt taken for contemplation. This is a process of purifying one's memory. One by one, distractions are dropped. The external object and the internal contemplation become identified into a single entity. Then consciousness is filled with what is presented without being dragged into any tangent of association. Therefore, there is no experiencing of confrontation, because the duality of the perceiver and the perceived comes to an end.

As the vitarka is no longer there, the savitarka samāpatti changes into nirvitarka samāpatti. In the yogi's sādhana (practice) this is a major crossing over. The most important thing to be noted here is the initial success of the aspiring yogi in liberating himself or herself from the clutches of memory.

Sūtra I:44

etayaiva savicāra nirvicāra ca sūkṣmaviṣayā vyākhyātā
etayaiva: by this also
savicāra: conceptual configuration of consciousness
nirvicāra: consciousness devoid of conceptual configuration
ca: and
sūkṣmaviṣayā: having the subtle for their objects
vyākhyātā: are explained

By this, savicāra and nirvicāra (consciousness with and without conceptual configuration), having the subtle for their objects, are also explained.

The four modes of mentation are compulsive repetition (cinta), linear movement through ideas (vicāra), vertical absorption or contemplation (manana), and stabilized absorption (dhyāna).

Vicāra is the linear flow of consciousness through ideas that are related to each other as cause and effect or in a syllogistic manner. Indian syllogisms are a little more elaborate than Aristotle's syllogisms. Apart from stating a cause, they also present an example. After establishing an argument, the mind goes to a consequent proposal or submission. When vicāra is taken for samāpatti, the linear movement of thought is verticalized until it becomes manana, which leads one to dhyāna.

Confrontation (vitarka) is presented to consciousness by the perception of an object. When an object is perceived with the senses and corresponding sensations are evoked, the afferent stimulation is immediately met with efferent reciprocation. Efferent reciprocation comes from interpreting the afferent stimulus in terms of concepts. When the outer form is presented through the senses it is reciprocated by a conceptual idea.

After a relationship is established between the formal perception and the conceptual interpretation of it by the mind (translated in the hypothalamus), it is not possible to say whether our experience resides entirely in the object outside, that is, the percept, or in the subjective consciousness in the form of a mental image or concept. These counterparts present a unified vision in which the somatic and psychologic are inseparable. At that point, a chain of reasoning can commence in the mind because the experience evokes previously associated memories.

For example, when a person's mind recognizes a percept such as a śivaliṅga as a here and now expression of the Śiva principle, a number of ideas come to her mind such as how the conjunction of Śiva and Śakti is the causal factor for the creation of the world, or the idea that Śiva is pure transcendence, belonging to the past, the present, and the future, followed by umpteen notions of Śiva lore. If her mind is allowed to get into the turbulent river of recurring thoughts, she will have no stable ground. An aspirant yogi does not want to be carried away by the multiplication of thoughts. To remain at the central locus of her consciousness and verticalize her mental energy to be concentered in a single idea such as that of Śiva, she can adopt a formula to merge deeper and deeper into her own Self with the aid of the *nāda* (sound vibration) emanating from the repetition of a sound system such as *namaḥ śivāya. Namaḥ* means "obeisance" and *śiva* means "supreme peace," so this is a practice of offering worshipful obeisance to the archetypal notion of peace.

The cultivation of *savicāra samāpatti* through such practices brings the aspirant to *nirvicāra samāpatti,* having no modifications supported by word images. Consequently, the recurring and repetitive modifications of cinta, the compulsive habitual function, automatically come to a close. That is a state of *niścinta,* having no thoughts. This leads to a state, which is as if the yogi has no mind, *amanaskata.* Here he or she enters *nirvicāra samādhi,* absorption without any thoughts. This sūtra introduces us to the depth of such a subtlety that can initiate us into the realm of transcendence.

Sūtra I:45

sūkṣmaviṣayatvam cāliṅga paryavasānam

sūkṣma: subtle
viṣayatvam: the province of concepts
ca: and
aliṅga: the noumenal
paryavasānam: extends up to, reaches up to

And the province of subtle concepts extends up to the noumenal.

When we walk on this earth we experience the concreteness of the ground beneath our feet. Earth is also called the supporter *(dhara).* We deduce the objectivity and tangibility of earth from the concreteness that we feel. Although it appears like direct perception, we are not perceiving the hardness but inferring it. That inference is a concept that is mentally deduced from an incomprehensible and unexplainable concomitance of certain types of evidence.

When we contemplate on what is very impressive as physical materialistic things, and so on, we come to see that our experience is constituted of a plethora of concepts. When these concepts are dropped one by one the mind will go to subtler and subtler areas until it comes to what may be called the very stuff of consciousness. When we contemplate on the mark of odor in the subtle particles of earth, taste in water molecules, form in the manifestation of heat, touch in air, and sound vibration in space, they all fall away from the integrity of perception and appear to be only modulated ideas in consciousness. When the concretization of the elements and the functional modification through qualities are all dismissed there remains only the value of pure awareness that exists. Through manana (contemplation), we ultimately reach the core of the phenomenon, which is only the noumenon. Then we say contemplation has gone from the specific to the non-specific and there is no mark (liṅga) to be observed. That also brings the contemplative to the void of manifestation.

Sūtra I:46

tā eva sabījaḥ samādhiḥ

tāḥ: these [are]
eva: only
sabījaḥ: seeded
samādhiḥ: absorption

These are only seeded absorption.

Even after the pollination of a flower, it looks fresh, as if nothing has happened. But the fact is that the pollen dust brought by an agent of pollination has gone into the ovary of the flower. It is seeded. When time passes and nature is favorable, the seed matures and will present itself through its germination and growth as a continuation of the species from which it has come.

Within us, the culture that has gone into the repository of an action propensity will ultimately present itself in the form of an action when the seeded impulse becomes mature. Such kind of seeding comes from the gross physical external environment. That is suggestive of vitarka, perceptual presentation. Thus even when savitarka changes into nirvitarka, the potential of the seed is not gone. Even before the physical mating of two people, the desire can remain in them and prompt them to actualize their desire. The subtle makes its impact on the gross. Even after the cessation of vitarka and vicāra, the seed for both can remain unhampered, albeit in a cloistered state. Hence, savitarka samāpatti, nirvitarka samāpatti, savicāra samāpatti, and nirvicāra samāpatti are to be looked upon as only seeded states of absorption. A yogi who has disciplined himself or herself to that extent still does not escape return to physical manifestation.

Sūtra I:47

nirvicāra vaiśāradye adhyātma prasādaḥ

nirvicāra vaiśāradye: [upon] the undisturbed flow of consciousness, consciousness devoid of conceptual configuration or cognitive function

adhyātma: the higher Self

prasādaḥ: clarity, lucidity, transparency

Upon the undisturbed flow of consciousness, clarity of the higher Self.

What is usually recognized as immediate perception is only mediate perception. For instance, when an object such as a red flower is directly seen with the eyes, we call it immediate perception. On examining this experience, we realize that the light reflected from the red flower is falling on the retina and causing certain agitations. It is the interpretation of those agitations that is recognized as immediate perception. Between the seeing subject and the object there is the medium of the apparatus of the eye and the biological and physicochemical intervention of the central nervous system. So such experiences should be termed as mediate.

When there is no cognitive function or cogitative reasoning, consciousness flows like a pure streak. The clarity of that consciousness is devoid of the impurities of an intervening medium. Hence what is present is only the pure light of consciousness. That is termed as a transparent vision of the Self, *adhyātma prasāda.*

Sūtra I:48

ṛtambharā tatra prajñā

ṛtambharā: pregnant with truth, truthful, truth-bearing
tatra: therein
prajñā: pure consciousness

Therein pure consciousness, pregnant with truth.

In our three states of consciousness—the wakeful, dream, and deep sleep—the stuff of consciousness is called prajñā. In the wakeful consciousness, the subject and object stand apart. Perception that is happening in the wakeful can easily be spoiled by various illusions. So the truth of wakeful experience is debatable. As we have noted, in that state consciousness is called viśvābhimāni. The individual self in the wakeful is the perceiver of the world, hence it is called *viśvātma (viśva:* universe; *ātma*: self).

In the dream state there is almost no truth. The dream that is seen is a perversion of memory in which many memory factors are untruthfully put together. The subject and the object are both happening within the dream consciousness called *taijasa*. The self in that state is called *taijasātma*.

In the deep sleep state consciousness is unmodified *(avyakṛta)*. The mass of consciousness in deep sleep has a pure and an impure aspect. The impure aspect comes from incipient memories. When these impressions are from the present life they are called samskāras and when they are from previous manifestations they are called vāsanās.

When all impressions of the past are flushed away with yogic disciplines, only pure consciousness remains. It has no impurity so it is absolutely truthful. Hence it is the ground for all truthful perceptions, inferences, and actions. The entire yogic discipline is to purge one's consciousness of all its impurities and make it pregnant with a reality that can be actualized in the here and now.

Sūtra I:49

śrutānumāna prajñābhyām anya viṣayā viśeṣārthatvāt

śruta: word-testimony
anumāna: [and] inference
prajñābhyām: [arises] from transparent consciousness

anya: [it is] different [from]
viśaya: objects of sensory experience
viśeṣārthatvāt: [as] the meaning of specific

It is different from word-testimony and inference, as the meaning of specific objects arises from transparent consciousness.

The state of *ṛtambharā* mentioned in the previous sūtra is further explained here. This sūtra implies the entire scheme of the contemplative discipline involved in the transference from vitarka to savitarka samāpatti, to nirvitarka samāpatti to nirvitarka samādhi, and from vicāra to savicāra samāpatti to nirvicāra samāpatti to a purificatory effect that the individuated consciousness undergoes.

A natural purification happens when the mind goes into the state of absorption. The fluctuating tendency of the oscillation of consciousness between subject and object is transformed into the fixation of consciousness in savitarka samāpatti or samādhi. Subjectivity becomes entirely identified with objectivity and the I-consciousness does not have a separate existence. Similarly, in savicāra samāpatti, the specificity of the object is replaced by the specificity of the species revealed by the concept. When both of these are transmuted into a harmonized or homogenized consciousness in nirvicāra samāpatti, mind becomes cleared of several impressions of the past. Thus a new transparency comes to it. After gaining that transparency, even when one is functioning in the wakeful and in the subjective consciousness, there is a transcendent vision that is not clogged by the specific inertia to which consciousness is usually subjected.

A lot of confusion about things happens because of the specificity of forms. A contemplative can exercise valid assessment of things without being caught in the fanciful imaginations of a non-yogi. For instance, if a contemplative is going to buy a gold chain or bangle, he or she also recognizes a chain as a chain or a bangle as a bangle. However, the specific attraction of formal differences is looked upon as a secondary aspect. Thus, the contemplative has another sense to appreciate the specificity of things in terms of classes. In the course of time, the breakthrough he or she makes in the appreciation of the general truth of the generic aspect of things enables him or her to see time as one stretch without breaking it into segments of past, present, and future. A similar breakthrough can also be made with regard to differences of masses and with regard to spatial separation.

Sūtra I:50

tajjaḥ samskāro 'nya samskāra pratibandhī

tajjaḥ: born from, arising from [truthful consciousness]

samskāra: registered and preserved impressions

anya: other

samskāra: the registration and preservation of impressions, formation of incipient memories

pratibandhī: prevent, impede, check, block, wipe out, inhibit

Registered and preserved impressions born from truthful consciousness prevent the registration and preservation of other impressions.

In India, it is a common custom to say "*AUM śāntiḥ, śāntiḥ, śāntiḥ,*" at the end of a prayer. In that invocation, AUM represents the ground of everything. The sounds A, U, M, have reference to the wakeful, the dream, and the deep sleep, respectively. To a yogi who is undergoing discipline, they refer to vitarka, vicāra, and samādhi. Samāpatti or samādhi comes when vitarka, vicāra, and all causal potencies have been cleared. The yogi's three references to śāntiḥ imply going from nirvitarka to nirvicāra to nirbīja (non-seeded) samādhi. In the state of nirbīja samādhi—as the yogi experiences a transcendental clarity of knowing the Self in its purest form—all residual potencies are thrown out and there is no chance for new potencies to be deposited.

This can be followed by a question as to whether the perfected yogi becomes incapable of functioning as a person. To this the answer is "no." It is like an actor who can accept the role of a king, a judge, a police officer, or a thief with full consciousness and deliberation. Then, when the play is finished, he can walk out of the theater without carrying with him the state of mind in which he was for a short while. The man who acted as king knows he has no regality when the play is over. The person who pronounced judgment knows he has no power or authority to judge anyone. The policeman need not be rigid or unfriendly to the man who acted as a thief. The actor who played the role of a thief does not carry with him any sense of guilt.

A yogi who has realized the Self looks upon the transactions of the world only as the role-playing that is assigned in the drama of life, without any false identity that can cause torment later. The transactions of life can continue without any new samskāra being created. A unitive discrimination *(akhaṇḍa viveka)* pervades the yogi's consciousness and thereafter he or she sees everything in the right perspective.

Sūtra I:51

tasyāpi nirodhe sarva nirodhān nirbījaḥ samādhiḥ

tasyāpi: of that also
nirodhe: by the restraint
sarva nirodhāt: all being restrained
nirbījaḥ samādhiḥ: [comes] seedless absorption

All being restrained, by the restraint of that also comes seedless absorption.

In the *Nirvāṇa Darśana* of the *Darśana Mālā* of Narayana Guru, the highest aspect of realization is described as that of the *brahmavit* (knower of the Absolute). If a brahmavit prefers not to retain the central locus of consciousness, then the last vestige of orientation also leaves and he becomes more established in the Absolute. Then he is called *brahmavidvara.* After becoming established in a state where bodily functions become negligible and consciousness is not affected by environmental factors or inner urges, the final state of *nirvāṇa* comes. Then the knower of the Absolute is called *brahmavidvariṣṭha.* When a person arrives at the last stage of not knowing anything by himself and others cannot rouse him to consciousness, no incipient memory remains to constitute a causal consciousness or causal body. Consequently he has no return to the cycle of birth and death, and is said to be completely burned out.

The state of nirvāṇa as described in Vedānta corresponds to what Patañjali calls the state of kaivalya. The word *kaivalya* is derived from *kevalam,* which means "aloneness." Individuation comes because of the proximity of puruṣa to prakṛti. In that state puruṣa is not alone. But the aspiring yogi disciplines himself or herself and withdraws from the impressions laid by perception. On transcending them, the yogi attains nirvitarka samādhi. But the memories already gathered in him or her can still cause trains of thought. With further self-discipline, the yogi transcends the dynamics of incipient memories and comes to nirvicāra samādhi. When such transcendence is maintained and the yogi denies further impact of prakṛti, the latent potentials to act or to desire are removed and he or she comes to a state of total liberation. Then the puruṣa is alone. Hence it is called the state of aloneness, kaivalya.

At the commencement of this first chapter of the *Yoga Śāstra, Samādhi Pāda,* Yoga was defined as "the restraint of all mental modifications." In the present sūtra, concluding the first book, we have come to a stage where all modifications are restrained. That is the final goal of Yoga according to Patañjali.

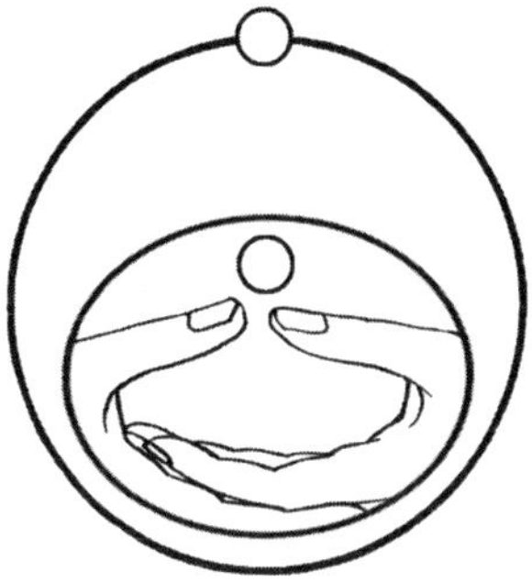

Chapter II: *Sādhana Pāda*

This chapter of the *Yoga Śāstra*—known as *Sādhana Pāda*—is specially dedicated to giving a functional understanding of our physical, social, moral, and spiritual dimensions so that a fourfold harmony can be established to perfect our discipline as yogis. When a desire comes to our minds, it is immediately followed by a question: "Is it possible to fulfill that desire?" If it is possible, we get the answer, "It is attainable." Attainment in Sanskrit is *siddhi.* The attainability of what is desired resides in its means. The means for attainment is called sādhanam. The person who endeavors to exploit the means of attainment is a sādhaka. The action or discipline that is implemented to actualize the attainment is sādhana. Thus, the possibility, means to be exploited, the aspirant who acts, the discipline or procedure of action, and attainment are five interrelated factors. This chapter of the aphorisms is also known as kriyā yoga (practical yoga). In that, the word *kriyā* comes from the root *kṛ*, which means "to act." According to Vyāsa, the unitive mind described in the first part of the aphorisms of Patañjali is given here as the goal to be attained by adopting the discipline of kriyā yoga.

Sūtra II:1

tapaḥ svādhyāyeśvara praṇidhānāni kriyā yogaḥ

tapaḥ: self-purification (literally "burning away")
svādhyāya: self-study
īśvarapraṇidhānāni: [and] continuous contemplation on īśvara (spirit par excellence, supreme spirit, noumenon, higher Self, designated by *praṇava, AUM*)
kriyā: practical, action
yogah: yoga

Self-purification, self-study, and continuous contemplation on īśvara constitute practical yoga.

As an aspiring student you are expected to adopt three steps in your action program. They are: the burning away of negative factors that hinder your spiritual progress (tapas), engaging in a thorough-going study of yourself (svādhyāya), and entering into attunement or at-one-ment with the nature of your higher Self (īśvara praṇidhāna).

Tapas is a purificatory function. The biologic matrix to which your sensory and motor systems belong and the inner dispositions of your individual personality are impressed with various negative conditionings. To purify gold, it is melted at a high temperature, which burns away the dross. Although the literal meaning of tapas is "burning," it is to be taken in a metaphorical sense, in which, for instance, a colored state can be decolored or a conditioned state can be deconditioned. A preceptor who has an insight into a disciple's personality flaws can expose him or her to situations that can change old habits; in their place new and harmonious functions can be instituted as habitual choices.

The culturing process of life as a whole is painful. That

pain is often experienced as something similar to a conflict or neurosis. In the present case, already existing pathological states are therapeutically corrected and the system as a whole is morally and spiritually replenished and nourished so you can live a well-examined life with values that are spiritually homogenized. When such corrections are made in body and mind the cogitating faculty becomes more efficient and its power of comprehension becomes clearer. Precision increases.

When your own nature is becoming more and more evident to yourself, the imperfections of your social personality will become more and more clear. In its place īśvara—the universal person not afflicted with the love/hate dualities of physico-social life—can be accepted as a better model for imitation or identification.

The word *īśvara* is derived from *īś*, which literally means "ruling from within." The life of an individual is not an amorphous chaotic structure that comes from the randomness of the physical world. It has a goal to achieve and laws to abide by. The innate law of everything that governs, controls, and maneuvers it to function for the purposeful attainment of a given goal is īśvara. If you know there is such a guiding principle in your life, life becomes all the more dear and an incentive comes to live as correctly as possible. Thereafter, the lower aspect of the self will always be in resonance with īśvara, the higher Self. That īśvara is looked upon as your true teacher or preceptor. Relating always with that īśvara to develop insight into the meaning of your life combines both the purificatory and educative aspects.

If you have lived for a long time with an undisciplined mind, allowing yourself to be conditioned with indiscriminate social habits, you cannot easily wean yourself from your established habits; you may find that the aloneness postulated by Patañjali's Yoga cannot be easily attained. The threefold method suggested here—purification, self-study, and continuous contemplation of Īśvara, the supreme model—is to enable your inner discipline to yield the desired result.

Inner impurities and spiritual absorption cannot go together. Diehard habits are the breeding ground of spiritual obstacles. If a seed is allowed to grow, in course of time, the stem of the plant will branch off and bring forth leaves, flowers, and seeds that belong to that particular species. In the same manner, each individual has many innate tendencies that can sprout. Hence, on the one side, new negative tendencies should not be encouraged to implant themselves in your personality formation and those that are already established, like parasites, are to be rooted out meticulously.

Just as you observe the world with your five senses and eradicate your wrong notions about things in your ordinary studies, you can adopt another field for study with another methodology. The field chosen here is your inner life, which is to be examined in the light of your preceptor's direction and the science of unitive life recommended by authentic books like the *Upaniṣads* and *Yoga Śāstra*. Further, precise understanding is to be established about your own self by making your words, thoughts, and actions concur with each other. The preceptor spoken of here is not a social person but the innate light of your own self and its voice. To begin with it is to your advantage if an experienced person explains how to familiarize yourself with the voice of the spirit. For this, see our commentary on verse eight of Narayana Guru's *Atmopadeśa Śatakam*, in *That Alone, The Core of Wisdom*, and *Neither This Nor That, But . . . AUM*.

Sūtra II:2

samādhi bhāvanārthaḥ kleśa tanūkaraṇārthaś ca

samādhi: absorption, equipoise in consciousness
bhāvana: bringing about, developing
arthaḥ: the purpose of
kleśa: afflictions, obstacles
tanū karaṇārthaḥ: for attenuating
ca: and

For the purpose of bringing about absorption and attenuating afflictions.

In the *Bhagavad Gita* Yoga is described as "sameness." The natural state of water is to be a pure and clear liquid with a surface like a sheet of glass. But a certain property of water makes its molecules very unstable and its surface is mostly uneven with tremors, ripples, or waves. Our consciousness is also like that. It is easily provoked and thus loses its transparency as well as restfulness.

Both Eastern and Western people have classical examples to illustrate the restlessness and cyclic function of the mind. The Greeks have the legend of Sisyphus and the Indians have the story of Narayanathu Bhranthan. As a punishment Sisyphus was condemned to roll a stone up a hill, but the stone would always escape him near the top and roll to the bottom. No one punished Narayanathu Bhranthan; he was pushing the boulder just for the fun of it. For Sisyphus it was very painful; to the yogi Narayanathu Bhranthan it was a sport. The summit of the hill is the symbol of victory, while the valley represents failure. Unlike Sisyphus, Narayanathu Bhranthan was a philosopher. He wanted to illustrate how difficult it is to ascend to the summit and how easy it is to fall to disaster. So, after painfully pushing the huge stone to the summit, he would let it roll down the hill. Then he would clap his hands and laugh hilariously to draw the attention of people to the fact that lazy bums are bound to fall, just like the stone.

Trying to reach the summit has three stages. First is exerting yourself physically and mentally (tapas). The second is understanding your own resources and applying your abilities to the best advantage (svādhyāya). The third is fixing your goal on the summit and attacking the problem by getting into a constant dialogue with the Absolute (īśvara praṇidhāna). When these three disciplines go hand in hand, you are disciplining yourself with kriyā yoga.

It is easy to imagine. It is a little more difficult to explain to another what you see in your imagination. It is even more difficult to act according to your word. That is why action is given primacy in the self-discipline that is recommended. Kriyā yoga has a positive goal. It also has a negative goal. The positive goal is to bring yourself into a state of equipoise and imperientially obtain absorption. When the mind is not disturbed by conditioned states, absorption naturally comes.

Physically and mentally we experience many distractions. Take the organs of action for example. Some people cannot articulate words the way they should be articulated. Some people irritate others as soon as they open their mouths. We see some people using their hands with great dexterity to paint, sculpt, or play musical instruments, while others have very little coordination between their eyes and hands. They fail to create anything. There are great gymnasts who can run or perform acrobatic feats, but some people cannot even stand on their two legs. While most people have control over their excretory organs, some are like leaking bottles. Every person is supposed to increase the species, but, unfortunately, some are impotent. Like that, in the sense organs also, many diseases can come such as being hard of hearing, insensitive to touch, blind, unable to taste or smell.

How many precious lives are lost in the pathological world. To retrieve those lives from their tragic situations and make them whole we need healing and therapeutic measures. At least for some people, kriyā yoga is of no significance until they are restored to normalcy. The secondary goal of kriyā yoga is therefore to adopt ways and means for healing and correction.

Vyāsa equates critical reasoning of a contemplative order with the flames of a fire. Fire purifies everything, and the same can be said about truthful reasoning. As dross leaves molten gold, so unwholesome emotionalism and wrong conditionings leave us when we insistently enforce our right reasoning. For example, you may be irritated by a person's word or action and flare up in anger; in this state of uncontrolled emotion you blurt out unkind words to retaliate. Later, when the emotion has subsided, right reasoning comes to your mind and you regret your behavior. In the light of this new reasoning you get a clear perspective of things. Tapas consists of taking full advantage of this sensibility you have gained, by using it as a beneficent frame of reference to keep calm on all such occasions in the future. In this way you can weed out the poisonous growths in yourself.

Sūtra II:3

avidyāsmitā rāga dveṣa abhiniveśāḥ kleśāḥ

avidyā: ignorance, nescience

asmitā: identification with the center of one's consciousness, ego identity, sense of individuality, I-consciousness

rāga: attachment

dveṣa: hatred, aversion

abhiniveśāḥ: lust for life, will to live, clinging to life, false infatuation *kleśāḥ:* the afflictions, obstacles [are]

The afflictions are ignorance, ego identity, attachment, hatred, and lust for life.

The Absolute as an idea is conceived of as the supreme truth, One without a second and unconditional. As just a statement, this has only a rhetorical significance. As individuals, our attempt is to experience the Absolute within the limitation of a living organism in which everything becomes conditional as soon as we try to comprehend it with our minds or senses. We are separated from the external world by the skin that is wrapped around our body. The skin is our sense organ of touch. So if anything registers its presence through the sensation of touch, we treat that stimulus as external to us. The corresponding sensation is felt as an inside factor.

All such sensations and accompanying judgments have a direct and immediate reference to the individual's central locus of consciousness that is recognized as "I am." When that I-consciousness relates itself to an external source of stimulus, three kinds of responses arise from our ego or I-consciousness. They are: like, dislike, and the volition to control the stimulus that is creating like or dislike. These are all caused by a veiling principle that obstructs us from knowing reality as it is in itself.

From the first and second sūtras we presume that our origin is the Supreme. We are compulsively shorn from that and come to identify with the psychophysical organism. Consequently we think of ourselves only as members of a society, all conditioned alike, with the physicochemical and physiological properties of a living body. Thus we are subjected to two misfortunes. One is our ignorance of our true Self. Second is identification with many conditional states.

From the very start of life, our conceptual beliefs are built upon unexamined and vague hearsay, false conjectures, and the propaganda literature of people with vested interests. Because of having lived in family and community circles of undisciplined people, our minds cling on to several prejudices. That state is generally called avidyā, being steeped in wrong prejudices and inadequate methods of right reasoning.

Avidyā generates wrong passions and uncritical fascination for sheer appearances. In our encounters with shallow and transient values, attachment to the unsubstantiated comes as a compulsion (raga), and it is followed by repulsive neurosis (dveṣa). False infatuation (abhiniveśa) can cause physical and mental torture which can disable a mind from taking up the challenges of life in a healthy manner. Several pleasure-giving incentives can lead to pain that cannot be easily alleviated. Insanity bubbles up for the first time in a person when he becomes conscious of his ego as an isolated existential being and wants to declare vehemently to the world, "This is mine!" When a person is completely steeped in his ego thrust the society cannot tolerate him any more so they put him away in an asylum or a jail.

Sūtra II:4

avidyā kṣetram uttareṣām prasupta tanu vicchinnodārāṇām

avidyā: nescience, ignorance
kṣetram: [is the] field
uttareṣām: for the others [whether they are]
prasupta: dormant
tanu: attentuated
vicchinna: alternating
udārāṇām: expanded, fully operative

Nescience (avidyā) is the field for the others, whether they are dormant, attenuated, alternating, or expanded.

Nescience is like a breeding ground. Egoism, passionate attachment, hatred, and infatuation grow in the field of nescience. Each of these afflictions has four states: dormant, attenuated, alternating, and expanded. The dormant condition is that in which the obstacle is present in a latent form. It is like a seed waiting for a favorable environment to express itself. The attenuated condition is similar to a sprout coming out of the seed, which has little strength to assert itself. It gets strengthened according to the stimulus it gets, gaining or losing momentum as the situation becomes more or less favorable. The alternating aspect is very much like ambivalence where two forces such as attraction and repulsion are alternately dormant and active. The fourth aspect is a fully operative stage where egoism, attachment, hatred, and infatuation become fully assertive.

When a person is in deep sleep he does not know who he is or what he wants. He has no idea of his likes or dislikes. Others also do not get any visible signs of that person's inner state of being. Deep sleep manifests in a person only for a very short period. Mind easily slips away from deep sleep either to wakeful experience or dream experience. The dormant state of the four aspects of nescience can be compared to the state of deep sleep. All potentials of personality expressions are residing within and are only waiting for the individuated consciousness to enter into a more congenial atmosphere. When the inconscient state of deep sleep exists, the ego has no awareness and therefore cannot will to act. The ego is devoid of any experiential enjoyment. But when volition and affection are operative, the afflictions also come to the forefront and become a personality feature of the individual.

In *A Thousand and One Arabian Nights*, there is a story of a fisherman and a genie. A fisherman went to the sea and cast his net. When he pulled it in there was a jar in it. He thought it was a treasure but when he opened it, a genie came out and threatened to kill him. Similarly, there are many dormant tendencies in us that are likely to bring the four kinds of afflictions or obstacles. They are like genies in jars, waiting to get out. Each of the four obstacles has four stages, so there are sixteen possibilities of exposing ourselves to different obstacles.

In Western psychology it was Kurt Lewin who introduced topological psychology for the first time. Unfortunately, he died before he was able to give it a full exposition. He gave the following example to explain the dormant state of obstructive tendencies. Suppose there are two people who are great lovers or two who are inveterate enemies who happen to be in a place, both masked in an unidentifiable form. If they do not talk and only sit around, the presence of the lover or enemy will not have any impact on the mind of the other. It is like all the possibilities are remaining dormant and inexpressive. That does not mean that the people concerned do not have within them the propensities to feel attached or hateful. It is this theme that is developed in a humorous and tragic way by Shakespeare in his plays, *A Midsummer Night's Dream* and *The Comedy of Errors*.

If a tiger is exposed to starvation for a long time and has no power even to get up, it may look at its prey with a sort of indifference. But if it is given a little more time, it will gather all its strength and pounce. Similarly, a man may starve his sensuous appetites for some time, causing his urges to become weak. But by merely starving one's appetites, deep-seated urges will not leave. When the environment becomes favorable, they will return with added vigor. Based on this theme, Rabindranath Tagore wrote the story of a sannyasi who thought he had transcended all of Nature's allure during his solitary meditations but found he had no taste for solitude after his hand and heart were touched by a young woman seeking his solace and protection from a cruel world.

In the *Bhagavad Gita* (II:59) it says: "Objective interests revert without the relish for them on starving the embodied of them. Even the residual relish reverts on the One Beyond being sighted."[1]

Most of the urges in us are like two-headed monsters. Two opposite tendencies come and we are dragged alternately in one direction and then another. This becomes vividly manifested in the case of schizophrenia. Even the very word *schizophrenia* shows a similarity to the Sanskrit word for alternating, *vicchinna*.

The last attribute, *udārāṇām,* resembles the generosity of a philanthropist. Here, however, it is not positive. It is the negative aggressiveness with which an urge or tendency asserts itself.

Sūtra II:5

anityāśuci duḥkhānātmasu nitya śuci sukhātmakhyātir avidyā

anitya: the non-eternal, the fleeting
aśuci: the impure
duḥkha: the painful, the miserable
anātma su: [and] the non-Self
nitya: the eternal
śuci: the pure
sukha: happiness, comfort, pleasure-giving, pleasurable
ātma: the Self
khyātiḥ: is taking to be, supposing
avidyā: nescience, ignorance

Nescience is taking the non-eternal, impure, painful, and the non-Self to be the eternal, pure, pleasurable, and the Self.

The most important discovery of modern science is that the stuff of the world is constituted of matter, and its primeval form is of a substance that can be described both as a particle as well as a wave. The science dealing with the mechanical pulsation of that energy form is quantum wave mechanics. One of the exponents of quantum mechanics was Erwin Schrodinger. In his famous book, *Mind and Matter*, he calls this world a construct of percepts, concepts, and relationships that is put together in a very private corner of the world, a brain concealed in a skull. When we take into consideration the awareness of the individual and the impressions registered in that awareness we have already referred to two thirds of what we may call the Supreme Truth. What remains is the concept of īśvara. In the first chapter of Patañjali's aphorisms, īśvara was equated with praṇava, AUM.

Praṇava is said to have four limbs: the gross, the subtle, the causal, and the transcendental. Or, to put it another way: the wakeful, the dream, the deep sleep, and the ground of consciousness on which the triple states of consciousness are superimposed. That ground is pure existence, which is self-luminous and the source of all values. Because of the altering states of consciousness, pure existence is obliviated by existential entities with phenomenal appearances. Knowledge becomes conditional and values relativistic. It is this transmuted phenomenality that is referred to here as nescience. It is experienced in the time-space continuum with name, form, and mass, which have existence only in relationship with individuated consciousness.

Here we are warned at the very outset of our search that every individual is subjected to a four-fold erroneous vision. The fleeting is looked upon as eternal. That which is conducive to bringing misery is seen as pleasure-giving. The impure or conditioned is seen as pure or unconditioned. The non-Self is mistaken for the Self. The very reasoning and cogitating faculty on which a person depends for discerning truth is vitiated by its own imperfections. Immanuel Kant puts it another way. He equates the individual with a person imprisoned in a castle from which he can look out only through stained glass windows. Albert Einstein gives the analogy of a clock that cannot be opened. All the workings of the clock can only be presumed with shrewd guesses. Such is the mystery of the phenomenality of the world to which we are exposed.

Let us take a closer look at the four errors that afflict us:

1. *Nitya/anitya*. On hearing the term *nitya* or "eternal," we tend to think of an entity that is infinite, both temporally and spatially, something without beginning or end, frontierless. But let us consider the glowworm, which can be seen at night. It flickers; its glow does not last for even a second. Yet poets from the very dawn of human civilization have adored the glowworm. Its glow is momentary but its reputation is eternal. The sense of wonder is so pronounced in every glow that it can certainly symbolize the self-luminous glow of our own consciousness.

From this example, it is evident that it is difficult to discern the eternal from the fleeting. Flowers that bloom in the morning may droop in the evening. That does not make a flower less adorable. The flower in all its glory represents the beautiful. A square meal can make us forget our hunger. That does not stop human beings from cultivating their farms and working hard to secure their bread. All human beings, from the moment of birth to their cessation from physical existence, are haunted by the fear of hunger. Thus hunger is at once fleeting and perennial. A yogi tries to make every approaching moment the most real moment of his or her life, as well as being concerned that it should be so all through life and even through several millions of lives if that contingency is to be accepted.

2. *Sukham/duḥkham.* Consciousness oscillates between sensations that are pleasurable and those that are pain-giving. Pain and pleasure are agitations of the nervous system. When the agitation is moderate, it is accepted as pleasure. When it increases or decreases, it is termed as pain. Even moderate agitation is not what is meant by sukham.

When we are fully awake, and functioning positively, we are oblivious of ten thousand functions happening in our very body. In those happenings there is no agitation. They are perfectly harmonious. But when one of our organs such as the spleen, heart, brain, or kidney even slightly malfunctions, we become very conscious of that faculty and describe our experience as painful.

It seems humans excel in their ability to cultivate masochistic tendencies. When a person smokes for the first time, it is far from being pleasurable. But many people cultivate pleasure in torturing themselves with agitation. Similarly, every so-called pleasure, when closely looked at, is a pain cultivated as a specialized form of pleasure. When masochism is complemented with sadism, personal agitations and disturbances are shared with the community and it is even eulogized as "culture."

3. *Śuci/aśuci.* Even the very commentators of the Yoga aphorisms are confused in defining purity. As an example of the impure they call the readers' attention to women because they have saliva in their mouths, blood in their blood vessels, dirt in their intestines, menstrual blood in their wombs, mucus in their decaying membranes, and secretions in their glands. It

seems that these medieval scholars have no sense of propriety. They are not only wrong in their assumptions but also cruel in their discrimination. Blood in the heart or blood vessels is not dirt but the most precious vital fluid. If the membranes of the skin, muscles, and other parts of the body did not turn into mucus, the body could never maintain its cleanliness. Saliva, bile, and all such digestive juices are precious to all human beings for the maintenance of life.

Where a thing is relevant it is not impure. Purity is to be maintained in the world by assessing the appropriateness of a thing and is not to be mixed up with social prejudices. It is not impure to have hair on the head or saliva in the mouth but it is certainly impure to have hair in the mouth and saliva on the head. Even memory, when it is misplaced, becomes dirt. A word said at the wrong time can be very destructive but when it is appropriate it is a pearl of wisdom. Those who want to maintain purity should look for relevancy and appropriateness.

4. *Ātma/anātma*. Discerning the Self is as difficult as discerning the eternal. As long as you live in a body and have to maintain bodily function with socially approved programs of action, conditionings—from autonomous reflex actions to biologic habits of all kinds—are to be accepted as part of your life. Only when you ultimately gain total absorption in the transcendence of Self will you cease to experience the reality of the conditioned self.

Exercise

Sit quiet with your eyes closed. Imagine there are others who are also not seeing or hearing anything. In your mind, try to describe your experience on the presumption that nothing has any name or form to describe.

After ten minutes, think you are dissolved away in an infinite consciousness as if you have no body, senses, or individuated consciousness. Leave it when you cannot remain in the quiet of your consciousness.

Sūtra II:6

dṛg darśanaśaktyor ekātmatevāsmitā

dṛk: the seer
darśanaśaktyoḥ: power of seeing or cognition
ekātmatā: identity
iva: as it were
asmitā: identification with the center of one's consciousness, ego identity, sense of individuality, I-consciousness

Asmitā is the identification of the seer, as it were, with the power of seeing.

In Western psychology the theory of perception is given as an external stimulus coming in the form of energy that is received and responded to by the central nervous system. In Indian psychology two poles are marked. From these poles two different kinds of energies are emitted; perception implies a confection of external energy coming from the object of perception and psychic energy coming from the perceiving agent. For example, the visual perception of an object is possible only when the object is illuminated by an external light. The perceiver is conceived to be the self that is going out to meet the external object through the sense organs, in the present case, the eyes. The awareness that is the intrinsic quality of the self and emanates from it is symbolically described as the light of the perceiver. The light that is reflected from the object of perception becomes the light of the object. When these two meet, the visual properties of the object are accepted as a mold for the psychic energy of the perceiver to transform itself and consequently perception arises.

The Indian psychologist holds the view that every object is perceived where it physically and temporally exists in the matrix of nature. Thus spirit and nature are counterparts of a binary system in which both aspects are of equal importance. One example given is of the Sun reflecting in a mirror. The mirror by itself cannot produce a Sun but when it is held against the Sun, it is capable of producing an image that has the qualities of the Sun such as radiating heat and light.

As we have seen, the four-fold inner organs conceived by the Indian psychologist consist of an interrogative aspect, a faculty of recall that presents all the associated exhibits that are helpful to identify a perceived object, a faculty of discernment, and affective dynamics. For these to manifest, nature's provisions have to be present, such as the five elements (earth, water, fire, air, and space) and the triple modalities (the sublime, the kinetic, and the inertial). If these are all taken away from a person's organism, no inner organ will function. Still, the inner organ is not merely a physicochemical and psychobiologic apparatus. It has to have a spirit or Self animating it, like the Sun reflecting in a mirror. If there are a million mirrors the Sun will reflect in all with different degrees of clarity and intensity. Similarly, the one spirit that is of the nature of awareness can manifest in countless millions of organisms.

Wherever there is a coming together of puruṣa (the Self) and prakṛti (nature), there is the likelihood of ego being presented. In the morning when the Sun shines it can be seen mirrored in all the dewdrops. If every dewdrop were endowed with a consciousness so it could say "I am," that would be the same as all individuated beings identifying the central locus of their consciousness as "I am." It is not the social ego that is referred to here but the simple dialectical fact of the one real appearing to be many. It is not a phenomenal appearance but an existential multitude in which each entity has an existential validity for a short span of time.

Exercise

Try to define nature and distinguish it from spirit. Examine your own psychosomatic system and its presiding consciousness. Remove one by one everything you can identify as belonging to nature. In the same manner, try to identify every aspect in you that you can attribute to the Self. See if any residue is left over.

Sūtra II:7

sukhānuśayī rāgaḥ

sukha: happiness, comfort, pleasure-giving, pleasurable
anuśayī: [is that which] accompanies, follows
rāgaḥ: attachment, affectivity, attraction

Attachment (rāga) is that which accompanies happiness.

The basic concept of the Indian psychologist, particularly of the Yoga-Vedānta school, is that there is only one existence in which everything finds its validity. There is only one knowledge and all piecemeal items of knowledge are instances of the modification of that one knowledge. One primordial value that is manifesting as all separate and distinct values. The human psychophysical organism is so structured that it can take only one item of existence, one modulation of knowledge, and one impression of value at a time. As in a kaleidoscope, attention can be shifted from one item to another in very quick succession.

An intriguing mystery is implied in the simplest reflection such as in a mirror. When we look at ourselves in a mirror, our left side is seen as the right side in the image and vice versa, but the top remains at the top and the bottom at the bottom. If we want to see the left side of our face in a mirror, we have to look at the right side of the mirror. We are so familiar with the phenomenality of reflection that we make an instantaneous correction in our erroneous vision. A similar anomaly happens in the process of individuation. Universal existence, wholesome knowledge, and the ground of value become fragmented and thereafter we see only the existence of this thing or that.

Form is like a tyrant. It dictates the individuality of things. Existence, subsistence, and value change into a spectrum that has several shades of validity in its existence, its truthful correspondence, and its value appreciation. Thus the agent of perception is thrown into a quandary and everything experienced is a challenge. When sunlight falls on a dewdrop, it glitters with all seven colors of the spectrum. What is seen as indigo this moment can change into an emerald green or a ruby red in the next. Thus there come flickering ideas of likes and dislikes. The dewdrop is only water. Similarly, when a value is projected on an object, it is very likely that the object is seen as precious. The perceiver does not recognize the fact that all three items—existence, subsistence, and value—are self-projected.

When the interest is catapulted by basic instincts like erotics, the intellect becomes very much assailed by the thirst of the ego. The beautiful and melodious voice of one's spouse, the joy that comes from fondling and kissing: all these look absolutely valid. But the slightest misunderstanding that arises between the mates can at once transform beauty into ugliness, a melodious voice into a harsh one. Touch can be a cause of nervous affliction. From this it is evident that the object by itself has no intrinsic value. It is in an attitude. Happiness comes when maximum harmony is established between the object and the perceiver. In Yoga, the nature of consciousness on such occasions is said to be sublime (sattva). The sublime causes an affliction that is of the nature of an indomitable affectivity (rāga). Affectivity causes attachment. Then you like to have a repetitive experience of the same, each time with added vigor and a variation in the form so that monotony may not dampen your interest.

Exercise

Listen to some very enjoyable music. Think of its affective quality, such as its melody, rhythm, and nuances, as projected by the peculiarity of your perceptual apparatus. Bring it back to your own self and think how much more melodious is your inner appreciation than the music you appreciate. The same can be done by watching a sunrise or sunset in which the beauty you admire can be seen as intrinsically identifable with your appreciative sense of color, form, and picturesque beauty. Thus, all the experiences of the senses can be summoned back to the central core of your own consciousness.

Sūtra II:8

duḥkhānuśayī dveṣaḥ

duḥkha: pain, misery, distress, sorrow, suffering
anuśayī: [is that which] accompanies, follows
dveṣaḥ: hatred, aversion

Hatred (dveṣa) is that which accompanies pain.

Hatred is a defense mechanism of the individuated self that becomes operative when we are exposed to misery or when we envisage the possible manifestation of pain. Happiness and misery are two faces of the same coin. To understand these two terms it is helpful to look into the Sanskrit words given in Patañjali's aphorisms. The literal meaning of the term for happiness, sukham, is "the space that is bright and beautiful," and its opposite, duḥkham, means "the space that is dark and infected with evil." We human beings alternate between these two living spaces, of which one is positive and the other is negative. The positive adherence to the bright and beautiful space of life has the quality of attraction. The struggle that is put up for the avoidance of the painful and evil forces is characterised by repulsion. The factor that brings repulsion can be from the environment or from the emergence of a thought or memory that fills the here and now with belching darkness.

From a microscopic entity like a virus or a bacteria to a powerful nation, all are again and again called upon to fight forces that are destructive to their continued existence. To change these basic responses in a living organism is as hard as changing the basic structure of the universe. Many people glibly say, "You should only love and not hate." These two polarized forces are the very warp and woof of life. Without understanding human nature, and not only human nature but the nature of all living organisms, you cannot change their operation. You have to watch continuously to see what attracts and what repels, what brings joy and what brings misery. You cannot transcend one without transcending the other. You cannot hold onto the pleasures of life and boycott the pains of it. The true happiness postulated by the yogi is neither embellished by pleasures nor embittered by pain.

There is the space in which the Sun, Moon, stars, and galactic systems exist. This we may call the grand space of outer manifestation. Part of our wakeful hours are lived in it. In our subjectivity—dreams, fears, expectations, deep sleep, and psychic and spiritual absorption—we live in an inner space. Outer space is illuminated by self-luminous stars, most much bigger than our Sun. When that light is cut off from us, our outer world sinks into darkness. Even when the Sun is blazing and the world is illuminated, if the inner space is tormented by an inconvenient memory or a tyrannizing urge, then we will be condemned to the darkness of the spirit. Thus we live in two spaces, the gross space ruled by the light of the heavenly bodies and the inner space illuminated by the light of our own Self. How we destroy the light within is narrated in verses sixty-two and sixty-three of the second chapter of the *Bhagavad Gita:* "Meditating on objects of sense-interest there is born in man an attachment for them; from attachment rises passion; in the face of passion (frustrated) arises rage. From rage is produced distortion of values, and from distortion of values memory lapse, and from memory-lapse comes loss of reason, and from loss of reason he perishes."[2]

Exercise

Recall to your mind its obsessions and inhibitions. Know these factors to be a product of your habitual thinking. Dismiss from your mind the reality of your obsessions and inhibitions. Remain quiet as a witness and not as a participant.

Sūtra II:9

svarasavāhī viduṣo'pitatha rūḍho'bhiniveśaḥ

svarasa: by the dynamics of one's own interest
vāhī: is sustained by, flowing
viduṣaḥ: the learned

api: even in
tathā: as in [the ignorant]
rūḍhaḥ: deep-rooted
abhiniveśaḥ: clinging to life, lust for life, will to live, false infatuation

Clinging to life (abhineveśa) is sustained even in the learned, as in the ignorant, by the dynamics of one's own deep-rooted interest.

The propensity that is expressed in all living beings as the will to live is compared in this sūtra to a fountain of irresistible interest that is governing the multi-faceted interests of life. The usual sense in which infatuation is understood is when young lovers aspire to possess each other for the consummation of love. In their wanting to relate to each other it is as if there exists between them a continuing gestalt. The instinct that governs such an infatuation is self-propagation. Self-propagation is the easiest and most popular way to attain immortality: even when we die, we continue through our progeny. When a river is in spate, it often becomes muddy and carries away anything that obstructs its course. Sometimes it is detrimental even to the trees or buildings that are on its banks. Similarly, when erotic passion is maximal, mind becomes disturbed and the power of discrimination becomes drastically lowered. Infatuated lovers are often uncouth and don't care into what tragedy they are leading themselves or how they disturb the social harmony of the society to which they belong.

Genetically speaking, the river of life has been flowing through millions of years and its power of persistence is almost unimaginable. All the interests of a person are interrelated and mutually supporting. Thus, the will to live becomes a mad frenzy when motivation is directed to the achievement of a certain goal. Even the trivialities of life such as wanting to have a cup of tea or coffee or a smoke can look so very important when the environment is not conducive to getting a drink or a smoke. In such situations people may even develop panic and anxiety. Love for life is expressed from the primal scream of a baby until one comes to the last pangs of giving up the ghost. Even someone so perfect as Jesus was obliged to say, "Father, Father, hast thou forsaken me?"

The deep rooted desire to perpetuate one's self in the memory of posterity is one way of gaining immortality. Lord Buddha, before entering into his final absorption of nirvāṇa, summoned all the elders to make sure they had all understood his teachings perfectly. He wanted to make sure that there would not be any mistakes in what his disciples would pass on to posterity as his word. Poets, philosophers, scientists, artists, and adventurous people like mountaineers and soldiers all are attempting to remain forever by immortalizing their names.

Once in a while we come across the example of a person who has freed himself even from such a desire. We do not know the author of the *I-Ching*. The author of that amazing book did not leave any trace of his or her identity. Even though *The Cloud of Unknowing* has been read with great veneration by aspirants all over the world, especially of the Catholic Church, no one knows who wrote it. The great author of the *Mahabharata* reveals himself simply as a black native of India (*Vyāsa*=writer; *kṛṣṇadvaipāyana*=dark-colored dweller of the island/subcontinent of India). Vālmīki is accepted as the author of the *Ramayana* but the name Vālmīki only means "one who is covered by an anthill." Kaṇāda, the rishi who expounded the philosophy of Vaiśeṣika, is so-called because his theory is an exposition of atoms (*kaṇa*=atom; *kaṇāda* =atom-eater). Such self-effacement is very rare, however.

The theory of reincarnation and the concepts of eternal life, hell, and heaven, are all symptomatic of the human fear of extinction. There is a sense of relief when a departed person is thought to be in another world such as Hades or Paradise.

Exercise

Before performing any action, think of the motivation behind it. See:

1. Whether it is the natural unfoldment of your intrinsic nature, from which you cannot withhold yourself. Then treat it as the unfurling of a flower and be a passive witness of it.

2. If the motivation is to increase your means for the purposive achievement of a certain goal, consider how beneficial such an act will be for all other sentient beings.

3. If there is a surging emotion that is blindfolding your discrimination, go slow and take time to reason it in terms of cause and effect to deplete the pressure that is compulsively accumulating in you. Reason gently and watch what others do without positive or negative exaggeration. Do not be in huste to establish your point.

Sūtra II:10

te pratiprasava heyāḥ sūkṣmāḥ

te: these
pratiprasava: a regressive reemergence into their origins
heyāḥ: [can be] removed, abolished, eliminated, destroyed
sūkṣmāḥ: attenuated (afflictions)

These attenuated (afflictions) can be removed by a regressive reemergence into their origins.

The five rudiments of obstruction—nescience, ego identity, attachment, hatred, and infatuation for life—do not reside in us as gross or subtle entities. They are causal factors. In a general sense, they are equivalent to what Freud and Jung call the unconscious. As causal factors are beyond the pale of consciousness, nobody knows where they reside. If they have a psychobiological and psychochemical basis, that is also not known to us.

In Western biology, certain chemical substances are postulated to be the vehicles of the information bits that are said to be hereditarily brought from the family tree into the embryo that has to develop into a fetus and subsequently into an individuated person. The Indian concept is not that of genes but of a causal body *(liṅga śarīra),* a subtle body *(sūkṣma śarīra),* and a gross body *(sthūla śarīra).* Just as in the Western concept of embryology, Indians also think of an evolutionary growth commencing from the causal body to the subtle body and from the subtle to the gross. The Self is said to develop different dimensions when it has to act as the supervising principle in these three stages of development and in the altering states of consciousness already mentioned as the wakeful (the consciousness that oscillates between subject and object), the dream (subjective or paraconscious), and the deep sleep (unconscious). The technical terms used to refer to these three roles of the Self are the empirical self (viśva), the creative self (taijasa), and the indistinct self of pure consciousness (prajñā).

Whether Western or Eastern, all psychologists presume that the cause of disturbance comes from a certain depth. Pioneers of Western psychology such as Freud, Jung, Adler, and Rank, were all convinced of this depth aspect. Pavlov, Skinner, and other behaviorists gave very little credence to the unconscious or subconscious and tried to interpret disturbances as well as learned habits as stemming from mainly from physicochemical conditioning of the biologic organism. Both the behaviorists and the existentialists therefore suggest measures for deconditioning a conditioned state. Both in psychoanalysis and in analytical psychology, bringing the dormant causes of disturbance from the unconscious to the conscious level is considered an essential feature of psychotherapy. Dream analysis and deciphering of symbols are considered as the main instruments of therapy.

Patañjali, on the other hand, suggests the removal of ignorance by flooding your interior with the true light of your own nature and transcending both pain and pleasure as the ultimate means of resolving psychological and spiritual maladies. Surface disturbances, personality maladjustments, and dysfunction of the psyche, including the physical organism, are all considered to be maneuvered by the built-in or deeply engrained maladies that can be satisfactorily corrected when you are provided with the right normative notion of a wholesome life and helped to have the right perspective of the unique features of your own personality make up.

It is not easy to have a regressive remergence into your own system without knowing how the microcosm is integrated into the macrocosm and what psychological forces are sculpturing the symbols of an inner secret language that is entirely individualistic. It is true that in the psychiatric classification certain patients show symptoms that are universally shared by patients of that particular classification. But the conceptual developments that happen in each person have varying external incidents and internal value-visions that interact differently. Thus, the symbol of one person's thoughts, dreams, and fantasies can be very different from the symbol of another. No psychologist can trace the entire development of the psychosomatic growth of any person to have a full understanding of their idiosyncrasies, antics, unconscious gestures, recurring dream symbols, and grouping of analogies on which basic concepts are hanging.

In India, the psychologist's place is assigned to a spiritual master, a guru. The usual time prescribed for therapeutic correction and shared growth between a spiritual master and a disciple is a minimum of twelve years of absolute bipolarity. It is through this bipolarity that the vertical parameter of the master's spiritual visions resonates with similar visions of the aspirant. They each have the opportunity to compare the differences in their reactions and behavior when they both react to the same situation and horizontal tendencies go in different directions. There is a constant attempt to verticalize the visions of both so that maximum resonance is established in their insights. Ultimately all personality differences are transcended until they come to a sameness of vision.

In the discipline of phenomenological reduction instituted by Edmund Husserl, further amplified by Martin Heidegger, and brought to a greater finish by Karl Jaspers, we have in the West a discipline very close to Patañjali's regressive remergence resulting in existential transcendence. How this can be applied in life we will come to know as we proceed deeper into kriyā yoga.

Sūtra II:11

dhyāna heyāś tad vṛttayaḥ

dhyāna: pure contemplation, even and harmonious flow of consciousness

heyāḥ: [are to be] removed

tad: their

vṛttayaḥ: modifications, oscillations, functions

Their modifications are to be removed by pure contemplation.

You actively enter into contemplative discipline after being initiated into Yoga. Initiation, technically called *dīkṣa,* is mainly intended to bring about the purification of the modifications to which the inner organ of individuated consciousness is subjected. Each of the aspects of the inner organ (questioning mind, recalling memory, reasoning intellect, and affective ego) has its specific kind of impurity. For instance, the curiosity to know spiritually and morally unprofitable occurrences outside yourself is an impurity of the interrogating faculty. Purity of the reasoning cogitation is dampened by the craving for pleasure. The impurity of the recalling faculty is the inability to discriminate essential memories from non-essential and irrelevant memories. The core aspect of the inner organ, the ego, is the most soiled and easily afflicted with moral and spiritual lacunae. In order to vacate all the four zones of your consciousness of the darkness of nescience, you should know how the mind functions.

The discipline called dīkṣa is essentially to keep all four aspects of the individuated consciousness free from blemishes. The Sanskrit term *dīkṣa* is very important because it suggests absolute bipolarity and continuing attention being given whole-heartedly to the persons, things, and events with which you are involved in the situation of your search. Only the most attentive can find his or her path inspiring. In such a discipline, you do not excuse yourself. Actually, initiation is from the side of the initiated rather than from the side of one who is initiating. The person who is seen to be ritualistically giving an initiation is at best only a witness. Absolute dedication has to come from the initiate.

In the *Mahabharata* Bhisma, the patriarch of the Kuru dynasty, is respected for being uncompromising in the pledge that he took upon himself, even when those who demanded it later excused him from it. It is easy to be excused by another, but if a person's conscience is always on the alert to be responsible, then we may say that person is an initiate. The guru or preceptor who is seen outside as a person is an exemplary model of moral excellence and a watchful conscience. In the contemplative life of a disciple he or she is always trying to look as perfect as possible to the watchful and critical eyes of the preceptor. The initiate is expected to be in a continuous state of contemplative dialogue with the Absolute which is spoken of differently as God, guru, or one's higher Self. The initiate has to bring his or her thoughts, words, and actions in a vertical line where each supports the other in maintaining moral integrity.

Nowadays dhyāna is loosely used to mean both "meditation" and "contemplation." Meditation is not dhyāna. It is only a serious form of pondering. Dhyāna is contemplation. In both discursive reasoning and critical examination, the mind goes from the center to the periphery or from the conclusion of one syllogism to another. In the contemplative discipline, consciousness is to be drawn from all sides to your own center with rapt attention and an attitude of devotion, which is as close as possible to intense love. In the *Bhagavad Gita* and such texts of contemplative wisdom, dhyāna is described as a state in which the mind is not invaded by imaginations or apprehensions of any kind. It is such a dhyāna that is prescribed here for the eradication of the impurities that come in the form of attachment or hatred, ego-identification with strong social emphasis, and the persistent will to commit yourself to programs that you think will ensure your name or fame or power over others.

Exercise

Take a piece of paper. In the center of the paper draw a very small circle and around it draw bigger and bigger circles, always keeping the distance exactly the same and making sure that the line is always equidistant from the circle that is next to it. This is to be done several times until you can draw all the circles with perfect precision. When that is achieved, reverse the order by drawing a big circle and then smaller and smaller circles until you come to the center point.

Still another exercise is to write four mantras—AUM, HRIM, SRIM, AIM—on a paper, leaving half an inch between each mantra in both directions, without using ruled paper. This should be repeated many times so that the mantras are in columns, each exactly below the other. This helps the mind to remain in one position and go deeper and deeper in its interest.

Sūtra II:12

kleśa mūlaḥ karmāśayo dṛṭādṛṣṭa janmavedanīyaḥ

kleśa: afflictions, obstacles
mūlaḥ: the root causes, origins [of the]
karmāśaya: [in] the reservoir of the conditioned or processed impressions of action, permanent features engraved on the mind
dṛṣṭa: [in a] visible
adṛṣṭa: [or] latent [manner]
janma: [in] life
vedanīyaḥ: are experienced

The root causes of the afflictions in the reservoir of conditioned or processed impressions of action are experienced in life in a visible or latent manner.

Individuated human life is born of processed or cultured impressions. These impressions pass through several life forms before coming to the present life. They can be compared to the propagating power of seeds or to the genetic continuation of whatever culture these life forms have experienced. What is termed as samskāra (culture) closely resembles the Western notion of neurobiological conditioning. The dynamics of an instance of conditioning are based on the accompanying pain or pleasure.

The general behavior of the various life forms that we see in nature is said to be guided by natural instincts. In Sanskrit this is known as *prākṛtam*. When the same is sophisticated, refined, cultured, and presented in a manner acceptable to others, it is called samskāra, a refined outcome or sublimated end result. The ethos or cultivated behavior of a regional culture can appear quite refined to the people of a particular geographical area or religious context. But the yogis are not thinking of social norms that please some particular group. They set their goal of refinement on the model of the purest of the pure Self, which is in no way contaminated by the physical, physiological, psychological, and sociological requirements of an individuated life.

The conditioning to which we are subjected is not a few random incidents of life. From the structuring of the hydrogen atom to the complex structuring of the human bio-computer that decides our action/reaction patterns, we have a story of several millennia. Thus it looks impossible to regress in the stream of life to arrive at the original nature of the spirit, which is only a triad of existence, subsistence, and value significance. Considering the closely packed information bits with which a gene is equipped through ages, they all hardly get a chance to become operative in one lifetime. It is postulated that everything we bring with us in the form of latent potencies is not lived in its entirety in one lifetime. So we think of the psychophysical organism only as a conveying vehicle that is given up when the life that is passing through it enters into another.

Like the momentum of a river decides the motion of the

stream, the quality of causal factors of action decides how we act or react as the stream of our life flows over changing contours of time and space. What is thus channeled through each one of us as an incessant flow is to be looked upon as the karmāśaya, the most subtle medium through which actions can be perpetuated and precipitated. From the karmāśaya there comes the desire to enjoy and to avoid painful situations.

A flowing river is always coming to a new situation, a new contour. Again and again the need arises to choose the pattern of action that is most appropriate to a given situation. The choice and reaction can be clumsy or efficient. Thus, the personality formation and development are a direct outcome of the action-reaction dynamic, which in turn gives expression to the innate propensities that are ever going through an endless process of evolution. It is as if our past is offering us the present and the future. The present is the only reality we live, and our response to the here and now is the link between the past and the future. Thus karmāśaya not only gives us the incentive act in a certain manner but also decides the uniqueness of individual responsibility.

Exercise

Write the hierarchy of values as it occurs in your mind. Then underline, with a colored pen or pencil if possible, the values that have great resemblance to your father's possible choices. With another color, mark the values that closely resemble your mother's choices. Underline the values that do not seem to be bright or praiseworthy. Mark the tendencies that are likely to lead you in the path of negativity and tragedy. Mark that which makes you conform to it obsessively with compulsion. By examining all this, conceive a value that you can adore as an inspiring goal to which you can return again and again.

Sūtra II:13

sati mūle tad vipāko jātyāyur bhogāḥ

sati mūle: as long as the root cause is there
tad: it
vipākaḥ: [must] fruition as
jāti: a class
āyuḥ: [programmed for] a certain duration
bhogāḥ: [and] experiences

As long as the root cause is there it must fruition as a class programmed for a certain duration and experiences.

In this sūtra, karma is to be understood in both its broad and precise senses. It is the action that decides the kind to which the organism has to conform. It is also what decides the time period the organism has to function in a certain manner. Again, as action is always value motivated, it decides for how long (and by interacting with what agency) the individuated person has to experience which value ensembles.

To understand all the implications of this sūtra, let us try to understand the evolutionary origin of classes. From the simplest particle onward, there are organizations of classes or kinds. In Sanskrit, class is called *jāti.* There are so many classes to which living beings belong. Humans are said to belong to the class of *Homo sapiens.* In the world of chemistry, basic elements are said to belong to classes that have universal characteristics that are mainly determined by the number of electrons and protons that constitute an atom and the patterned arrangement of the atoms in a molecule. The atomic number and weight of elements like hydrogen, helium, sodium, and carbon are different, so they belong to distinct classes. If karma is the cause of quantifying electrons and protons by which a certain class has come into manifestation, whose karma is that and from which agent do such actions come? What is the meaning to be assigned here to the word action (karma)?

Wheat, corn, and beans belong to different classes. What kind of action has caused these special species? Humans, rhinoceroses, and frogs all belong to different species. A species has homogeneity; class difference comes from heterogeneity. That is why Narayana Guru, in his work, *Jāti Mimāmsa,* writes, "Within a species, is it not, that offspring truly breed? The community of man thus viewed, to a single caste belongs." Although various terms to categorize different racial groups of human beigns have been used, even among these groups other categories can be seen because of geographical and other differences. Among the blacks of Africa there are tiny figures, the pygmies, and the tall people of the East and the North. Among the so-called Aryans there are contemplative brahmins and aggressive Nazis. Even in the same family one man may bc introspective while his own brother is a very outgoing extrovert.

When we analyze class on the basis of karma, we can see two incentives to act. One is that which marks the character of an individual and the other is that person's allegiance to the clan or racial group or ethnic community to which he or she belongs. Also, historical, cultural, and political ideologies decide group behavior. Geographic and climatic conditions can even affect with compulsion the gait and movement of a person when he or she walks. When snow is falling and cold winds are blowing, nobody can have a lazy, leisurely stroll down the streets of New York, London, or Frankfurt. One has to walk with quick paces to keep the blood circulating and the body warm. In South India where the temperature is almost always very warm, one will get tired if one walks very fast. So it is even considered a virtue, especially for women, to move around like an elephant or wobble like a goose. Considering all this, in the *Gita*, we read that even for great scholars the path of karma is difficult to discern. India is a country where even villages are divided in terms of caste. And yet, so far no scientific study has been properly conducted to discern what caste is and how, in spite of its irrationality, it has such a strong hold on the minds of people so that one cannot rid another of his or her prejudices.

Action and the experiencing of pain and pleasure are both value-oriented. For the realization of certain highly coveted values one needs a whole lifetime. A virus, on the other hand, does not have to retain its identity for a period longer than a few seconds. Once it gains entry into a living body, it automatically replicates in a fraction of a moment. Its action of replicating its class and being nourished by the host cell has a fleeting nature. For the functioning of such a being no voluntary deliberation is required. It can fully submit itself to automation. It has no questions, no cogitation, and no memory recall. It is not the same for an oak tree. Immediately after sprouting from an acorn it cannot produce a similar acorn. It takes years for it to grow into a mature tree, for branches to stretch in different directions and new acorns to come. Thus the karma of the oak is bound to be complex. It has to function through many parts of the tree such as the root, leaf, bark, ascending and descending saps.

For other species, symbiotic actions are required for the perpetuation of two species such as between a flowering plant and the insects that feed on its pollen and help it pollinate. The karma spoken of here thus has a wide range, from the assemblage of particles to the highly organized and programmed action of a responsible member of a sophisticated community.

The duration spoken of in this sūtra is not that of an organism's bodily existence but the unit of time required for an action to evolve from the first inception of a desire to the fruition of a programmed action in results. In certain species like that of human beings, there can be the concept of an action that stretches beyond the duration of a lifetime. A far-off goal sought by an entire community can involve the death of the old, birth of the new, and maturation of the young in new awakenings of consciousness as part of one national action. In a historical action in which countless millions of people are involved, the development of a socio-economic and cultural action can stretch through several centuries, such as the revolution started by Lenin and others in Russia. Just as the continuous birth of many cells and death of many cells in a human body seldom affects the integrity of a whole person's identity, in group life also, while individual action is contributory to national action or universal action, the universal action has a decree to make with regard to the modus operandi of each individual's choice of field and execution of action.

The chance element that religious people recognize as grace or the providential factor is again something to reckon with. When one is fortunate to be grafted on the action programs, thought streams, value vision, and goal orientation of a great person, such as Plato emerging as an inseparable continuator of Socrates or Marx revising and restating the political philosophy and epistemological stand of Hegel, the quality of action that is so intertwined with the value significance of the goal chosen can completely transform even the personality make-up of a person who is brought to toe the program of a great visionary.

Vyāsa gives an elaborate commentary to this sūtra. If the cause for conflict resides as a dormant tendency in the karmāśaya, it will mature in the course of time. To abort that possibility, the nucleus of that cause should be squashed. If wheat or paddy rice are husked, they cannot germinate again.

A fried seed also loses its potential to germinate. Such is the relationship between the potencies of impressions laid by previous actions and the conflicts that arise from the maturity of those impressions. Nescience, ego-identity, attachment, hatred, and infatuation should be carefully discerned and rendered impotent with the practice of opposing energy channelization.

Right knowledge is the means to destroy these negative forces. If that is not done, then these tendencies will assume three evolutionary forms of development. One is that the accumulated tendencies will get into relationship with each other through permutations and combinations and will assume the format of a fresh individuation, which thereafter becomes the main mark of the class to which one belongs.

The various tendencies that line up, one behind the other, to present through the organism will decide the period that is required for all the unfinished karmas to complete their sway in life. That decides the longevity of the individual.

Also, the faculties that are to be developed by the organism are intrinsically connected with the experiences that the individual is expected to have. If there is nothing in you that draws you to become a connoisseur of music, there will not be any incentive for you to develop a high sensibility in your listening power. In the same way, the variety of experiences that you are eventually to be exposed to can only happen through a long period of organizational growth.

These three kinds of formations and fruitions are called the three-fold maturation *(trivipāka)*. Vyāsa recommends that we look into certain important questions that can be asked in connection with the three-fold maturation of the tendencies that are brought over from the previous life. First, does each karma necessitate a subsequent birth to work out all the details of that karma? Is it true that even one karma can precipitate many births? Do many karmas bring in their train several births or are we allowed to live the implications of several karmas in living one life?

Vyāsa does not think that each karma requires a separate life. The urges to act, born of previous impressions (vāsanās), are not presented to the conscious mind and volition in any definite order. The priority of a certain karma to perform comes more as a reciprocal polarization between incipient memories and environmental factors that are conducive to the performance of the required action. There are also incipient memories that, when not given opportunities to actualize, wear out their potential and become defunct, unable to present again. A number of incipient memories belonging to different orders can be presented in the same life because the external world is presented to the individual in a kaleidoscopic manner and a variety of interests can meet with satisfaction as the individual goes from one context to another.

What matters is mainly the dynamics that find their inclusion in the causal body that is transferred from the present life to the next, both as a witnessing principle of the entry of life into the sperm of the father and egg of the mother and as the architect of the manifesting embryo into its maturation. If multiple interests are already present and if they are seeded as separate package programs in the causal body (liṅga śarīra), it is possible that in the next life the person may have a schizophrenic personality that can be a simple split, as in the case of a dual personality, or a fragmentation, as seen in multiple personalities. In spite of the multiplicity of interests, if a person has a unifying principle that governs the whole being, he or she may develop the personality of a genius like Leonardo da Vinci and show several interests and talents where each is promotive of the other. Incipient memories, like biological genes, are the net products of several lives, whereas the karmāśaya is the sum total of the mutations that have come into the personality development and evolution of a single lifetime.

There is no rule that all the potentials of causal consciousness should be lived and fructified in the same life, just as all the genetic potentials that a person has are not developed or lived during his or her lifetime. Death is the best of all purificatory disciplines imposed on every individual by nature. A number of half-attempted action programs and values of lukewarm interest are all nullified by death. It is like the night sleep that comes each twenty-four hours and wipes away most of the unprofitable memories and eradicates the toxic formations of several biochemical products in the body. Thus, suṣupti (deep sleep) and death are our best friends to make us again and again fresh and replenished to return to the arena of life.

Sūtra II:14

te hlāda paritāpa phalāḥ puṇyāpuṇya hetutvāt

te: they [the seeded carriers of action propensities]
hlāda: [have] joy
paritāpa: [or] sorrow, suffering
phalāḥ: [for their] fruit
puṇya: virtue
apuṇya: [or] vice
hetutvat: in accordance with

They (the seeded carriers of action propensities) have joy or sorrow for their fruit in accordance with virtue or vice.

Modern commentators have done a great disservice to the study of karma by oversimplifying the course of action, conceiving of it in a linear manner and restricting the cause and effect relationship to be of one-to-one correspondence. Karma is not linear. It propagates its energies in different directions. It has a vertical implication as well as horizontal modifications. It is also naive to believe that one person's action boomerangs only on that person. When Jesus Christ stood before Pilate as innocent as a lamb, a crowd of unthinking religious fanatics shouted, "Crucify him!" Being overwhelmed by numbers, Pilate ordered him to be killed. Thereafter Pilate washed his hands, openly declaring that he did not want the sin of murdering an innocent man to be on his hands. Thus, there were a number of people on the causal side of the crucifixion and the bitter fruit of the plurality of causes was experienced in anguish only by Jesus.

Mahatma Gandhi, loved universally by all those who care for human virtue, was shot in his chest by a single man. On the side of the cause there is only one man and his action was the simple pulling of the trigger of a gun. The effect of that murder was to throw a nation of millions of people into tears. Unable to bear the pain of the injustice done to Gandhi, several Indians committed suicide. This is a case of one cause and several side effects. Thus several causes can culminate in a single effect and one cause can lead to many chains of events.

The Yoga aspirant should see puruṣa on one side and prakṛti, its counterpart, on the other. Where prakṛti, provoked or stimulated by the presence of puruṣa, becomes transmuted, the triple qualities of nature (the sublime, the kinetic, and the inertial) are operative. Quintuplicated elements operate in nature as subtle energy forms *(tanmātras)*. In each element—such as earth, fire, water, air, space—only one half of its pure energy is maintained. The rest is supplemented evenly with the energy quantums of the other four elements. Thus, each element is to be understood both in its purest form and as a compound with the other four forms.

For a psychophysical organism to evolve and function as

an individual, there has to be the bonding together of the gross (compound) elements and the pure elements. The puruṣa or spirit finds its inseparability in such a constellation of gross and subtle elemental structure. At the various levels of the spirit's impact on the elemental body, organs of perception and action manifest. They are all coordinated by the binary principle of consciousness called manas, which plays the double role of consciousness and unconsciousness. The one energy that comes to all these as animation (citiśakti) is a quantum that is pulsating from the spirit.

In this complex organism a two-fold projection is happening. Inertial matter appears to be conscient and the conscient principle of the spirit appears as if it has physical limbs. Where these two projections overlap, the individual experiences ego-identity. This ego-identity takes upon itself the agency to perceive, conceive, judge, and react. The interrogating aspect of mind is like a specially deputed watchman and caretaker of the individuated house of consciousness. Even before the senses and the mind come into a full encounter with an externally present object, the questioning aspect of the mind signals the indication of an object to be verified.

Identifying a certain object as something being presented in the here and now holds out two challenges: how to react to that object in the present and how to know what the significance of that object will be in the near or far future. The present and the future are manifesting out of the past. Hence, all scrutiny for identification comes from a comparison with the past through the recall of memory.

While the sensory system is bringing in stimuli from the outer world, the motor system that controls the organs of action has to carry out the response to the stimulus even when the stimulus is partial. The five-fold actions are: articulation, manipulation, mobility, excretion, and procreation. For each of the five faculties to function, the relevant areas of action are to be roused and a lot of energy is to be channelized into the organs of action. The response given to every stimulus can have the special quality of being virtuous or vicious. If we take, for example, the faculty of articulation, a single word that escapes from a person's mouth can sometimes cause something so disastrous as a world war. Similarly, a word uttered in sympathy can pacify a nation. In the same manner we can see the importance of the other four faculties. Our actions are rendered painful or joyful through wrong or right identification in which the five obstructions in the path of Yoga—nescience, ego-identity, attachment, hatred, and infatuation with life—operate in various combinations.

Sūtra II:15

pariṇāma tāpa samskāra duḥkhair guṇa vṛtti virodhāc ca duḥkham eva sarvam vivekinaḥ

pariṇāma: resulting from change
tāpa: anxiety [and]
samskāra: the registration and preservation of impressions, formation of incipient memories
duḥkhaiḥ: [on account of] the pain, misery, distress, sorrow, suffering
guṇa: [of] the three qualities, triple modalities, or primary constituents of nature *(sattva, rajas, tamas)*
vṛttiḥ: the functions, modifications, oscillations, modulations
virodhāt: [on account of] the conflict between
ca eva: as also
duḥkham: [is] pain, misery, distress, sorrow, suffering
sarvam: all

vivekinaḥ: to those with unitive discrimination

To those with unitive discrimination all is misery on account of the pain resulting from change, anxiety, and the registration and preservation of impressions, as also on account of the conflict between the functions of the triple modalities of nature.

This sūtra is given with special reference to the attaining of absolute aloneness, which is considered to be the final goal of Patañjali's eight-limbed discipline of Yoga. The dialectical situation in which an aspiring yogi is placed is between the ever-increasing plurality of nature and the unitiveness of the spirit. The discrimination of a person who comprehends the unitiveness of the entire system is also said to be unitive *(akhaṇḍa viveka).* What is subject to change is the projected picture of existence, modulated consciousness, and the transient form of interest specified by names and forms within the frame of the time-space continuum in which subtle causes manifest into gross effects and the agent of action is incessantly identified as the knower, doer, and experiencer.

In pure spirit, there is nothing specific. The projected specificity of each gestalt that is presented to consciousness not only hides the unitive reality of the Self but also alienates us from our absolute nature and brings us into encounter after encounter in which the time sequence is very pronounced. As Plato puts it very succinctly, the pure light of the Absolute is hidden away and the individuated person has access only to the images cast by reflected light.

This indirect illumination of the Self that we experience as a conscious awareness of mentation is further vitiated by the triple qualities of nature. Even in the most grotesque projection of a shadow there will be a one-to-one correspondence between the original and the image because the very act of reflection comes from the sublime quality of nature, sattva. But in actual or empirical experience, this correspondence is distorted by the ever-moving and ever-changing mechanism of the world phenomena, causing the object and the subject to flicker in such a way that when one is seen, the other is hidden. Also, all previous conditionings are focused on each image so that it becomes highly exaggerated as either very dear or very hateful. The subtle veil that hides reality is magical; it operates without giving any glimpse of its interception. As a result, we are almost oblivious to the numinous that shines forth as value in everything.

When the same light is focused on two different bodies of biochemical structure, the light that falls is immediately affected so that the reflected rays are considerably different in their radiating frequency and amplitude. Consequently, the eye that receives the reflected light from the two objects will see them as considerably different in their colors. The old proverb says that there is many a slip between the cup and the lip. Between the changing structure of the external world and the reciprocal disturbance happening in the human brain, many truths are annulled, many lies are added, and the poor organism has to contend with what is allotted to it by the niggardly provision of a step-mother-like nature.

Taking cognizance of the sad fate to which we creatures are subjected, the *Gita* describes this world as a home of suffering *(duḥkhālayam).* The Buddhists, as if in one voice, register their protest and say in a sweeping manner: "everything is painful *(sarvam duḥkham).*" The Christians call this world a world of crosses. Thus, there is a universal depreciation of the world of names and forms.

This world is a flux. Heraclitus said, "No one can step in the same river twice." Everything is subjected to change and evolution. The playful fawn has green meadows to run about and graze in, pure water to drink, sunlight and moonsheen to illuminate its pretty world. But no one can say when there might be a brushfire that will burn the fawn alive in a conflagration. In the fishpond there is crystal clear water and beautiful lotus flowers. The fish that play hide and seek in the water have enough larvae to feed on. When spring is gone, summer comes. In the hot Sun, water evaporates away. Finally a day comes when the bottom of the pond cracks and the fish die without a drop to drink.

When we are children our mothers rock us to sleep singing lullabies. They feed us with bread and butter, milk and porridge. Not knowing any care of this world, we run around with our playmates. But as we grow up we become strangers to this world. There is no one to believe, no one to love. For an ounce of love that one receives, a pound of freedom is to be bartered. Thus every change in life ultimately brings us to an uncompromising doomsday. This world is full of contradictions. The housewife forgets to hide away a piece of cheese. The smell goes to the far-off field and brings the bright-eyed mouse to the kitchen. Seeing the cheese he rejoices. To the tomcat of the family, the mouse smells more inviting than the cheese. Before reaching the cheese the poor mouse is gobbled up by the cat. There is deception everywhere.

Although Indians see only the negative side of life, the plus and minus, yin and yang, are actually well balanced. The most exhaustive and penetrating study of change in time was made by the ancient Chinese people. We have the best testimony of this study in the *I-Ching* or *Book of Changes*, a book that has never been rivaled any time anywhere in the world. Although nobody knows who the author was, it is revered around the world as a flawless book that explains the relationship of the individual both to the elements of the changing social matrix and to the cosmic flux of time. This book has no local, fixed emphasis and is of perennial importance.

Eight symbols are accepted to form the basis of the *I-Ching*. As in the Jewish tradition, the family is the model for all relationships in the Chinese tradition also. A family unit is considered to be constituted of eight persons: Father, Mother, First Son, Second Son, Third Son, First Daughter, Second Daughter, and Third Daughter. These eight family members are represented by eight trigrams, each with a name, attribute, and image. Sixty-four hexagrams are formed from various combinations of these eight trigrams. A numerator trigram is given and complemented with a denominator trigram.

In the Western world, the law of causation is considered very important and therefore the main relationship that is reckoned is that of the effect relating to cause. Psychologist Jung calls our attention to the fact that the Chinese way of looking at the relationship of things in this world is different. A one-to-one correspondence between cause and effect is not acceptable to the Chinese people. The wise men of China were humble enough to accept that both the structure and function of truth are beyond the comprehension of a rational mind. Truth is to be approached with an open mind to have a general notion of the particular manner in which Heaven and Earth come into conjunction.

Thus, there are three main approaches to truth. One is the pragmatic approach of the West regarding the actualization of certain events for which one cause is considered a premier cause and a certain effect is considered consequential to that cause. The Indians, who are more concerned with the realization of truth than the actualization of pragmatic events, refer the multitudinous effects to a primal cause and their method is, as already mentioned, one of regressive remergence. The Chinese people are not afraid to face the enormity of the challenge of life and they are therefore willing to accept each situation as a paradoxical coming together of two opposites, which they call the yang and the yin.

The model given in the aphorisms of Patañjali goes very much with the Vedāntic notion of treating this world as illusion and therefore the resolution sought is one of transcendence rather than living the given life in the here and now.

Sūtra II:16

heyam duḥkhamanāgatam

heyam: is to be avoided, is to be removed
duḥkham: the pain, misery, distress, sorrow, suffering
anāgatam: [that] has not yet come

The pain that has not yet come is to be avoided.

Before a child is conceived, the mother provides an egg that can be thought of as an empty chair. When a sperm comes to sit on the chair, the sperm and the chair become riveted into one person. After sitting in the dark of the mother's womb for nine months of preparation, the person comes out and is seated in the theater called the world. A large screen seems to be before the child, but it is actually inside. This screen is the mind. The first projection on the screen is that of the child's mother, feeding and suckling. Then comes the father and perhaps brothers and sisters. The child does not merely see them, but is tied, bonded to them. These bonds are made of ropes with two strands, one of love and one of hate. These dual bonds are felt toward every item of attraction and repulsion.

The first major cause of misery is forgetting that these are all projections on the screen of the mind. It is just like weeping when you see a beloved actor in a sad movie. You forget that it is only a projection of colored film on a screen. In Indian philosophy this is called avidyā, basic ignorance. You are aware of only the projections and forget that the seer, the seeing, and the seen are all one. This ignorance of the whole story of your physical manifestation in this world is the first cause of suffering.

The next two causes of misery are thinking that love and hatred are constants. Your interests alternate. That which attracts one minute can repulse the next. If an object of love is forced, it becomes an object of displeasure. For instance, a mother gives her breast to her child with great love and it gratefully suckles when it is hungry. But if the breast is given when the baby wants to enjoy something else, the child will avoid it with signs of displeasure. Objects thus do not have intrinsic value to be attractive at all times. However, some interests, such as eating, drinking, and sleeping, recur regularly in a consistent pattern. In the ever-changing pattern of interests, love and hate are generated by your states of mind, not by the things outside, but you forget that you are projecting your values and aversions on to things and then loving or hating them.

Interest is like an electrical charge. After the quantum of energy comes to an end, the charge wears off and the interest wanes. You go from one train of thought to another, without being aware of it happening. For example, you may be thinking of A: AAA. A is dominant in the pattern but B slips in occasionally: AAAAAABAAAAAABAAAAAA. Very subtly B starts to infiltrate: AAAABBAAABBBAABBBBABBBBB. Like A changing imperceptibly into B, love is not a constant reality; it can change into hatred. The mother can kiss and hug her child in great affection, but if this is prolonged too long, the child tries to struggle away. Neither love nor hate are permanent values, but are two sides of the same coin.

The fourth cause of suffering is asmitā, I-consciousness. The ego is exposed to the ambivalence of love and hate, happiness and misery. They are alternating experiences of the ego. When the ego is pampered by love, it experiences happiness. When hatred is there, it experiences the darkness of misery. Without the ego, neither is there. The ego is raised by relating to another ego. When another shouts, we also shout. When two egos get into conflict, anger builds into anger.

Once Balarama, Krishna's brother, was fighting with a huge demon. They were raging with each other and the demon was growing bigger and bigger. Then Krishna came along and said, "Let me deal with him." He said to the demon, "Brother, why are you fighting?" The demon was humbled by his gentle manner and kindly approach. He became smaller. Then Krishna said, "Let us be friends," and the demon became even smaller. Krishna patted him lovingly and he became only one inch tall, sitting on Krishna's hand. Balarama was astonished. Krishna said, "Do you know who this demon is? He is anger. If we feed anger with anger, it becomes gigantic, but if we feed anger with love, it disappears."

The final cause of misery is abhiniveśa, the will to live. You forget that you have only come to the world for a short period. Like a beautiful mango that conceals a worm in its pit, you may have come from your mother's womb with the seed of death sitting within your life, such as a genetically inherited disease. Certain diseases camp within you and only start to peep out when you reach thirty or forty years of age. At age fifty or sixty, the disease comes to stand with you, causing you to panic and try to push it away. With proper diet and medication, it may withdraw for awhile, only to return with greater force. Then the disease says: "My friend, from birth I was always with you. It is now time for me to walk in front and for you to follow."

You forget that death is inevitable and you put up a

valiant fight all the time. But you cannot go on forever, so when the time for death comes, your suffering can be great if you are possessed by abhiniveśa, the spirit of never wanting to leave this world.

Patañjali reassures us that all five causes of suffering can be corrected. First you need to understand the screen on which the play of life is projected and that you are not different from the experiences you are projecting, or the projections you are experiencing. A drug addict looks for drugs, an alcoholic for drink, and a lover of books for a library. Each of us creates our own world and then complains about the environment.

You can create a conducive environment by carefully structuring your world. You can withdraw your mind from the marketplace where it gets easily soiled. Nightmares come out of you because you have irrational fears lurking in your mind. By going deeply into the areas of the mind and illuminating them with the inner light of the Self, this darkness will go.

Once you can see the impermanence of the five causes of misery you will gain the capacity to distinguish between the avoidable and unavoidable situations of life. If rain comes, you must wait for it to stop. Although a situation is unavoidable, it may be possible to improve it. If it is wet and cold outside and it is possible to sit by a warm fire or in bed between woolen sheets, then do so. Gandhi used to say that you can't remove all the thorns from your path before you start your journey, but you can wear shoes to protect your feet. There are many disharmonies in the world, but you can be a peaceful person in a peace-less world.

You can use your intelligence to mitigate the suffering coming from unavoidable situations. If a mad dog rushes at you, don't challenge it. Move out of the way, shut and bolt the door. Learn where danger is hiding and how it can pounce on you. Then don't give it the opportunity to pounce. If certain situations or foods disagree with you, avoid them. Be discriminating. Make a distinction between love and infatuation. One person was suffering and sobbing and depressing everyone around him. He called it lost love but it was really infatuation, not love, because he wanted to kill the woman whom he swore he loved.

You can keep emotional stress states from creating compulsions in your behavior. If someone has stumbled and harmed you, give up your hatred and forgive them. You will find that the demon flies and love comes in. Ninety percent of the time, you can avoid that which can be avoided, mitigate that which can be mitigated. Life will be more peaceful if you live simply. Yoga does not offer a solution after death; it is showing us how to live in the here and now.

Sūtra II:17

draṣṭṛ dṛśyayoḥ saṁyogoheya hetuḥ

draṣṭṛ: of the seer
drsyayoh: of the seen
saṁyogaḥ: [is the] conjunction, union
heya: [which is] to be avoided, to be removed
hetuḥ: the cause [of that]

The cause of that which is to be avoided is the conjunction of the seer and the seen.

To most people, dreams, deep sleep, and moments of inner absorption do not appear very important. They think they live only when they are wakeful and engaged in transactions. In wakeful consciousness, the seer is the subject and the world interacted with or encountered is the object. The stuff of the seer is consciousness. What you recognize as awareness of your mind is only a peripheral aspect of the self-luminous light of your own Self *(ātman)*. From this peripheral consciousness, as you move inward to the depth of your consciousness, you pass through the regions of preconscious or semiconscious areas, a non-differentiated region of consciousness where there is no distinction of the subject and the object, and finally you come to the pure homogeneity of your deeper Self.

This deeper aspect, in the view of Patañjali's Yoga aphorisms, is the puruṣa or spirit. The puruṣa does not act; it has no limbs, and it is indivisible. Just as a light has its own luminosity and is capable of illuminating other things, the puruṣa can know and can also make things known. Puruṣa can be considered as the bright dynamic energy of consciousness. When we look at this world from the side of the spirit or puruṣa, it is first seen as a noumenon surrounded by the consciousness of mind, having for its adjuncts the senses and a body equipped with sensory and motor systems.

Individuation of the person comes to be with the interaction of the spirit and nature. We have already seen that in nature there is a quintuplication of elements and the functioning of triple modalities. When we study this body, we see how the physical laws that control and operate it are important. When the physical energy is seen as packages of varying quantums, the reference is to the manifestation of the chemical stuff of matter. When the mechanism that is seen in physical and chemical energy is looked upon as active units and interacting principles, the biologic factor evolves. When the same, in its complex organisation, has within it both a principle of awareness and a conscious manipulation of its destiny, biology is supplemented by psychology. Here the individual is seen more as a psychosomatic system programmed with definite purpose.

In this universe Earth is an insignificant speck. Among the sentient beings habitating Earth, humans are only one of many kinds of living beings. Out of the skin that covers the whole area of the body, two tiny spots have the ability to mirror everything outside and enable the person to think of the whole world as an object of perception. These little spots called eyes have the power to see not only the objects immediately presented, but also can see objects of the past that have been shining in the firmament as brilliant stars several thousand light years away. Thus stars many times bigger than the Sun, which exist at a far-off distance both in space and time, find their counterpart in the human eye. The world is, as a visible entity, only in the eye of the person who apprehends it. It is this coming together of the world outside and the vision of the person inside that forms the ground for all experience, where life is lived in all its richness and its negativity of pain and misery.

An image seen in a mirror is a transitory phenomenon that will not cling on to the mirror when the position of the mirror is changed. But the inner organ of a person is such that whatever image is projected on it will leave an impression that can remain in the depth of consciousness to the very end of life. Thus you are not only suffering from what is immediately projected on your senses and inner organ, but also from the stored impressions that remain with you as painful memories or inviting visions. Patañjali is of the opinion that, pleasant or unpleasant, these memories are the source of misery and should not be encouraged. According to him, all programming is to be avoided and he prescribes the abolition of the conjunction of the seer and the seen. But this is not always considered to be the greatest ideal. His two commentators—Valmiki of the *Yoga Vasistha Ramayana* and Vyāsa of the *Bhagavad Gita*—give the alternative of positive programming, turning to what is good for you.

Sūtra II:18

prakāśa kriyā sthiti śīlam bhūtendriyātmakam bhogāpavargārtham dṛśyam

prakāśa: illumination
kriyā: activity
sthiti: [and] stability
śīlam: consists of
bhūta: the elements
indriya: [and] sense organs
ātmakam: is of the nature of
bhoga: experience
apavarga: [and] liberation
artha: for the purpose of
dṛśyam: the seen

The seen consists of the elements and sense organs, is of the nature of illumination, activity, and stability, for the purpose of experience and liberation.

In our everyday life experience we have on one side the self, the subject, "I." On the other side is the physical world. Between the experiencer and the experienced, three functions are involved: cognition, reaction, and registration for recall. First, the cognizing faculty comes in the form of illumination. After the "I" cognizes, it reacts in the form of an action program. Then the confection of these two as an experience is stored for future reference. According to Indian schools of philosophy, these three functions come from nature: sattva provides clear illumination for cognition; rajas gives the dynamism to respond to situations; and tamas provides the memory storage that is absolutely necessary for one to know how to deal with the world. Patañjali says we are thus equipped for two opposing reasons. We can experience the world and bind ourselves to it or we can free ourselves from all its knots. It is up to us whether we want to be free or stay in this world of happiness and sorrow.

Illumination, knowledge, programs you to feel many things—anxiety, curiosity, urges, drives—that make you restless. This restlessness is not a disease to be cured. It is needed for all the activities of life. Once you are disturbed, you are stimulated to accomplish and experience. Maturity depends on the amount of stored experience you have. Theoretical knowledge is to be followed by practical experience in order to bring stabilization. For example, in learning to play a musical instrument, you first observe the proper finger movements as demonstrated by your teacher (illumination). Then, you practice the movements again and again (kinetics), which enables you to retain what you have learned (inertia). You become a cultured person when you have taken pains to get practical experience.

A planted seed can elaborate itself into a tree with trunk, branches, leaves, flowers, fruit, and finally another seed that can be planted to produce the same kind of tree. Hidden in the seed is the stored essence of the roots, trunk, flowers, and so on. In the same way, the essences of our experiences are stored within us. Freud and others say the storage is in the unconscious; Indian philosophers say it is in the deep sleep aspect of tamas. This storage is most important for the continuity and stabilization of culture.

If you want to be emancipated from all the effects of the culturing you have undergone, the horizon of the application of your values needs to be expanded. For example, you would share what you have acquired not only with your own family but with the whole world, like Einstein who studied and worked very hard and then shared the results of his labor with all. To transform your value system you have to use the same faculties you used to acquire it, such as your brain. The same equipment that you use for experiencing is to be used to transcend that experience. First you accept your bondage, then seek and find emancipation. A true yogi can experience transcendence in immanence and immanence in transcendence, first making himself or herself bound, then enjoying that bondage for the benefit of the world. He or she works day and night as an example, being happy and sharing that happiness with all.

In life there is a magical element that can also be real. We have two worlds, the world of light and the world of darkness. Life is generated between the Sun above and the Earth below. A seed needs both to grow. A seed is so small yet magically it can become a whole tree. Even if a heavy stone is above the seed, the sprout will circumvent it and find a way to come up. Similarly, a root that is very tender and soft can even break a wall that is in its way. Life has this magic power of being able to make a breakthrough. This is *pradhāna*, a very forceful energy. It is magic because it achieves things you don't think it can. Its domain is the actual, where action can take place. The actual belongs to the present; the real is the essence of the actual, a philosophical abstraction of present, past, and future.

Each day, the actual aspect has to break through all the impediments of life. To channel energy to action is very important. Energy is inertial, but can assume a momentum. Jung asks the question, "When a mother sees her own child trapped under something heavy, she is able to lift more than she usually has the capacity to lift. Why?" Her great interest, her love for her child, enables her unactualized potential energy to become dynamic. Jung also points out that many people's energy is blocked, frozen. Most people do not know how much energy they have because they don't know how to have a goal-oriented life and how to direct their pent-up energy to their goals. Many young people in India, eighteen to thirty years of age, suffer from depression. Their energy is pent up and they do not know the magical power within them. They need to know how their essence can be brought into conjunction with their motivation to bring that essence out as actions and then stabilized as a seed bed for future occasions.

For example, in our potato cultivation here, we took a risk because we invested in the potatoes for seeds, the manure, and tilling the soil, but if the rain hadn't come at the proper time, we wouldn't have gotten a crop and our investment would have been lost. But the rain did come and the ten sacks we planted will become sixty sacks. That fruition can be used for a continuation in a bigger way: it will be enough to eat, to share with the workers, and to put all of the land under cultivation for the next crop, without having to buy any more seeds. In a similar way in all our small matters, we can see how work will flourish in the next stage. That initiates motivation to grow into momentum that melts the blocks.

Narayana Guru wrote sixty works that can fit into a small book. Then Nataraja Guru devoted himself to explaining and elaborating those teachings. He wrote five thousand pages on only nineteen of the original works. I am studying and writing thousands more pages, but there is still so much untapped, left for others to continue. So much came from one man, like radium that goes on radiating. Such great geniuses change the world. We need to begin with changing ourselves. If we find the unperishing truth within us, we can go on tapping that forever.

In this sūtra Patañjali is drawing our attention to the pradhāna, the power we have within us, and asking us to perfect our lives and bring our potentials out to finality. To aid that process, yogis have given attention to the synergic centers (cakras) that run in a vertical parameter from between the brows to the base of the spine.

Ājña is the synergic center that is most well known to us. It is placed between the two brows. *Ajña* means "to command," a very appropriate name for this center because all of the commands that we give to our organs of action originate from here. Even to move your little toe the message has to go from this area of the brain.

The ājña has the triple agency of the knower, the doer, and the enjoyer. Even the most difficult tasks are assigned to the body from this command area that has the ability to release energy to both the faculties of perception and faculties of action. The doer carries out messages in accordance with what is known.

Ajña also has a penetrating power to go into the details of all the data presented to the senses and mind and know a thing from within with its identification. After considering the quality of the sensory data, the command area can refer the data of perception to the intellect (buddhi), which applies its discriminative power by associating the present data with previous experiences. The intellect flashes back the message of affirmation or negation. If the message is affirmative, then the ājña flashes a message to the organs of action to react. When the agency of action gives a command to the organs of action, it also provides a flow of energy by connecting all the appropriate glandular secretions and enzymes.

The third function of the command area is that of consciously appreciating the experience, either through its power of obsession or its negative power of inhibition. The whole function can be compared to planning, cooking, and eating a meal.

One cannot think without the use of words. So before the ājña is ready to give a command, appropriate words are to be coordinated and presented to consciousness. This very intricate action happens in the *viśuddhi*, in the area of the larynx. Although words come from the throat plex, it is programmed by the incentives of the four cakras below it: *anāhata* (heart), *maṇipūra* (navel), *svādhiṣṭhāna* (genitals), *mūlādhāra* (base of spine).

In the vertical parameter ranging from the ājña to the mūlādhāra, three divisions are to be made. The two upper cakras (ājña and viśuddhi) comprise the articulating area. The two middle centers (anāhata and maṇipūra) form the coordinating area. The third area, which includes the two lower cakras (svādhiṣṭhāna and mūlādhāra), is that of the creative urges. The mūlādhāra is the physical-electrical-chemical foundation of the individual that controls the supply of energy, both by channeling and regulating. The svādhiṣṭhāna is the psychic foundation of the individual that provides for the personality structure.

The nutritional system of the maṇipūra is to be bracketed with the blood supply of the heart. But the designation of anāhata as the heart is not to be taken literally. The brain, liver, thyroid gland, pituitary and adrenal glands, and sometimes the gonads are all to be included. When the anāhata (meaning "the unbroken") is supplied with the interests of the lower cakras it immediately understands the purport of the interest. It is ready to supply the limbs with the required energizing blood and other energy-releasing biochemicals of the body. The heartbeat increases or decreases in response to plus or minus behavior being indicated.

In the articulating area, the transition is from idea to word. This is the great magical performance of the spirit articulating through matter, the process of semiosis. The norms and noetics of semiosis are organized at three levels: pragmatics, logistics, and syntactics.

We can thus see how the six synergic centers are well coordinated to function in accordance with a purposive program of life. It is for this reason that the yogis of India have given their attention to each of the centers to make sure they are functionally correct and not afflicted by blocks that can cause malfunction. The furnace of the maṇipūra is to be fed with proper fuels so it can provide the energy needed for the disciplining of the conscious and unconscious urges unfolding from the physical and psychic bases of life. The anāhata (unbroken) thus will be fueled to apply a continuous, even pressure of discipline in life. That will enable the purificatory action of the viśuddhi to aid the command area with discrimination in choosing commands without errors. Together, the six centers tell the story of pradhāna, the magic of melting frozen energy and growing into a person with wider horizons and higher visions.

Sūtra II:19

viśeṣāviśeṣa liṅgamātra aliṅgāni guṇa parvāṇi

viśeṣa: particular, specific
aviśeṣa: universal, generic
liṅgamātra: differentiated, with a recognizable mark
aliṅgāni: undifferentiated, without mark
guṇa: [of] the three qualities, triple modalities, or primary constituents of nature *(sattva, rajas, tamas)*
parvāṇi: [the] stages, phases

The stages of the triple modalities of nature are the particular, the universal, the differentiated, and the undifferentiated.

In a desert land there are many small grains of sand. When the Sun blazes overhead, sunlight falls on the faces of each grain and reflections shine in various directions. The composite effect is a mirage. The mirage created by the reflected light appears like a lake with ripples or waves of water in it. The very Sun that produces the illusion reflects in that "lake." The blue sky and clouds that float in it are also reflected in the illusory water surface of the mirage. Thus, an entire world, without the least substance, is projected by the light of the Sun. However false is the Sun reflected in the mirage, it has the characteristics of the actual Sun such as concentrated bright light and radiating beams. The light that is reflected from the mirage also has the warmth of sunlight. Thus the mark (liṅga) of the Sun is also the mark of the reflection.

In a similar way, the all-filling light of consciousness, puruṣa, lends its own light to the individuated consciousness. The desert represents nature. Instead of the grains of sand, there are the five elements and the three modalities (guṇas). The mere association of nature with spirit causes a mirage-like individuation. In this individuation, a personality is reflected. The pure light of consciousness before individuation is called *pratyak ātma*. When the same is reflected in the mirage of its own light, it is called *cidābhāsa*. Even though it is illusory, the individual functioning as I-consciousness has the characteristic mark of puruṣa, just like the Sun reflecting in the mirage has the characteristic mark of the actual Sun. Thus, in the cidābhāsa I-consciousness, there is the mark of individuation, liṅga, whereas when it is referred back to its source, the pure state, it is aliṅga, without a mark.

In the *Chandogya Upaniṣad* these liṅga-aliṅga aspects are referred to in the presentation of the great dictum *(mahāvākya):* That You Are *(tat tvam asi)*. You *(tvam)* has a mark; That *(tat)* has no mark. Relating the specific to the universal is relating the wakeful, the dream, and the deep sleep to the fourth state, which is no state and is transcendental. This marks the transcendence from conscious absorption to transcendent absorption. In the phenomenology of Edmund Husserl also, the transcendence of the existential ego into the transcendental is given. This sūtra is to be taken as an a priori instruction to the aspirant. The imperiential verity of it is to be established through the disciplines given in this chapter to actualize the union of the relative with the Absolute.

The epistemology of Yoga is the same as that of the Sāṅkhya Darśana of Kapila which is based on the binary principles, puruṣa and prakṛti. Later the Yoga discipline of Patañjali became associated with Vedānta. Such an interpretation came primarily through Vyāsa and Vācaspati Miśra rather than Patañjali. The plurality of puruṣas originally postulated by Kapila and accepted by Patañjali became more generalized in the form of a universal person bereft of all the disqualifying limitations of individuated puruṣas; this universal puruṣa was equated with Īśvara.

In the later discipline of Yoga, puruṣa assumed the position of ātma, especially *jīvātma*. As in Vedānta, later schools of Yoga also recognize jīvātma as having the triple aspects of pure existence (sat), subsistence in pure consciousness (cit), and the basis of all values (ānanda). The sat-cit-ānanda aspect of the puruṣa is referred to as the numinous aspect. A distortion of the original Sāṅkhyan epistemology that has crept into interpretations of this sūtra has been overlooked by critics and commentators alike. The plurality of puruṣas has been superceded by the unity of the puruṣa.

In any case, puruṣa is the only luminous principle. Even though Patañjali does not recognize the unity of a single Self for all individual beings, he also finds it necessary to have a luminous principle to illuminate the four inner organs and the instrumental aspect of the five organs of perception and five organs of action. He relates the functional aspect of the living organism (jīva) primarily to a numinous aspect of the puruṣa.

The psychosomatic system is fashioned out of the primal

characteristics (tanmātras) of the five gross elements—smell in earth, taste in water, sight in fire, touch in air, and sound in space. The five-fold qualities of the elements and the three operational modalities of nature are all unspecific except in maintaining the principles of their main characteristics such as the element earth retaining in it the characteristic of odor in conjunction with the other qualities of taste, form, touch, and sound. The faculty of mind is fashioned out of the pure essence of illumination. When the psychosomatic system and the mind are put together, they make a living organism that is ready to have experiences.

When the five sense organs and five organs of action are activated in continuation of the latent tendencies laid in the system by karma, non-specific cognitions such as hearing, sight, taste, touch, and smell become specifically related to objects with empirical qualities that have validity in the wakeful world of transaction. The non-specific experiences do not hold out vivid distinctions between individual items, but in the world of empirical encounter with objects the marks of individual items are clearly seen.

Prajñā, the very stuff of consciousness, can have two aspects: manifest (samprajñātam) and unmanifest but potentially manifesting (asamprajñātam). The manifestation of prajñā comes as individuals and species of the concrete, objective world and as assumed names and forms in the subtle realm. In manifested consciousness the stuff of consciousness assumes shapes and hence it is called *vyākṛtam (ākṛti*=shape). In the unmanifest, it is *avyākṛtam* (bereft of shape). There is no thick line between the manifested and unmanifested. Everything happening in the avyākṛta or unconscious state is not totally lost to us. Certain indications help us to conjecture and make inferences about imperiential aspects of consciousness.

The mechanism of the mind operates differently in the different states of consciousness—wakeful, dream, deep sleep,

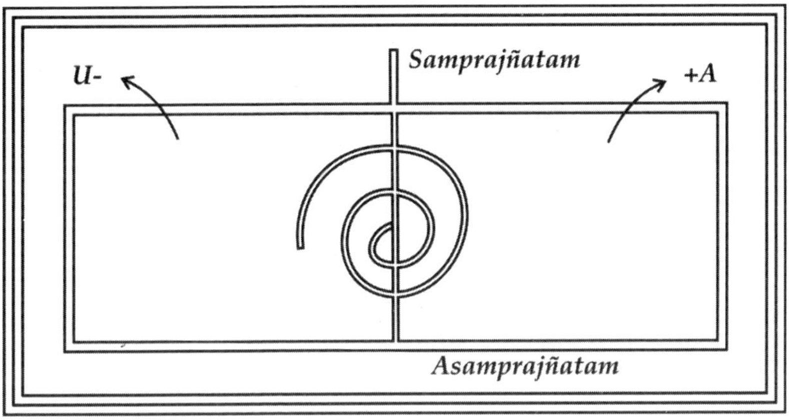

and transcendent, which are represented by the four limbs of the praṇava, AUM. The experience that is related with the consciousness in the wakeful, represented by A in AUM, is vitarka, which literally means "specifically presenting an encounter." The vitarka, or fully horizontalized presentation of consciousness, comes with a general indication that one's consciousness is going to be bifurcated into the knower and the known.

The entire consciousness withdraws from its amorphous state to a centralized focus of consciousness. The first indication of the modification of unmanifested consciousness is the occurrence of a central locus at which consciousness is focused. Consciousness comes to have both a locus and a periphery. The convergence of consciousness to the central locus causes a new throb of consciousness at the center, which is recognized as I-consciousness. As soon as I-consciousness manifests, it simultaneously differentiates both objects and ideas as "this."

Thus the first bifurcation of consciousness is into "I am" and "this is." "This" provides the stuff for cogitation and "I" functions as the cogitator. In the act of cogitation a challenge is thrown to the I-consciousness to come out of its subjective enclave and relate with what is presented as an object. A question arises from I-consciousness: "What is this?"

When consciousness is called to attention, it has to converge to several levels before it comes to the object of consciousness in an acute and intense manner. At the first level we know that something is presented, then that it is a moving body, further, that it is an animal belonging to the canine species, then that it is a Pomeranian. Then we recognize that it has white fur-like hair and is looking at us with loving devotion. Thus, step by step, we come to the center and our consciousness has the quality of concentration. Finally, we forget ourselves and see only the loving look of the dog. This is vitarka.

The coordinated consciousness that envelops the self is psychophysically supplemented by cogitation, which commences with an interrogation of any encountering element

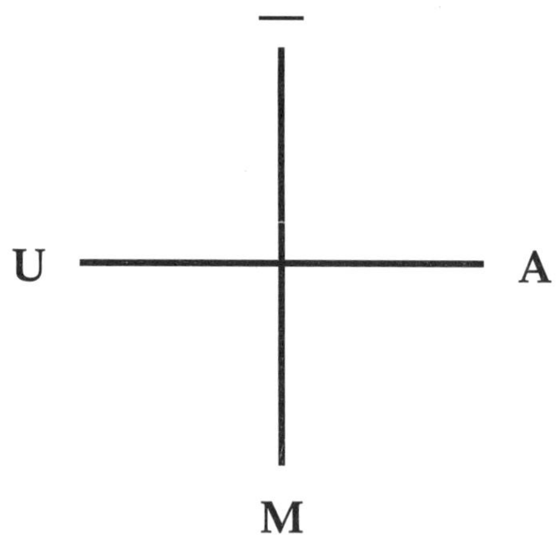

A	gross	*vitarka*	morphology	phenotype
U	subtle	*vicāra*	histology	genotype
M	causal	*ānanda*	mutation	personal
__	transcendental	*asmitā*	consolidation	spirit/individuation

to which a person is exposed. It ultimately culminates in the certitude of a judgment that is the basis for a number of major factors that build up the personality such as the finalizing of concepts, the structuring of the hierarchy of values, preferences adopted for consistent behavior, and the normative notion of values both for personal guidance and interpersonal relationship. This is an area where consciousness of the self is interwoven with the physicochemical properties of the body and the dynamics of vital forces called prāṇa. In this area we have located, our consciousness withdraws itself from its vague and amorphous permeation to a centrally accepted object of interest, which we have noted is called vitarka.

Vicāra corresponds to the subtle states of imagination and ideational composition that happen exclusively in the subjective consciousness, represented by U in AUM. The cogitational impact on the transformation and consolidation of concepts takes place as the structuring of reason. Without giving up the pragmatic interest of the individual, we here go into the logistics of the expression of our interest both verbally and overtly through action. Just as we encounter external objects, molecular manifestations of ideas arise in mental awareness. From that point consciousness grows into more and more associated areas of the idea until it becomes a very elaborated system in which individual items get lost in the characteristics of their species. From the species, consciousness traverses into the generality of the genus, and from genus into the fundamental principle that governs the genus. This process is vicāra.

Unlike in vitarka, consciousness moves centrifugally in vicāra. As it establishes more and more in generic consciousness, its significance is more universal, both spatially and temporally. Vicāra culminates in the certitude that gives both contiguity and consistency in value appreciation and behavior, and is capable of creating permanent marks in personality. Although vicāra is like spirit, mainly consciousness in character, its basis is established in energy supplied by vital forces like prāṇa. Thus vicāra is placed between the psychosomatic individual and the spirit, where there is a reciprocal relationship between body and spirit. In its purest adherence to the primary principle that governs ideas, it is given the status of absorption into reasoning consciousness (savicāra samādhi).

Ānanda does not mean pleasure of the sense organs or the mind, but rather the value-measurant. In the concealed state of deep sleep, corresponding to M in AUM, experiences that have happened in the perception of the wakeful and the reasoning of the subjective and dream states are processed. They then remain as both information bits and the causal elements of future drives and propensities that govern emotional life.

In the experiencing of the physical world, the emphasis is on morphology (form and structure), whereas in the analytical study of inner relationships, histology (minute structure) is given priority. When one comes to the state of the unconscious or causal consciousness of deep sleep, mutation, which is mainly of an evolutionary purport, becomes significant. Each time an experience produces in us an affection or affliction, the stimulus bringing the experiences that are related to an external body or an internal idea causes a conditional state by which our future interests are positively or negatively tied up with the stimulus that has produced pain or pleasure.

From the most intense pain to ecstatic blissful experience, everything is covered by the norm called ānanda. When a child first sees the bright flame of a burning candle, it may try to hold the flame. If, consequently, the child's fingers are burned, it feels great pain. After the incident of the painful burning the child's mind retrospectively goes into the whole incident and looks upon burning flame as the cause of its pain. Thus the child gets negatively conditioned and will no longer try to catch flames. This process is happening through a process of mutation. Thus, suṣupti or causal consciousness is a sort of factory where the personality is manufactured through a series of evolutionary mutations.

The consolidation of personality (asmitā) that gives maturation to the individual takes place in the final state of absorption, corresponding to the fourth limb of praṇava. The transcendental state is permeated with silence. As the psyches of most people are frequently disturbed, they hardly experience any absorption. Hence, the formation of the personality happens at the level of causal consciousness and the mutation caused by the pain/pleasure principle affixes characteristic love/hate attitudes to personality.

The self is individuated when it is expressive in the form of a commanding, maneuvering, and directing knowledge that has its grip on the discerning and cogitating mind, the volition that is giving directives to the motor system, and the selectively structuring inner faculty that is creating endless coordination between the sensory and motor systems so that the individual can become proficient in talents. This matrix of consciousness is called vijñāna, fully coordinated knowledge. The aspect of talent that marks the characteristic specialties of an individual's personality does not leave the individuated self even when the physical and mental apparatus withers away. Thus, vijñāna has a two-fold significance. It is the deeply ingrained conditionings, both of affliction and affection. To that extent, it belongs to the causal consciousness. It is also the greater reservoir of talents, part of the continuing history of the self in the future.

Sūtra II:20

draṣṭa dṛśimātraḥ śuddho'pi pratyayānupaśyaḥ

draṣṭa: the seer
dṛśimātraḥ: [is] consciousness only
śuddhaḥ: pure
api: even though
pratyaya: cognition, content, consciousness
anupaśyaḥ: [it] witnesses

The seer is consciousness only; even though pure, it witnesses cognition.

We have to think of three spheres to understand this sūtra: the seer (A), the seen (C), and, in between them, an apparatus (B), which functions instrumentally to provide the seer with a replica of the seen. The puruṣa is an undifferentiated seer. In conjunction with the inner organ (antaḥkaraṇa), a false identification is made between the spirit (puruṣa) and the I-consciousness (ahamkāra or asmitā) of the

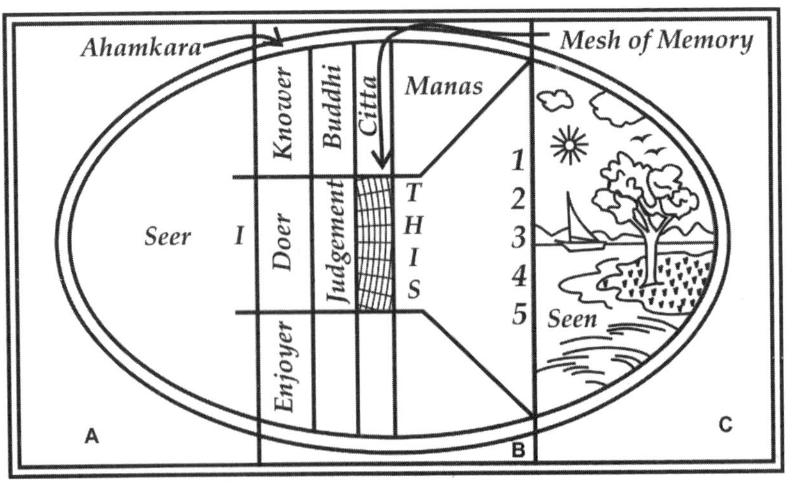

inner organ.

When the external senses perceive concrete objects in the world of the time/space continuum where bodies are in motion and a process of evolution is going on, the interrogating faculty of the mind (manas) presents the theme of perception to the psychic inner organ. It is immediately reciprocated by the I-consciousness as an agency who is interested in the object of the senses. The presentation of the object is termed "this." The reciprocating inner faculty is identified as I-consciousness. There is a spontaneity in the functional togetherness of I-consciousness (aham) and "this"-consciousness (idam).

Whatever is presented as "this," belonging to time and space, with the triple qualities of nature, has to pass through a matrix of previous memory (citta). As the incoming stimulus percolates through memories, both of a highly reduced incipient type as well as of more recent conditioned states, the intellect (buddhi) is provided with a number of data to be processed. After some fluctuation of doubt, the intellect decides the nature of the presentation.

The intellect has no direct relation with the percept. It has only a processed replica to deal with. But when it makes a judgment, it triggers ramifications in three directions: the registry of knowledge; the stimulation to react with appropriate action; and an affectivity of attraction or repulsion, joy or distress. The combination of the three can be compared to a holographic effect. The mystical sense of wonder and the mystery of a hologram are experienced along with the psychosomatic composition.

The purpose of this sūtra is mainly to give us the discriminative knowledge that the spirit is not a participant in the game that is played by the jīva, even though the game is only possible because of the proximity of the apparatus of life to the self-luminous spirit.

Sūtra II:21

tadartha eva dṛśyasyātmā

tadarthaḥ: [is] for the sake of that (the seer)
eva: alone
dṛśyasya: of the seen
ātmā: the very being, essence, nature

The very being of the seen is for the sake of the seer alone.

Patañjali's Yoga Sūtras were given with the intention of enabling a person to disentangle himself or herself from the many types of conscious or unconscious bondage that are essentially of a psychological nature. It is not a book intended to explain the cosmologic phenomena of this world that seems to be of great temporal and spatial magnitude. As an individual you have a finitude to which all your faculties belong. Your world of visible perception extends only to those stimuli that affect your visual faculty from moment to moment, comprising only a small fraction of the cosmological world. Even though the vision of a given time does not cover the entire world of physical existence, psychologically it is a complete experience. You can only cope with that much perception in the given circumstance with the faculty you are endowed with.

Even though several sounds are simultaneously filling the atmosphere in which you live, you are concerned only with a few sounds that are interpreted as pertinent to your welfare or detriment. There is a vast amount of physical energy knocking around you but you are concerned only with what you experience as heat or cold, touches that are soft or hard, or physical pressures of varying degrees.

Even though delicious dishes are cooked and served in all the dwellings of human beings, you are only concerned with the food and drink that you partake of at your meal time. Similarly, only those molecules that enter your nostrils and knock against the olfactory receptors are experienced as good or bad odors.

It is as if the immeasurable vastness of the cosmos in its temporal and spatial magnitude is of no consequence to the individual. Your mind is a receptacle like a plate or cup in which you receive a limited share of your world. Patañjali confines himself to that world of psychologic significance, and to the study and evaluation of it in terms of a person's happiness or misery. That is why it is said that the perceptual world of nature is what is given to the individual spirit (puruṣa) to experience for its own meaningful search and progression into ultimate fulfillment.

Sūtra II:22

kṛtārtham prati naṣṭam apyanaṣṭam tadanya sādhāraṇatvāt

kṛtārtham: one whose purpose has been fulfilled
prati: for
naṣṭam: [it becomes] non-existent
api: although
anaṣṭam: does not cease to exist
tad: that (it)
anya: to others
sādhāraṇatvāt: because of being common

Although it becomes non-existent for one whose purpose has been fulfilled, it does not cease to exist because of being common to others.

This sūtra is only to answer a rhetorical question. Puruṣa in Sāṅkhya philosophy is a circumlimited numinous principle that is one among many. It is only in its relationship with prakṛti that the status of a seer comes to puruṣa. According to Sāṅkhya and Yoga realization is the attaining of a certain disillusionment so that the world that is seen becomes of no consequence. With that, the world ceases to be for that puruṣa.

What then is the status of the world that seems to be there if it has ceased to exist for the liberated person? The answer is that the puruṣa in the Sāṅkhyan philosophy is one among many puruṣas. With the realization of one puruṣa, only that puruṣa's world ceases to be. As there are many other puruṣas who are not realized, their worlds continue.

Similar questions are raised in Vedānta also. Certain realized persons who continue to live in their physical bodies until death comes seem to approve of the empirical validity of the world in and around them. The Vedāntin would say that this is because, even after a rope is burned to ashes, it still looks like a rope. Only when it is rudely shaken does it disintegrate.

In his *Advaita Dīpika,* Narayana Guru gives the example of a person who, although freed from an earlier confusion about the directions of a place, such as mistaking the east for the west, will continue to see the directions as before. Another example that can be cited from our common experience is that of a straight rod which, when put into a glass of water, looks bent where it enters the water. From experience we know that this is only a visual error caused by the refraction of light in the medium of water. Although the appearance remains the same, a person who has such knowledge is not affected by the illusion.

A similar problem was taken up by Bishop Berkeley when he said that everything is born of the percipient's idea. He said that the world is there because you see it. To the question, "What happens to the world when you do not see it?" he answered that someone else would be seeing it. When questioned about the contingency of nobody seeing it, he answered, "God will be seeing it."

This sūtra is not as important as the rest. Its only significance is that it helps us to conceive that the discipline of Yoga is like entering into a pupa state. The silken thread that is woven around a silkworm is of use to it only until the caterpillar grows into a butterfly. Then it can discard it. Similarly, for the yogi, the seen world is a means to attain the yogic perfection of kaivalya. When that state is attained, he or she becomes a *kṛtārtha* (one whose purpose is fulfilled) and thereafter needs no world.

Sūtra II:23

sva svāmi śaktyoḥ svarūpopalabdhi hetuḥ samyogaḥ

sva: of it (prakṛti)
svāmi: of the owner, master (puruṣa)
śaktyoḥ: [and] powers of both
svarūpa: the essential nature
upalabdhi: the apprehension [of]
hetuḥ: [is the] cause
samyogaḥ: the conjunction, union

The conjunction of puruṣa and prakṛti is the cause of the apprehension of the essential nature and powers of both.

In every individual there is a spirit core (puruṣa) ensconsed in nature (prakṛti). Spirit is the indwelling owner of the individuated spirit/mind/body complex. As we have seen, in nature there are three modalities: the pure-clear principle of the mirroring or replication of entities; the kinetic principle of bringing transformations to replicated objects; and the inertial or freezing principle of giving static representation to whatever is experienced. Through its relationship with prakṛti, puruṣa comes to experience the transactions of the wakeful world, the composition of dreams from memory elements, and the feeding in of action potentials and memory tags that can compulsively bring a feedback dynamic to it. All put together, these can be called the state of bondage.

When puruṣa is unrelated with prakṛti, it is in a state of aloneness and liberation. So, essentially, there are two states: being bound to nature or being free of nature. These can also

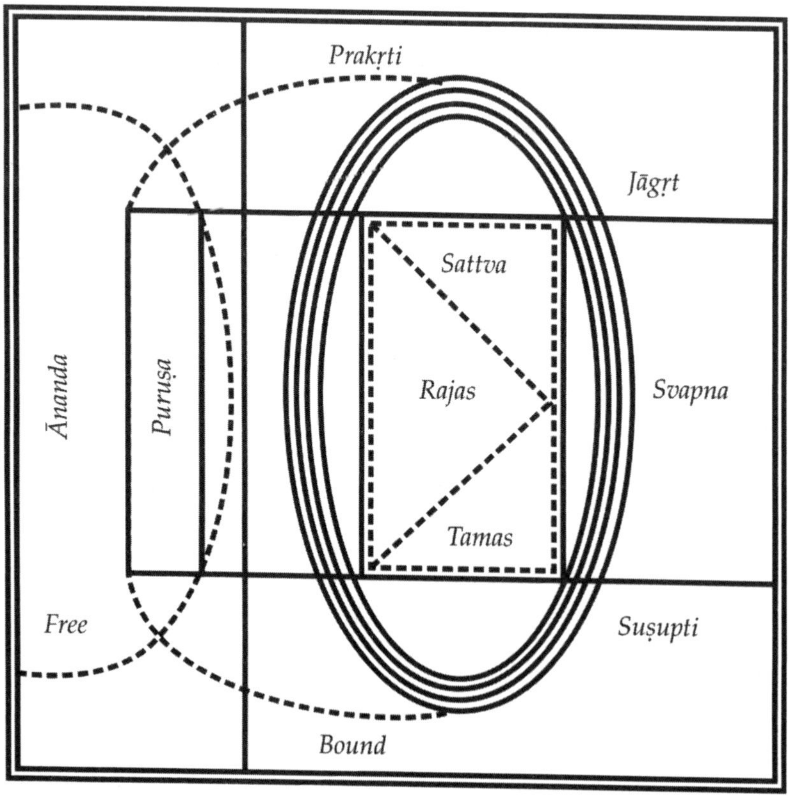

be termed as transcendence and immanence. Both are only of partial value, so far as individuated beings are concerned. The ideal state is when the individual is conversant with both immanence and transcendence. The *Īśā Upaniṣad* has presented this theme in its most excellent form.

There is a wholesale liberation when the master of the individuated life feels free within the frame of reference of the immanence in which the puruṣa is placed and carries out the dictates of immanence even when in perfect resonance with the freedom of transcendence.

All implications of bondage and liberation become evident through the comparison and contrast of the two sets of norms with which we are equipped. One set of norms is given to us to play effectively and pragmatically in the world of empirical facts, the world of relativity or relativistic values. The other set is to reveal the falsehood of relativistic experiences so that we may have a unitive understanding. Thus this sūtra holds in its grip one of the major mysteries of life.

Sūtra II:24

tasya hetur avidyā

tasya: its
hetuḥ: cause
avidyā: [is] nescience, ignorance

Its cause is nescience.

The world stands divided into three groups. From the humblest forms of life like bacteria to those animals not endowed with the faculty of reasoning, all live in the present, caring only for the here and now. Among human beings also we find people of that category whose maxim is "Unknown tomorrows and dead yesterdays, why fret about them if today be sweet?" There are others, especially those influenced by religion, who do not see any meaning in the present. They say, "Vanity of vanities, everything is vanity." They forgo the present for the promised land of tomorrow.

There is a third group of people who see the relativistic imperfections of the given world but at the same time see how beneficial it is to use all the faculties of this body/mind complex and enjoy the vast changes of this world. They want to live in the transcendent and the immanent at once.

A question may arise: why bother at all about a transient world and its relativistic values? Why doesn't the seer remain unperturbed in its own nature? The present sūtra is an answer to that question. Puruṣa is susceptible to avidyā or nescience. That is the price one has to pay for being individuated. The puruṣa is of such nature that when it is attracted to the mirrored image of its identity, nescience comes and blindfolds it. Thus, until it recaptures its freedom, it will remain as an imprisoned splendor in the mesh of nature.

Sūtra II:25

tad abhāvāt samyogābhāvo hānam tad dṛśeḥ kaivalyam

tad: that [nescience]
abhāvāt: the non-existence, absence, negation [of]
samyoga: [the] conjunction of prakṛti and puruṣa
abhāvāḥ: the non-existence, absence, negation [of]
hānam: [is through the] elimination, abandonment [of]
tad: that [its]

dṛśeḥ: of the seer
kaivalyam: [is the] liberation, aloneness

The absence of the conjunction of prakṛti and puruṣa is through the elimination of nescience; its absence is the liberation of the seer.

To understand this sūtra we should compare and contrast the two possible states: that of prakṛti and puruṣa being in conjunction and that of their not being in conjunction. Most people living in their individuated embodied state know only the state of the conjunction of prakṛti and puruṣa. Although deep sleep gives a semblance of a separation of puruṣa from prakṛti, it does not bring a real aloneness of puruṣa even though the agency of the knower, the doer, and the enjoyer is lowered to the minimum.

No state of consciousness is absolutely free from other states of consciousness. Even when the gross is experienced there can be subtle elements in it. Similarly, there can be gross elements in the subtle. When the causal is experienced, it can accommodate the subtle. Even so, the causal can incorporate the gross. In the wakeful state there can be intervening spells of dream and some elements of the wakeful can percolate in the dream. In deep sleep also there can be intermissions of dreams and the gross physical can even act without disturbing the rationale. All these make the field of the knower very complicated.

In the transactional world, the five organs of perception receive stimuli from objects outside. The stimuli pass through a matrix of memory and, consequently, the intellect is poised to respond to the quality of the stimulus. In conjunction with the ego factor, the motor system is pushed into service to react adversely or in favor of the oncoming stimulus. Here the intellect is empirically acting, taking into account full cognizance of physical and chemical laws. In addition, the socio-biologic factor and ethics are also considered by the intellect. Thus the responses are made to conform as closely as possible to morally recognized social norms. In Freudian language we may say the ego and the super-ego are holding the id in check.

If the spirit is not interested in the transactional world, it can refuse to illuminate the intellect. When such a negative withdrawal is made by the puruṣa from the instrumentality of the mind and senses, it is called *pratyāhāra* by yogis and *uparati* by Vedāntins. For instance, a person may live quite close to a tavern or liquor shop without having the least awareness of what goes on there simply because he is not at all interested in what happens in such a place. Thus, every person, to some extent, unconsciously exercises withdrawals of the light of the spirit.

When we are in subjective consciousness, the intellect is freed of all rigid laws, not only of biochemical factors but also those relating to social approbation. The intellect is free to choose its areas of operation on the basis of the pleasure principle. When the causal factor is shaken out of its structured orientation, only the uncertainty of nescience prevails and it is as if the individual is in limbo. There is a fourth state in which the individual is acted upon by the collective consciousness. There, the function of the intellect is pushed away from conscious deliberation to reflex conditioning.

A yogi who is fully disciplined and completely cut off from various exposures can remain bereft of all past impressions. In that case, the individual escapes from the structured function of organisms. Then we may say the spirit is separated from nature and it is free.

Sūtra II:26

vivekakhyātiraviplavāhānopāyaḥ

viveka khyātiḥ: the discrimination [between the Self and the non-Self], discriminative light, discriminative function
aviplavā: unbroken, unceasing, unwavering
hānopāyaḥ: [is the] means of eliminating [nescience]

The unbroken discrimination between the Self and the non-Self is the means of eliminating nescience.

The life of a yogi can be compared to driving a vehicle on the highway. To the yogi, one-pointed attention or total devotion is the path in which he or she is driving the vehicle of his or her life. When full attention is given to any theme of life or to any situation, it is only natural that the yogi would exercise caution and mindful discrimination in relating to the other with perfect knowledge.

This mindfulness needs to be applied to all four frames of reference of human experience. In the first frame of reference—the transactional world—a person is physically awake and mentally alert, facing one encounter after another. There the discrimination is that of a subjective identity and an objective consideration of polarity.

In relating with other things in the wakeful world, the yogi exercises two complementary aspects of discrimination. On the one hand the yogi recognizes the unity of all things in the Absolute and that he or she is not different from others. What is seen as beneficial to the self is seen as being beneficial to others also. Consequently, the yogi will not deny another's access to what he or she aspires to. Secondly, the yogi will also recognize that, as physical entities, all bodies are distinct and each person is a sovereign principle enshrined in a particular body with likes, dislikes, and preferences that should not be overridden.

Even people who do not know anything about the value vision of a yogi exercise several discriminative cautions in their daily life. We like to hear the pleasing and melodious voices of the people whom we love and those who are specially trained in their voice culture. But we request another person to speak or sing only when we know our demand is not an imposition on them.

It is very pleasant to be fondled by a lover, to embrace a dear person, and to be excited by a loving kiss. But in our transactional life we have made certain ethical restrictions and such indulgences are allowed only rarely at convenient places when circumstances are congenial. Sexual cravings are sometimes very strong and may provoke us to cut across social restrictions. To avoid such longings every society has its definition of incest and physical relationships between most people are considered immoral.

Certain forms are very attractive to look at, especially a handsome or beautiful face. But there is a person behind that face or form whom we do not want to offend by staring. Our tongues are not satiated by enjoying delicious food. To restrict our greed and avarice we program our eating times, observe many table manners and give due consideration to the needs of others. Fragrance has its attraction. All the same we know fragrance comes from bombarding molecules of matter and we do not like our air to be polluted by again and again contaminating it with chemical substances.

Thus, the transactional world is full of restrictions and every member of the community is expected to exercise discrimination. Otherwise many professions would become impossible such as the relationship between the teacher and the taught, the therapist and the patient, the coach and the trainee. There are several magic circles around a person that are not to be transgressed by another. Only with a high degree of sensibility can we decide how far we can go and where distance should be maintained to be honorable.

In the dream state or when we are in the subjective realm of engaging in creative work, we are mainly concerned with ideas and imaginations. They do not have any empirical validity so we have to exercise caution not to mix up facts with fictions. There are many unconscious and autonomous functions in us that are meticulously carried out for our biological and social welfare. In such cases both attention and discrimination are instituted by nature.

Ultimately, there is an all-embracing reality to which we belong that is most peaceful and unbroken. Sustaining it all through life is the prime requirement for a peaceful life. So the yogi attunes to that reality and maintains equilibrium with it. This is the highest form of keeping our discrimination alive at all times.

Sūtra II:27

tasya saptadhā prānta bhūmiḥ prajñā

tasya: its
saptadhā: sevenfold way
prānta bhūmiḥ: [is the] final stage
prajñā: wisdom, unmodulated consciousness

Wisdom is the final stage of its sevenfold way.

This sūtra is such that it is not to be explained because it is only anticipatory of the following sūtras.

Sūtra II:28

yogāṅgānuṣṭhānād aśuddhi kṣaye jñāna dīptir ā viveka khyāteḥ

yogāṅga: the limbs of Yoga
anuṣṭhānād: by the practice [of]
aśuddhi: the impurities
kṣaye: are destroyed
jñāna: knowledge
dīptiḥ: arises
ā vivekakhyāteḥ: [which] leads to discrimination between the Self and the non-Self

By the practice of the limbs of Yoga, the impurities are destroyed, and knowledge arises, which leads to discrimination between the Self and the non-Self.

The Self has its pure form and its phenomenal aspect. What is considered as the pure state of the Self in Vedānta is equivalent to what the yogis term as puruṣa in a state of aloneness. When individuation happens and puruṣa is in conjunction with prakṛti, the body/mind complex becomes contaminated with the projected qualities of nature. This happens to such an extent that the puruṣa forgets its pure nature.

When an aspirant, wanting to return to the purity of aloneness, undergoes a rigorous discipline of the eight instructions given, he or she sheds all impurities until clarity comes. When all the impurities are washed away with the discipline, consciousness becomes clear. Consequently the puruṣa becomes capable of clearly seeing the pure as distinct from the impure and what pertains to the Self as distinct from the non-Self. This inner awakening is the beginning of realization. Thereafter, there prevails in the aspirant yogi clear knowledge that can keep discrimination alive. When such a clarity is established, the yogi is considered to be stablilized on the irrefutable foundation of Yoga.

Exercise

The first indication of impurity is I-consciousness. To remove that dirt, consciousness is to be neutralized so that it does not oscillate between the subject and the object. Then both object-consciousness and subject-consciousness leave. To bring about that neutralization, the distance between the knower and the known is reduced by focusing on the neutral zero between the incoming and outgoing breath. Physically the mind is kept at the throat plex (viśuddhi), the purificatory center.

Sūtra II:29

yama niyama āsana prāṇāyāma pratyāhāra dhāraṇā dhyāna samādhayo'ṣṭāvaṅgāni

yama: self-restraints
niyama: observances, carrying out of positive programs
āsana: posture, seat, steady position, foundation
prāṇāyāma: regulation of vital forces, regulation of breath
pratyāhāra: withdrawal from distraction, withdrawal from the instrumentality of the mind and senses
dhāraṇā: holding the focus of the mind, the consistent focusing of consciousness, retaining or sustaining an idea or principle
dhyāna: contemplation, even and harmonious flow of consciousness
samādhayaḥ: absorption, equipoise of consciousness
aṣṭau aṅgāni: eight limbs [of Yoga]

Self-restraints, observances, posture, regulation of vital forces, withdrawal from distraction, holding the focus of the mind, contemplation, and absorption are the eight limbs of Yoga.

You have two opposite kinds of propensities that actualize with different modes. They may be termed as propensities with horizontal tendencies and those with vertical tendencies. Although their functions are opposite and distinct, they are also complementary forces, reciprocating with each other, which can be harmonized to your advantage. The horizontal forces are such that in the here and now action incentives gather momentum and exaggerated importance is given to your performance. Gratifying desires becomes more and more emphasized and you forget to restrain. The vertical propensity takes into account the past, the present, and the future and is always value-oriented with a long-term consideration.

As most of your energies are lying dormant in the unconscious, you need to make a conscious effort to cultivate values of perennial or long-term significance. As the restraints and performances or observances are complementary with each other, *yama* and *niyama* can be taken as counterparts of one yogic discipline.

If you, as an aspirant yogi, have the intention of undertaking a thoroughgoing self-discipline, you are recommended to choose one interest rather than pursuing many interests. When full attention is given to that chosen interest, body, mind, and ego are all interlinked in one line. That means you have placed yourself in a set that involves both the physiological and psychological. To indicate this the word *āsana*, "steady position or posture," is given. That does not necessarily mean sitting with a certain physical posture. When a cat is preparing to pounce upon a rat, it assumes a posture

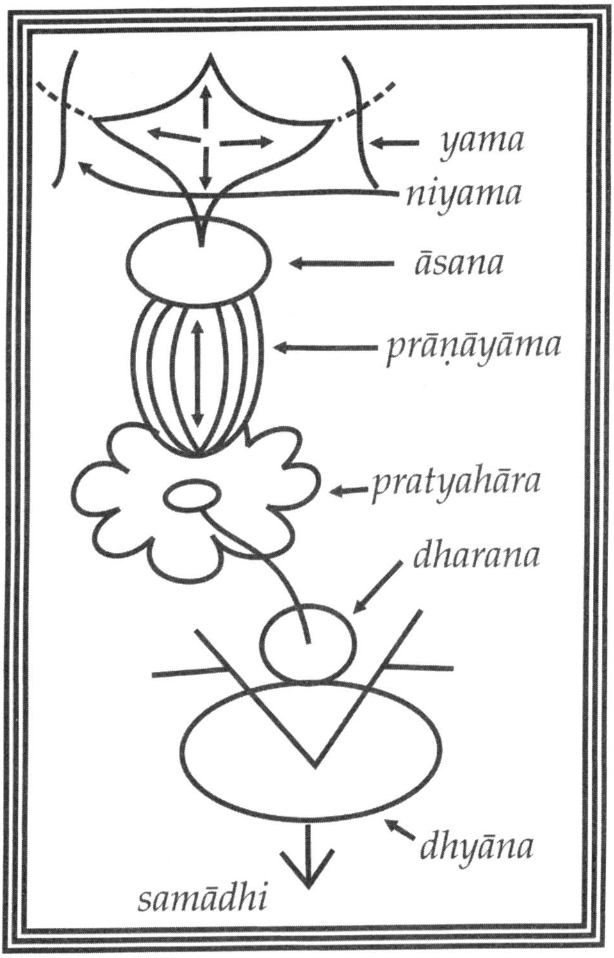

that is more an attitude than a special contortion of its body. Similarly, posture here is to be understood as posing yourself in the most congenial manner to be able to give full attention.

The body/mind complex is an aggregate of inertial substances and animating spirit. There are energies to be released and energies to be restored. When outgoing energy and its restoration are brought into a single discipline, that is regulation of the vital forces, *prāṇāyāma*.

Nature has its own program of proliferation and abundance. Even to produce one seed, countless grains of pollen dust are put on the stamens of a flower. Similarly, your mind bristles with desires. When the most appropriate is singled out and the others are discouraged from occupying the central focus of consciousness, you get into a position that is conducive to programming a future possibility in a systematic manner. This singling out of one interest and warding off of distractions is *pratyāhāra.*

When you have a steady state of mind you can choose a value to nurture as the central piece of your psyche. It will retain the quality of your life. That is called *dhāraṇā,* sustaining a certain idea or principle for a considerable length of time. For that, the fluctuating interests of your mind are to be brought back to the same challenge again and again. That kind of repetitive practice is *samyam.*

When a chosen value of life is fully identified with and that prevents other mental modifications from coming, dhāraṇa changes into a contemplative state. Then it is called dhyāna. Once the mind has attained the tranquility of a non-modulating state, the intellect is no longer deputed to act upon the bid of the ego to examine the external world. Instead it becomes fully established in the blissful state of the Self. That is indicated here as *samādhi.*

In the coming sūtras, these eight limbs of Yoga will be separately treated in more detail, to enable us to both understand and practice the eightfold discipline of Yoga.

Sūtra II:30

ahimsā satyāsteya brahmacarya aparigrahā yamāḥ

ahimsā: nonviolence, non-hurting
satya: truthfulness

asteya: non-misappropriativeness, non-stealing, honesty

brahmacarya: adhering to uprightness in life, walking in the path of the Absolute (*brahman*)

aparigraha: non-acquisitiveness, non-possessiveness

yamāḥ: are the self-restraints

The self-restraints are nonviolence, truthfulness, non-misappropriativeness, adhering to uprightness in life, and non-acquisitiveness.

To observe yama, you have to establish yourself in five states of integrity: *ahimsā*, observing compassion in love and serenity; *satya*, holding fast to the pure and clear notion of your true Self with wholeheartedness and not deviating from its integrity; *asteya*, never considering anything outside yourself to be the source of the truest joy; *brahmacarya*, walking always in the path of uprightness; and *aparigraha*, consistently and continuously giving up the attitude of ownership of any object of pleasure.

Ahimsā: Nonviolence

The first-born in this world was hunger. The hunger of an organism is to be appeased with another organism. Thus the very first need is to eat, which simultaneously necessitates the killing of another. Life is nourished by life. The imperativeness of killing precedes eating. If eating and killing are not acceptable, dying is inevitable. This is the greatest enigma of life. Should I not kill but simply die? Or shall I kill so that I may live? It is inevitable that the taking of one life is necessary to save another life. Such being the basic law of life, how can the very first restraint of non-killing be actualized?

In smaller animals there is no morality attached to killing or eating. Whatever is inevitable is done. Only human beings have attached moral significance to the food they eat. The first consideration is reverence to life. Am I displacing someone else to perpetuate my existence? To exist means to exist in the body that is composed of the five elements and operated upon by the three modalities of nature. Yoga is a program to disassociate the spirit from the clutches of nature. That being the ultimate goal, the very first suggestion is to overlook the need to live in the body. What is ultimate cannot be immediately implemented. Hence a series of disciplines are given to guide one to the acceptance of the ultimate.

The instinct to kill and eat is very deep. However, to have love and preserve those whom you love is an equally deep instinct. There are a few kinds of animals that, immediately after begetting their children, kill and eat their progeny. But most living beings refuse to eat their own young, even when they are starving. Many animals refuse to eat their own kind. Thus, most beings manifest the general principle of selective killing. That principle operates when people refuse to kill and eat the animals that live with them as pets, even when other animals are not available, or when they choose not to eat animals but to exist on the abundant offerings of plants, or when they choose to eat more prolific species instead of sparse ones. A widening circle of empathy brings more and more discrimination in the selection of foods. That means love and caring for other living beings are placed higher in the hierarchy of values than the satiation of hunger.

The aspirant yogi wishes to preserve other beings as much as possible while finding a solution to his or her own hunger. As you also want to sustain life until realization comes, you should regulate the need to eat in such a way that the least violence is given to the organic system of the world. At the same time, to compensate for what little necessary destructiveness you engage in, you give your own life for the preservation and propagation of other forms of life. It is thus in a very wide yet restricted sense that the ideal of non-violence is to be looked upon.

The physical body encased in skin marks the separation of one individual from another. It is the physiological scaffolding of the psychic interior operating mechanism called the antaḥkaraṇa, which functions as a liaison between sense organs as well as between the sensory and motor systems. As we have seen, the four aspects of the inner organ are:

1. the mind (manas)
2. the structuring of associations of memories with an inquiry as to their relevancy in presenting with a will to know (citta)
3. the crucial judgment that is to be made about every situation to which attention is given (buddhi)
4. the affectivity registered for the future retention of a memory that can always hold out a memory tag to caution the jīva of its affective importance, pleasurable, painful, or indifferent (ahamkāra)

The impressions that come to our sense organs can act as preserved memory through a particular symbolic device, such as a spoken or written word or a physical form. A recorded memory can be kept alive for the rest of our life. This memory tag is equated to the fragrance of chemically functioning materials and is called vāsanā. The mind then manipulates the new programs that are being conceived on the basis of the memory.

From the very beginning we have learned that the word is our handle to prod the mind. From early childhood memory has functioned as our compendium of information. As this storehouse of knowledge is the vehicle for all thoughts and actions to be kept ever relevant in our personal life, learning is given the foremost place in human life. The legibility, clarity, and consistent interpretation of the symbols of language help us to build up our character. Any dysfunction or malfunction can cause aberrations in our personal behavior, mental as well as physical. The aberrations that come to the mind can result in confusions of values, a mixing up of morals, and disorder at several levels, emotional, rational, and functional. One result of disorder can be seen when a person tends to become emotionally disturbed and consequently violent. That is why the very first preference in yama is given to ahimsā, the discipline of nonviolence.

Ahimsā is not merely to be understood as non-hurting. Its positive counterpart is being compassionate and helping others whenever someone is in need of help. Both compassion and the tendency to hurt come under affectivity of the organism. Affectivity can be of a physical, biological, psychological, or sociological order. There is self-hurting and hurting of others with whom a person comes into encounter. There can be benevolent affective encounters such as in love-making, parenting, companionship in team operation, and nursing the weak and aged. In voluntary encounters, discriminative judgment connected with intelligence plays a large role. Such happenings mostly occur in the wakeful consciousness in which all senses are focused on the receptivity of incoming energy and directing of the output of energy for programmed action. The human body, senses, mind, and functional devices are conceived both on the protective side and the destructive side of defense.

A discriminative maneuvering is usually taken up in the agency of affective knowledge as well as motivated behavior. According to the Sāṅkhya philosophy, affectivity is connected with the modalities of nature recognized as sattva, rajas, and tamas. Sattva is generally described as a pure, clear prevalence of spirit that regulates the mind in its discriminative power. Rajas is a translucent agitated emotional state, and tamas is one of obscuring opacity. The common cause of all bondage is the pleasure principle in affectivity. As the mind works in a contradictory manner according to the pain-pleasure signals that it gets, the thwarting of pleasure can bring a spectrum of rage, from simple depression to the criminal programming of mind toward retaliation. The behavioral pattern that implies masochism, sadism, and planned hurting tendencies is difficult to understand and even more difficult to correct.

Further, most social groups have developed a sophistication that bypasses many ethical considerations wherever it is necessary for society to condone publicly approved destruction of life for what is considered the welfare of the society. Using pesticides and insecticides, the killing of fast-proliferating animals, and even the sanctioning of abortion by modern society are all against the ideal of ahimsā propagated by the Yoga philosophy of India.

A method suggested in the *Upaniṣads* and the *Bhagavad Gita* to modify vāsanā is to entertain positive thoughts and attitudes that can wear away negative tendencies and potentials, and to cultivate benign thoughts and sublime value appreciation.

Satyam: Truthfulness

In life there are certain things that are experienced by all sentient beings as irrefutable. The irrefutability of a thing is felt by all concerned as an imperativeness that cannot be explained away. Hence all people agree it has an existential status. This is very pronounced when the existence is gross or concrete. Suppose a bus, traveling through a gorge between two cliffs, comes to a landslide that has left a huge boulder blocking the road. The passengers may have all sorts of differences in their religious faiths, political ideologies, personal prejudices, and so on. But they will all agree to one thing — they cannot continue their journey until the road is cleared. This is an irrefutable fact that does not depend on anyone's opinion. Such an encounter is an existential encounter.

Truth is not always presented as an irrefutable existential factor. There are subtle situations where the pros and cons of everything involved or implied cannot be easily traced. Then it is possible to hoodwink another or tell blatant lies, pretending one is more in the know than others. This is a clear case of deception. Untruth is passed on for truth in many situations that are elusive and subtle.

In such a case, if you dare to make a pronouncement, you should take the responsibility to go into all available data and, through the application of verifiable methods, arrive at truth with the conviction that what you are going to say is nothing but truth. It is that kind of truth spoken of here: by speaking truth, you are directing a fellow being in the right path; and, by withholding that truth, you are allowing a fellow being to be duped.

The Sanskrit word for truth, satyam, has three syllables: *sa, ta,* and *yum.* In the *Chandogya Upaniṣad* it is said that sa and yam stand for absolute truth but between them comes the evil influence of ta, tamas (blinding darkness). Thus, pure truth never manifests in total clarity to a human mind. Suppose we say that the shortest distance between two points is a straight line. There is a logical compulsion to believe the truth of it. But suppose the two points are as far apart as two stars at two extremes of the galaxy. If a line is drawn from one to the other, it can never be a straight line because space itself has curvature. So even a mathematical truth can become falsified. This is the ta of which the rishi of the *Chandogya Upaniṣad* is speaking.

To compensate for this, the yogi is not expected to learn the intricacies of physics and mathematical logic. You are simply advised not to distort the truth for convenience. Throughout the religious world of belief and dogma, uncouth lies are precipitated and perpetuated by people for vested interests. Hence this warning that, even unintentionally, out of sheer ignorance, you may lead another to wrong consequences by distorting truth. The yogi makes every effort not to be a howler telling untruth or a simpleton believing in something because somebody said it or it is written somewhere.

In the last days of Lord Buddha, he told his disciples: "Do not believe in a statement because it came from an ancient tradition. Do not believe because many believe. Do not believe because it is said by someone far more aged than you. Do not believe because somebody is threatening to kill you unless you believe. Diligently inquire, deeply ponder, and, if after careful examination, you are convinced of the irrefutability of the truth before you, accept it and stand by it." This is probably what Patañjali also means: that you should adhere to truth at all costs.

Asteya: Non-misappropriativeness

The discipline of asteya is to be understood by taking full cognizance of the disciplines of nonviolence (ahimsā) and truthfulness (satyam). Ahimsā is not doing violence to the harmonious setting of the world order. Satyam—appreciating the existential verity of everything in its natural setting—is complementary to the appreciation of innate harmony.

In *steya* (misappropriativeness) two grave epistemological violations are made in understanding the whole truth to which you belong. First is that of thinking that you are the possessor of things. If the entire universe is an expression of the Supreme Self, the Absolute, nothing belongs to any private person because persons also belong to the Absolute. Secondly, if you think that you are void of any value that belongs to yourself, that is a blindness of truth from which you suffer. You feel envious of another's possession and want to grab it from them only when a value manifestation is considered as belonging to them and not to yourself. If you do not separate yourself from the totality of being, then there is no room to feel that you are an unfortunate wretch who lacks something that is cherished.

A holistic vision makes a double correction so that you neither feel alienated from a wealth of values that you see manifested elsewhere nor do you feel the internal hankering to possess what is wrongly identified as an external factor.

Brahmacarya: Adhering to Uprightness in Life

In India a person's life span is described as having four complementary aspects in the pursuit for the actualization of the higher values of life. The four stages of life are said to be: studentship, the married life of a householder, weaning away from household obligation, and, ultimately, living as a renunciate. In fact, the intrinsic values of life are such that the four aspects cannot be completely distinguished or separated from each other.

The first stage of life is designated as *brahmacarya*. That is a time when a person is to be fully instructed in the normative notion of life. The norms are spiritual, moral, social, obligatory, and transcendent. *Dharma* is the main ideal stressed during this period of self-discipline and instruction in the science of life. Dharma is that which sustains life and all its potentials in the here and now. Hence it is specific. As years pass, the horizon of value interests expands from the here and now consideration to the eternal. The expansion intends to bring within it the good of all.

At birth a person is said to be of very little knowledge *(kimcitjñatva)*. The path to perfection is to become conversant with the omniscient *(sarvajñatva)*, the omnipresent, and the omnipotent. Movement from the small world of little knowledge to the infinite world of omniscience is a logarithmic spiral in which the microcosm and the macrocosm become harmonized. The unbroken growth of persistently relating the individual to the Absolute is indicated by the word brahmacarya. Many have missed this point.

As brahmacarya is intended to provide an aspirant with a fully enlightened path that will ever lead one from finitude to infinitude, brahmacarya is identical with the prayer given in the *Bṛhadāraṇyaka Upaniṣad:* "Lead me from untruth to truth, from darkness to light, and from death to immortality." From the first cognizance of the inflow of stimuli through the five senses to the final merger in the all-transcending imperiential unity of the Absolute, brahmacarya is the only path that one has to tread. Any deviation is *vyabhicarya.*

The restraints given by Patañjali include brahmacarya to caution the aspirant that there are false paths and temptations from which you should recoil. One who truly understands what brahmacarya is has already attained the highest mark of discrimination that justly qualifies one to be an enlightened person. With that wisdom-insight, one confers on oneself rishi-hood, Buddha-hood, Christ-hood, and the peace of Islam.

Aparigraha: Non-acquisitiveness

As brahmacarya is a life-long discipline to transcend the compulsiveness of ego—with the intention of ultimately identifying oneself with the Absolute—non-acquisitiveness is its natural corollary. Although the literal meaning given to aparigraha, "non-grabbing," has reference to the brute form of robbery, when you understand its full import, you will see it as the most graceful behavior of a lover of humanity.

The beautiful attitude that is implied in the teaching of aparigraha is given in the story, "Mokusen's Hand," told by Paul Reps in his *Zen Flesh, Zen Bones*:

> Mokusen Hiki was living in a temple in the province of Tamba. One of his adherents

> complained of the stinginess of his wife.
>
> Mokusen visited the adherent's wife and showed his clenched fist before her face.
>
> "What do you mean by that?" asked the surprised woman.
>
> "Suppose my fist were always like that. What would you call it?" he asked.
>
> "Deformed," replied the woman.
>
> Then he opened his hand flat in her face and asked, "Suppose it were always like that. What then?"
>
> "Another kind of deformity," said the wife.
>
> "If you understand that much," finished Mokusen, "you are a good wife." Then he left.
>
> After his visit, this wife helped her husband to distribute as well as to save.[3]

The same teaching comes in the *Bhagavad Gita* in verse 22 of chapter IV: "Satisfied with chance gains, unaffected by conflicting pairs of interests, non-competitive, remaining the same in gain or no gain, he remains unbound in spite of having been active."[4]

There is a universal benevolence that can be noticed in nature. Even a seed sprouting in the crevice of a rock gets enough water to moisten its roots. Such is the bounty of nature that whatever is due to each being is apportioned. If you identify yourself with the Self of all and see yourself as indivisible from the Absolute, you enjoy the sharing of your bounty even when it is as small as the proverbial coin that an old woman gave to Jesus. When you understand that there is no need for any anxiety, many negative feelings will go away. You will see only friendship and charity coming from everyone and will feel like reciprocating the graceful behavior of all. This is aparigraha.

Sūtra II:31

jāti deśa kāla samaya anavacchinnāḥ sārvabhaumā mahāvratam

jāti: class
deśa: place
kāla: time
samaya: occasion, circumstance
anavacchinnāḥ: not conditioned by, not limited by
sārva bhaumāḥ: [the] universal [restraints]
mahāvratam: [constitute] the great vow

Not conditioned by class, place, time, or occasion, the universal restraints constitute the great vow.

A yogi has to be a law unto himself or herself. A life without adherence to law and discipline can be very chaotic. In the *Manu Smṛti* and other books of injunctions, we see models of individuals and societies who framed laws to discipline themselves. For instance, in the *Manu Smṛti* we read that a virtuous and wise person will take the vow not to spit in an open place. This may seem to be a very trifling thing, but in a country like India, even in the time of Manu, people might have been untidy and unhygienic in their personal behavior. So he thought he should caution people to set laws for themselves, which he called *vrata*.

Most of the injunctions given in the *smṛtis* have relevance only with regard to certain classes of people at certain times, places, and occasions. But here Patañjali says that the five disciplines of restraint (yamas) should be observed by all aspirant yogis as a great pledge or vow *(mahāvrata)* all through their lives. That is why we said brahmacarya is not only for the period of studentship. It is to be continued until one's death. A person may make a rule for himself that he will not take tea or coffee. That is not a great vow. Certain people consider their vows to be very superior such as Jews and Muslims who take the vow not to eat pork. These are only conventional adherences to custom. But the resolves never to hurt another person, never to fashion or falsify truth, never to misappropriate, never to deviate from the path of righteousness, and never to violate the rightful provisions that naturally belong to others are great vows.

In both Yoga and Vedānta, ethical morality is not established on religious scruples. Holding yourself in a state of restraint should be based on a clear knowledge of your perfection. There is nothing really existing outside yourself to be aspired for or needed to make yourself perfect or complete. A person who has very clearly enunciated the restraint that is spoken of here is Henry Bergson. In his book, *The Two Sources of Morality and Religion*, he describes two kinds of morality and two kinds of religion. He says that in open morality, you remain steadfast to the principle of truth because you find that it is not possible for a person of integrated character to resort to falsehood. Here you are honest to yourself, not because honesty is required by the law of the country or the mandate of any religion. A truthful person is fearless. It is not fear of punishment that deters such a person from doing wrong, but simply being unable to concede to evil. If you are such a person you are a law unto yourself, living in your own opinion and not in the opinions of others. Then your love, honesty, compassion, generosity, and peaceful nature are characteristically your own. You do not look for any reward for honesty or absolute dedication to truth.

Closed morality is when a person holds back from untruth or dishonesty because of the fear of the punishments with which religion and government threaten their votaries.

Jesus Christ refers to people physically restraining but mentally becoming infatuated. In the *Bhagavad Gita* also we read that a truly honest person does not have a separate outside distinguished from his inside. Such a person is meritorious both within and without. In the second chapter of the *Holy Qur'an* also, the hypocrite is condemned in strong language. To maintain a cloak of virtue in public, the average man is tempted to be dishonest and hypocritical.

With regard to ahimsā a person may not literally hurt anyone physically, but he may cause the misery of someone else because of his cunning ways. That is why we hold dear the examples of teachers like Lord Buddha or Jesus Christ. They have rightly interpreted ahimsā in their personal lives and have stood firm with the heart that dictates the law for a person in this world. In our own days, Mahatma Gandhi has equated ahimsā with satya. You can be truly non-hurting only when you realize your Self and fully dedicate yourself to the truth of your Self. This principle is derived from two famous mantras of the *Īśāvāsya Upaniṣad:*

> The one who continually sees
> all beings in the ātman (Self) alone,
> like that, in all manifested factors the Self also,
> never becomes repulsed.
>
> In whom all beings
> are known as the Self alone,
> what delusion is there
> or what sorrow
> to one who beholds this unity?

Every religion has a central axiomatic principle on which the morality of that religion is established. In the *Upaniṣads* the axiomatic teaching is given as the unity of the one Self that is in the heart of all. It is this realization that leads us to both ahimsā and satya. Then we will have no private world. When we look inward we will see the entire infinitude of consciousness as our truth, the only Absolute. We will not see another there. When we look outward, from the blade of grass under our feet to the far off invisible galaxies also, they are all one. So there is nothing to be privately desired or grabbed. Then the truth itself stabilizes us in our belongingness with all. It is this vision of oneness that cancels out all pairs of dualities in a realized person's life. The basic nature of life is the knowledge of a single existence, which is not—even for a second—different from the total value or ānanda of life. Thus the yogi is a person of open morality whose religion is a dynamic religion and not a static, structured one.

Sūtra II:32

śauca santoṣa tapaḥ svādhyāya īśvarapraṇidhānāni niyamāḥ

śauca: inward and outward cleanliness or purity
santoṣa: contentment
tapaḥ: self-purification, austerity
svādhyāya: self-study
īśvara praṇidhānāni: continuous contemplation on īśvara
niyamāḥ: [are] the observances

Purity, contentment, self-purification, self-study, and continuous contemplation on īśvara are the observances.

The instrument of search and achievement of a Yoga aspirant is composed of the four inner organs, the ten organs of perception and action, and the physical body with a nature in common with that of the external world. In the attempt to attain aloneness, the seeker is liable to be hampered by various obstacles. In the present sūtra we are given the modus operandi by which the search can be effectively made and the desired goal reached through a five-fold methodic exploitation of the body/mind complex in which the possibility inheres.

Śauca: Purity

Suppose we have before us a certain destination. Before commencing our journey, we naturally ask about the condition of the road: Is it well maintained and clear? Are the weather conditions conducive to travel? If these factors look favorable, then we turn to the vehicle: Is a reliable car available, does it have a good seating arrangement for all the travelers, are the parts well lubricated, are the tires in good condition, is there enough fuel, is there enough water in the radiator to cool the system, is the battery well charged? Then, even more importantly, the driver is to be considered: Is she reliable, experienced, sober? Only when positive answers for all these and many more questions are arrived at do we begin our journey.

Similarly, at the commencement of the long journey to aloneness, the yogi wants to know how to maintain the body/mind system as a good vehicle to go from where he or she currently is to the ultimate goal. The first requirement enumerated here is *śauca,* purity. There can be different models of seeking enlightenment. The principle of starting with a purificatory process is a traditional method. It proceeds from the environment to the instrument to the programming to the programmer.

The first concern is with environmental factors. In order to sit comfortably for a long time in one place to regulate the incoming and outgoing breath and ponder over a certain contemplative subject, the environment should be conducive. That place should not be infested with disease-causing germs;

the air should not be polluted; there should not be too much humidity or dust in the atmosphere; there should not be distracting noises from sound pollution; and the peace of the place should not be marred by squabbles and fights of unruly people.

If your home environment is filled with filth and has various kinds of insects or reptiles in it, and you continuously wear the same soiled clothes because you have no clean clothes to change into, there is no physical purity. To begin the search, you need purity of home and clothing. But even a person sitting in a very clean house wearing costly clothes may be unclean if his body is not clean and the dirt coming out of the body is not properly removed. To efficiently conduct a Yoga search, your body as well as your clothing and environment need to be clean.

Physically, your inner as well as outer cleanliness is important. Even if your body is clean, if you eat or drink unwholesome things, your blood can become contaminated. Consequently your brain will be affected. Your body may not get sufficient rest because your sleep is disturbed. All kinds of emotional disturbances can come from psycho-chemical pollutants. Thus it is an essential part of physical and mental hygiene to have only wholesome food and drink.

Even when you are physically disciplined to have a clean life, if your associates are not wise and sober people, they can create many distractions that drag you away from your motivation. Great care should be taken in what you feed your mind with. Purity of mind comes only when you listen to words of purity and engage in actions of purity. It is a vicious circle: if your words and actions are evil, your thoughts will be evil, and if your thoughts are evil, your words and actions will be evil. A high sense of spiritual purity is to be maintained to have a disposition pure enough to always inspire you to have a longing to attain the highest.

The old proverb says: "Cleanliness is next to godliness." Here you should know that being clean in environment, clothes, body, food habits, associations, actions, words, thoughts, and spirit are all interlinked. Śauca, keeping yourself pure, is the first step in your onward march to identity with the Absolute.

Santoṣa: Contentment

The second item of discipline enjoined by niyama is that of normalizing your subjective needs by which a natural equipoise can be maintained as a preliminary to the great pilgrimage you make to kaivalya. The mind can be compared to a pool of water. The slightest disturbance can create ripples or waves on the surface. Dirt on the shores can easily pollute the water and make it murky or muddy. The mind can also lose its tranquility from external causes or the surfacing of certain needs and urges. For this reason, Vedāntins recommend both *sama* and *dama* to maintain the tranquility of the mind. Sama is not succumbing to disturbances coming from within; dama is restraining provocations from outside. Santoṣa is a state of mind that comes only when sama and dama are properly exercised and the mind is freed of all its agitations.

There is a more positive aspect to santoṣa than just being tranquil or contented. It is also being cheerful and creating around yourself an atmosphere that is pleasant to yourself and to others who join you in that environment. Santoṣa requires moderation in accepting the pleasures of the world so that they are not followed by the hangover or aftermath of hedonistic indulgence. Gentle sharing of loveful thoughts, showing one another the appreciation of the good values that are manifested in people's thoughts, words, and behavior—these do not bring any evil after-effects that cause a person to regret or repent. Activities such as listening to gentle music, pondering over thoughtful poems, and seeing performances that create only love for aesthetic values can all be conducive to santoṣa.

The natural fulfillment of a need makes a person happy—this is santoṣa. But if you are stung with greed, your pursuit for acquisition will have results that will be far from making you truly happy. Although santoṣa is a cheerful state, maintaining it is difficult. You have to cultivate a very high sensibility to preserve your santoṣa in the right spirit and enable it to be a harmonizing catalyst in maintaining equipoise in society. According to Indian literati, time spent profitably is that devoted to pursuits in science and poetics. They call the worthwhile use of time in exploring the realms of science and the humanities *vinoda*. Vinoda is not merely having fun for some time. It is the precipitating of interest in values that make a person rejoice both in heart and mind. This is the same as what is recommended in this sūtra as santoṣa.

Tapas: Self-purification

Tapas is the third item in the discipline of niyama. At the beginning of this chapter, we stated that tapas, svādhyāya, and īśvara praṇidhāna constitute kriyā yoga. The word *tapas* means "warming up" or "bringing to a white heat." Metals like gold are purified by being melted. If an alloy such as bronze is to be made, copper and tin are to be melted and blended. If rice is to be made edible, it is to be cooked in boiling water. Thus we are familiar with the application of heat for various constructive purposes. In the present case, warming or heating up is to be taken both physically and metaphorically.

Heat has two powers. One is of fission, which separates two entities that otherwise seem to be inseparable. The other is fusion, the blending of two entities into one. In Yoga, we want to apply the principles of both fission and fusion. As we are psycho-physical organisms with the inner organs, sensory and motor systems, and a physical body in which all these faculties inhere, systematic heat is to be applied to all parts of the body/mind complex.

The first entry of the world into a person is through the faculty of hearing. Hearing has the immediate impact of placing a demand on the mind to create a concept to account for what is heard. When the intellect provides the mind with a conceptual counterpart for every sound it hears, citta (the memory faculty) holds on to it. A child picks up words and concepts during its first three years so diligently that it gets all the useful words of its mother tongue that are thereafter used all through life.

The words that enter our systems have conceptual connotations that can inspire us, elevate our minds, and be beneficial to all. In the same way, there are certain words with vulgar meanings that can demoralize us. It is not easy to root out a conceptual meaning from memory. So civilized societies are very careful to teach children words of the right kind. What is obscene is not allowed to be expressed in a cultured society. In Sanskrit, acceptable words are called *sabhya,* which means "worthy of being uttered in a congregation." Obscene words are called *asabhya,* "not worthy of being uttered in a congregation."

The first austerity recommended is that of using words of an inspiring nature with the right intonation at the appropriate time. Part of that tapas is holding your tongue and keeping golden silence when your vocal expression is not going to help another. Like the arms and legs of the body, the word is a useful limb of the person in you. Just as mothers hold the hands of their children to guide them, you can hold a person with words and lead him or her in the right path. We need good roads to travel safely; parents and teachers provide good paths by paving them with right words.

Using words to teach, direct, conduct, inspire, console, and encourage another is a positive value of the tapas of speech. Even when a person is far away you can stretch your spirit to that person by writing appropriate words. All expressions of love that are physically possible can be given to another with words in a very intimate and intense way. That is also tapas of the word.

The world comes to us in the form of heat and cold. The faculty of touch is not confined to any part of the body. We can touch and feel the world with the skin in which our bodies are wrapped. No sense organ is greater in area than the faculty of touch. We cannot live in icy cold or in burning flames. There is a proportionate blending of heat and cold that pleases us but the entire world does not always remain at that ideal temperature. So we have to acclimatize and be somewhat indifferent to heat and cold. A yogi is therefore expected to show sameness to heat and cold, of course, only to the extent that it is not detrimental to the body.

The heat and cold we experience can be physical and mental. Relationships between people can be cold or warm. Just as it is necessary to protect ourselves from extreme heat and cold, it is also necessary to avoid getting into bizarre attitudes of hatred or sentimental attachment. Moderating between extremes in attitude is also a tapas pertaining to sensation.

Most people live, even amidst beauty, without having a sensibility to discern the beautiful. Wordsworth complained that we waste our time getting and spending and do not have the sensibility to stand and stare at a beautiful daffodil or violet. To discern the beautiful, to create and protect it with the intention of sharing it with others is another tapas with which we can train our eyes.

It is so intriguing that in our mouths we have a tongue that can relish a variety of tastes ranging from bitterness to sweetness and that the tastes are kept in fruits and various other kinds of foods that nature provides us with. Most of our tastes are cultivated. Human health is intrinsically connected with what we eat and drink. Yet most people have cultivated wrong tastes and harmful addictions that not only bring physical disease but also mental aberrations. Addiction to alcohol and drugs is not rare. Restraining the palate and guiding it to partake only of things that are beneficial to the body/mind complex is another tapas.

We also have the capacity to smell, which may seem to relate only to temporary experiences, but this is not so. We bring with us the fragrances (vāsanās) of the many lives we have lived before. To rid ourselves of our vāsanās or residual memories is another important item to deal with. Life is rectified and saved when we can discern what memories we should cherish and what we should not carry with us.

Just as we restrain our sense organs to make our lives wholesome, we can also keep our organs of action engaged only in pursuits that are beneficial to the world. Then we can say we are doing proper tapas. Thus tapas is a very important discipline.

Svādhyāya: Self-study

Fourth in the series of niyama is svādhyāya. In wakeful consciousness, perceptual mentation is happening with the oscillation of awareness between the central focus of our subjective consciousness and any object of interest outside our being. I-consciousness does not have a mathematical location. Although it has no substance as such, from childhood we are so reared that we associate all ideas with thing-ness, so I-consciousness is even projected on certain intimate aspects that are focused in the consciousness called "I." The identification of the area that is recognized as belonging to oneself is "mine." All of empirical experience is therefore dichotomized into "mine" and "not mine." As the return path to aloneness does not warrant anyone carrying with them anything not their own, only that which a person recognizes as one's own has relevance in the present study.

When you enter into the discipline of preparing yourself to achieve aloneness, the most appropriate questions to ask are "Who am I?" and "What is truly mine?" When people came to Ramana Maharishi and asked him for instruction, he always had one question to ask them, "Who wants instruction? What is it in you that says, 'I am' and 'Who am I?'" Whatever your question, need or problem, as a preliminary to knowing what is yours, you need to ask, "Who am I?"

The *Brahmavidyā Pañcakam* of Narayana Guru gives the two classic questions that a disciple is expected to ask his or her guru: "Who am I?" *(ko'ham)* and "Whence this world?" *(kutojagad)*. You have only to know who you are, what you are not, and how you are connected with what you are not. In his *Brahma Sūtra Bhāṣya,* Śankara enters into the mainstream of brahmavidyā (science of the Absolute) by raising the question, "What is this thing called 'I am'?" and "What is it that is termed 'you are'?" In Patañjali's Yoga Sūtras we have now also come to this study of oneself.

Svādhyāya is studying "Who or what am I?" and "What is mine?" "Who am I?" is not a question that can be replied to with an answer that will remain intact throughout one's life. We live in a world of transient names and forms. What we know at this moment disappears in the next. Suppose in this moment you recognize yourself as the perceiver of a beautiful rose laden with dew drops. In the next moment that image doesn't remain. You may then be recognizing yourself as a person who is confronted by a furious cobra or a charging wild animal that wants to pierce you with its sharp teeth. The answer to "Who am I?" in one situation doesn't hold good in another situation. As relativistic conditions continuously change and move, you need to know what the condition of the next moment will be. That is why it is said that a single answer does not solve the problem of *samsāra* (phenomenal world). The vision of the Absolute is not static so that you can hold on to it. Only when the vision of the Absolute is continuous and contiguous is the merger into the eternal of any use.

Svādhyāya is generally recognized as the study of words passed on by seekers who have gone before. The records of the experiences of wise people are available to us as compendiums of great works. It is worthwhile to study those books every day. Further, it is very wholesome to spend at least some time each day with an enlightened person, listening to his or her word directly. It is not possible to gather wisdom all in one day, but each day you can learn a little. Wise persons teach with their words, their modes of action, their thought processes, and, above all, with their silence. Attuning to all these aspects will bring conviction.

When what you experience, what you hear from great people, and what is recorded in the scriptures from time immemorial all come in one line, then you can be sure that your svādhyāya has been profitable. Such is the royal path in which you are confirmed that whatever you have been doing as sādhana (practice) is ultimately successful.

Īśvara Praṇidhāna: Continuous Contemplation on Īśvara

In kriyā yoga—which is re-emphasized here in the fivefold discipline of niyama—īśvara praṇidhāna is contemplation on the nature of īśvara with a view to keeping yourself in absolute unition with the pure and transcendent ways of īśvara. In the *Yoga Śāstra,* īśvara is not presented as the God of the Semitic religions, nor as similar to the deities of the Śaiva and Vaiṣṇava religions. Īśvara is defined as a special spirit unaffected by any evil. The role of īśvara is that of the supreme teacher. In one sense the īśvara of Yoga is identical with the īśvara of Vedānta—they are both designated by praṇava, AUM.

Praṇidhāna is an act of dedication by which you do not consider yourself to have any foundation other than īśvara. We can put it another way: although each person is said to have an individual puruṣa that is in conjunction with nature (prakṛti), the individuated puruṣa should be looked upon as a spark of īśvara. That spark undergoes certain transformations, at least superficially, to accomodate whatever the puruṣa is witnessing because of the three modalities of nature, sattva, rajas, and tamas.

This concept of the puruṣa as both the individuated consciousness of the finite being and the transcendent spirit is difficult to comprehend, so it is simplified by the *Bhagavad Gita* as two kinds of nature (prakṛti) and two kinds of spirit (puruṣa). In the *Gita*, the manifested and immanent aspect of nature is called *aparaprakṛti* and the unmanifested and transcendent aspect is called *parāprakṛti*. Similarly, the numinous principle that is in active participation with the wakeful, dream, and deep sleep experiences of the individual is called *kṣara puruṣa,* the transient spirit, and the pure, transcendent principle of the noumenon is called *akṣara puruṣa.*

To tide over the implied duality of prakṛti and puruṣa, Vedāntins offer a third concept called *puruṣottama,* the superior person or transcendent spirit. The kṣara puruṣa or transient individuation is treated as a reflected person whose reality is derived from the unaffected and transcendent noumenon. To work out the scheme in the *Gita,* Krishna advises Arjuna to raise this lower self by the higher Self. The lower self can be contaminated by nature and is equivalent to the reflected or image-like puruṣa. The Self that can restore or raise the lower self is the same as īśvara, the unaffected noumenon.

Even when a snake is seen in a rope, the ground of that

illusion is the only reality that is. Similarly, when you see that the ground of your being is īśvara, the supreme spirit, you are having īśvara praṇidhāna. You are expected to cultivate a transparency of vision that can cut across the illusions created by the nature modalities so that you do not take them for reality. The Yoga aspirant continuously forgoes all the ramifications of what is perceptually presented in the phenomenal world and adheres only to the truth represented by the true spirit, īśvara.

That means you have to keep vigil over the three states of consciousness that cyclically present as waking, dream, and deep sleep, ever seeing īśvara as their ground, known as the fourth (turīya). Usually there is a compulsiveness to validate the objectivized world of the wakeful as a reality "out there." That validity is shattered when its place is taken by a dream, but the consciousness of the individual has no power to recognize a dream as a dream when it is going on. It lacks the critical acumen to compare and contrast what was originally validated by wakeful experience and what is given in the dream. This incapacity to recognize the true nature of a presented state becomes much worse when you are pushed to the unconscious depth of deep sleep.

Only when these trappings of individuated consciousness are torn away do you see the changing states as aspects of phenomena. When that discriminative power is achieved you will continue to see—in the wakeful, the dream, and the deep sleep—the formless and the timeless without any subject-object differentiation. Until you come to such a state, you have to meditate on the true nature of īśvara. The reality of īśvara effaces from your mind all the wrong impressions with which you identify as the knower, the actor, and the enjoyer of the wakeful and dream states.

Tapas and svādhyāya will bear fruit only if they are fully complemented by īśvara praṇidhāna. There is a finality achieved only through the continuous contemplation of the pure being, īśvara, as your own higher Self and, for that reason also, your truer Self. Although at the beginning of this chapter, īśvara praṇidhāna was given as permissive and not mandatory, when we consider the value of the model presented by īśvara we can see how important īśvara praṇidhāna is in kriyā yoga.

Sūtra II:33

vitarka bādhane pratipakṣa bhāvanam

vitarka: confrontation, conflict
bādhane: when disturbed by
pratipakṣa: the opposites
bhāvanam: cultivate, ponder

When disturbed by confrontation, cultivate the opposites.

Vitarka (confrontation) is a constant occurrence in the world of transaction. When the normal flow of your consciousness is obstructed by a frightening incident of a person, thing, or event confronting you, you cannot move forward without resolving the ensuing problem. If there is a roadblock you cannot pass that way unless the block is removed. The block in your path may be so formidable that you cannot handle it on your own. Where one person fails, ten people coming together can succeed. A quantitative force is met with an equal force. Physical blocks can be physically removed if a force is organized that is sufficient and skillfully applied.

Vitarka occurs in our personal lives more as conflicts of

mind than as physical encounters. There are a number of dialectical situations in life such as the relationship between guru and disciple, husband and wife, parent and child, ruler and ruled, master and servant, and so on. The bipolarity between the pair is to be established on positive love and mutual understanding. If disadoption comes in the mind of the guru or disciple, no wisdom transaction can occur between them. If husband and wife lose their mutual respect and think of each other as a burden, a nuisance, and a drag, their life together becomes miserable. These are causes of greater conflicts than physical confrontations.

Our personalities unfold in our life situations. The unfoldment comes both from within and without. An inner dynamic decides the form of the individual's personality. It is like a die that is fastened to a lathe. Whatever is worked by the lathe can only come in accordance with the die. It is here the real problem comes. Our personalities are such that they are like clay pots and bowls that are preformulated and prefabricated. There are unique distinctions between personalities. Often, however much is the need for two people to live together, they cannot get away from their egoistic stances to make a common cause. To resolve such riddles, a psychological device that is basically spiritual is given in this sūtra.

A pot and a bowl can be blended into a new form, but first the prefabricated vessels have to be reduced to the state of clay. Then the clay is to be made into the desired shape. Like the basic clay that can be fashioned in many forms, our personalities have sprung from the common spirit in which there is no difference. A yogi who is very conscious of the empirical and transactional peculiarities of the world of things and persons decides to leave aside his or her ego and approach the problem from the starting point of manifestation. At that level there is only īśvara. If you put yourself in the position of īśvara and look at things with a neutral mind and no vested interest, you will perceive them from a catholic, altruistic, and compassionate ground. As you then have no ego, your counterpart can also loosen his or her grip on the ego. This is just like disarming a rival. The Zen Buddhists call this "listening to the clap of one hand."

When clay is put on a potter's wheel it does not become a pot by itself. It is the potter's intention that fashions the lump into a beautiful pot, jar, or mug. The intention of the potter is not physical. It is a vision in the spirit of the potter. We are all in some way fashioning the other according to our spiritual visions. If the clay put on the wheel is too moist, it cannot be fashioned. If it is not sufficiently pliable, then also it cannot be fashioned.

Suppose an evil-minded person is always being an aggressive nuisance to you and you cannot but hate him. You can look at that person from another angle. When he sleeps he is like a helpless child lying in the cradle. However bad he is to you, the most compassionate God is supervising his circulation of blood, his respiration, his metabolic balance, and a million other things that make his existence possible. If God cares for him so much and you share the mind of God, you can also care for him. Even though in the given empirical situation and social structure, you may not be able to literally hug and kiss him, all the personal bickering will disappear from your mind.

Krishna asked Arjuna to be of his mind—not the social mind of an individual in confrontation—but the mind of all. In that, friends and foes are all merged into the one fantasy of a universal dream. There is no anger or attachment there. When we are identified with this universal mind, God's mind, the person who is spitting venom or kicking at us is seen only as a patient with a malady. Suppose a mother is watching over her child who has a high fever. If, in his delirium, he speaks evil words and curses his mother, she doesn't react. Her compassion only increases and she gives even greater care to her child to bring him to normalcy. This is how we can change the world by changing ourselves. You change yourself by establishing yourself in a spiritual position and becoming equipped with God's vision. The yogi who is ever engaged in īśvara praṇidhāna has no other identity and thus transforms himself or herself to transform the world.

Sūtra II:34

vitarka himsādayaḥ kṛta kāritānumoditā lobha krodha moha pūrvakā mṛdu madhyādhimātrā duhkhājñānānanta phalā iti pratipakṣa bhāvanam

vitarka: confrontation, conflict
himsādayaḥ: such as violence [whether]
kṛta: done by oneself
kārita: instigated, caused to be done [by others]
anumoditāḥ: abetted, approved
lobha: greed
krodha: anger
moha: [or] delusion, confusion
pūrvakāḥ: precipitated by, caused by, preceded by
mṛdu: mild
madhya: medium
adhimātrāḥ: [or] intense
duḥkha: pain, misery, distress, sorrow, suffering
ajñāna: ignorance
ananta: endless
phalāḥ: result [in]
iti: thus
pratipakṣa: opposites

bhāvanam: cultivate, ponder

Confrontations such as violence, whether done by oneself, instigated, or abetted, whether precipitated by greed, anger, or delusion, whether mild, medium, or intense, result in endless misery and ignorance; thus, cultivate the opposites.

Even when a person wants to live a very righteous and peaceful life, many obstructions get in the way, making life a chain of conflicts. No one is blessed with a path that is straight and wide where they can walk fearlessly. From childhood we have seen people exterminating anything believed to be harmful. As humans have an intense fear of snakes, even the most innocent of that species is ruthlessly killed wherever it is seen. One of the most profitable multinational industries of our own age is the manufacture of insecticides and pesticides. The psychological extrapolation of this is the termination of anyone who opposes you. This can even be extended to your own brother. According to the Bible, the history of this approach began with the first human family when Cain refused to be his brother's keeper and even eliminated his brother Abel out of sheer jealousy.

Those who have hardened their minds can cause violence to others and be worse than brutes. There are others who have the prick of conscience, so they induce others to do violence to those with whom they are displeased. Then there are those who neither inflict violence nor induce others to commit it, but rejoice when their adversaries are exterminated in a fateful manner. We have legislated laws against violent crimes and even the crime of aiding and abetting violence. But those who secretly appreciate or rejoice in the ill-fate of those they do not like escape the attention of others.

In India every year several hundreds of innocent young women are burned alive when their parents fail to give the dowry they had offered to get their daughters married away. Sometimes even those who have fully paid are burned because the husband sees another prospective bride who is willing to give a more lucrative dowry. In the committing of this kind of crime there are all three kinds of agents: those who directly kill, those who induce to kill, and those who rejoice that death has come.

Yoga is not a passive way of closing one's eyes to injustice. If the yogi has a moral conscience, he or she has to challenge all three kinds of involvement in violence.

Three things are indicated here as instrumental in causing violence. The first is greed. The concern for security is instituted in us from early childhood. A baby in the arms of its mother is scared whenever there is a quick movement around it; then it clings to the body of its mother. When the nipple of the mother's breast is pulled out of the child's lips it screams as if it is going to lose its sustenance forever. Later in life we identify our security with valuable things such as food and shelter. When we grow in sophistication and understand that exchange value has an advantage over use value, we learn to hoard money or gold with which security can be bought.

This fear as well as conviction is looked upon as a commercial proposition by the greedy vultures of society who have instituted devices like banks, insurance companies, agencies for surveillance, and concealed accounting systems like those for which the Swiss banks are notorious. Greed has become an octopus that induces us to rate everything in terms of money. Even sacred institutions like marriage are wrecked by the greed of the participants.

The second cause of violence is emotional disturbance that eclipses a person's rational power. Even small children throw tantrums at a very early age and behave like monstrous dictators. Later that becomes a personality factor in some people. It begins as a defense mechanism and becomes a habit.

The slightest provocation can cause an avalanche of glandular secretions which make such people forget all sense of proportion and propriety. They forget the exact nature of the relationships that exist between them and others when they are stung with pride and prejudice, anger and animosity. They engage in animal behavior like baring their teeth, mauling, biting, shouting, or shrieking. Such behavior not only disturbs the person doing it but also fills the whole atmosphere with feelings that are so scary and evil that they can cause the death of a family. In the politics of crime precipitated in a family, some are directly involved, some are agents, and some secretly rejoice in the crumbling of the family.

Some people never grow up. They always remain as deviant or perverted children, full of fear and suspicion. They live in perpetual paranoia. There are a number of people who—even when already saturated with their illusion and fantasies—intensify their delusion by becoming alcoholic or heavily drugged. They give themselves into the hands of mischief makers.

Greed, anger, and delusion all cause people to behave like slaves of passion. Even the little spark of intelligence in them is forged into a weapon of the devil. The conscious self—which should always be raising one to one's higher Self—goes in the opposite direction and pulls one into darkness. That is why the previous sūtra recommended an attitude of annulling the negativity that afflicts the mind of the ill-fated. The true nature of the Self and the reality of īśvara are not different. They are both one hundred percent opposed to these three kinds of darkness. By establishing oneself in pure existence, subsistence, and value, īśvara becomes sufficient to counter the darkness of ignorance. If we do not reform ourselves, ignorance will precipitate more and more darkness and we will suffer endlessly.

Sūtra II:35

ahimsā pratiṣṭhāyāṃ tat sannidhau vairatyāgaḥ

ahimsā: [in] nonviolence, non-hurting
pratiṣṭhāyāṃ: firmly established, grounded
tat sannidhau: in the presence [of one]
vaira: hostility, enmity
tyāgaḥ: ceases

In the presence of one firmly established in nonviolence, hostility ceases.

In this sūtra we are led to the very source of our actions and thoughts. As we go closer and closer to the Self, the homogeneity of selves becomes clearer and more evident. The ego of a person is one of the four inner organs. It can have two identifications, one with the individuated social member of a community and the other with the inner organ (intellect) that is receiving the light of the Self.

The social factor manifests when you take upon yourself the agency of action or of a person who intends to prevail upon others with your words. If you withdraw from the sense of agency, both of action and speech, then your I-consciousness remains only as a recipient of the light of the Self. If that state of consciousness is maintained for a long time, you will come to stay more in unity with the Self, which by nature is pure existence, subsistence, and bliss.

You can go to a still deeper anchoring of contemplative at-one-ment when you recognize your absolute union with the life of all, especially through īśvara praṇidhāna. There is no question of wanting to show any violence to anyone because there is no one apart from yourself. A person who has cultivated a positive attitude of union with others—not only humans but all sentient beings—affects others just like a magnet affects a piece of iron by magnetizing it. The peaceful silence of a yogi will affect the entire atmosphere around him or her with a unifying and pacifying magnetism. In the yogi's silence everyone is disarmed. If you walk into a room and find a person sitting there in a state of meditation, you will immediately experience an aura of serenity. It can have such a telling effect on you that you feel spellbound and wouldn't dare to cause that person any disturbance. Just as anger and madness are contagious, peace and silence are also.

There are many true stories that illustrate how, in the presence of a deeply loving person, even wild animals become affected by their love. Paul Brunton recounts such an incident at the ashram of Ramana Maharshi. One day he saw a cobra raising its hood and hissing at him. He ran out to get a gun. A silent mendicant of the ashram came in. On seeing the snake, he lovingly went near it and, like a guide, showed it how to retrace its path to the jungle. Brunton thought that the mendicant had cast a magic spell on the snake. But the mendicant, who did not speak, wrote in the sand with his walking stick that when a person casts fear away from his mind completely, all those who come into contact with him also become fearless.

It is a common experience of many yogis that they become a center of attraction for others. People are drawn to them with great love and affection. This is especially so when they are wandering in lands where they have not gone before and where people are total strangers to them.

Sūtra II:36

satya pratiṣṭhāyām kriyā phalāśrayatvam

satya: [in] truth, truthfulness
pratiṣṭhāyām: [for one] firmly established
kriyā: action
phala: fruits, results
āśrayatvam: rests on, depends on [truth]

For one firmly established in truth, the fruits of action rest on truth.

Truth is to be understood from the relativistic position of the empirical world where it has transactional validity and also from the absolutist point of view in which truth remains the same for all people all over the world irrespective of the time factor or space factor. Persons who enter into the path of truth will initially only become conversant with the relativistic aspects of truth. Soon they will find out that there is a degree of untruth that enters into both the perceptual and conceptual comprehension of truth. Then they do not fight in the name of relativistic truth. If they are bent on knowing what truth is, they will find out that in all things held as valid for transactional purposes, there is a common factor of homogeneity by which empirical truth can be discerned from illusions. They will also recognize that there is a non-physical reality that provides for the truthful existence of things.

For example, if ten or a hundred people are present in a place where all of them see several objects such as a tree as a tree, a stone as a stone, the sky as the sky, a cloud as a cloud, and so on, the specific differences between the things does not matter in the recognition of each element as truthful. This is what is called the irrefutable existentiality of things. In Sanskrit this is called the *satya* that makes truth valid. When the yogi becomes conversant with the unmanifested substratum of truth and the manifested modification of truth, his or her mind can easily go between the ground and the figure.

Truth has a value dimension as well as an existential dimension. However true a thing is, if an exposition of it is detrimental to the common good, then priority is given to the collective value rather than to the existential factor. One is not deemed a liar for not revealing to the world a socially detrimental truth. It is very difficult to draw a line between absolute truth and the relativistic evaluation of truth. But it is taken for granted that truth need not necessarily be harshly presented. Hence the old adage, "Speak truth, speak it sweetly."

In a person with far sight and insight, in whose consciousness existence and value blend as a holistic apprehension, both truth and goodness manifest in knowledge as the adorable or the beautiful. Consequently we can say that person is not confined to the limited field of the body/mind complex. Such a person is called a *mahātma,* one whose Self (ātma) has reached the highest magnitude possible, which implies the good of all. A person who has matured into that state gains a prophetic vision of foreseeing things, the capability of forewarning and of predicting future good. All great reformers and all who are the saviors and prophets of the world first speak the truth. In the course of time, what they have said comes to be true. This is the mark of a person being established on truth.

Sūtra II:37

asteya pratiṣṭhāyām sarva ratnopasthānam

asteya: honesty, non-misappropriativeness, non-stealing
pratiṣṭhāyām: [for one] firmly established
sarva: all

ratna: precious things, valuable things
upasṭhānam: present themselves

For one firmly established in honesty, all precious things present themselves.

Of all the vices that a person can cultivate, the most subtle is the stealing of virtues, values, and advantages that do not naturally belong to one. Pilfering, stealing someone's valuables, and so on are all *steyam* in some sense, but the kind of stealing from which a yogi has to desist is not the thieving of a highway robber. There are incomparable masters of the world like Lord Buddha, Jesus Christ, the Prophet Mohammed, Guru Nanak, Śankara, Ramanuja, Madhva, and, in our own days in India, Sri Ramakrishna, Dayananda Saraswati, Swami Vivekananda, Narayana Guru, and Mahatma Gandhi, who all represent precious values in the hearts of people. It is common knowledge that these glorious names have become commercial propositions and that, all over the world, very subtle forms of thieving the glories of great people are precipitated.

The great number of Buddhist vihāras, churches of all kinds, masjids, and so-called spiritual and welfare institutions that have risen in several parts of the world are the best example of the subtle way in which people make a living on the reflected glory of great people. One has to wean oneself away with great care from such dishonest sharing of the booty of religious and spiritual exploits. The great masters have given up everything for the sake of their love for all sentient beings and they are naturally held in great glory by humanity moved by gratitude. When, through historical chance, others assume the positions of these great ones, they are verily great deceivers who don the raiment of glory without paying for it.

Think of a great guru who toils for several years, mounts

rugged peaks with great earnestness, and, after years of penance and prayer, comes to realization. Most naturally, he is worshipped by humanity. If a person who incidentally stood by him is acclaimed by his friends as the successor to the guru, does he have the same inner worth? If he repeats, parrot-like, what his guru has taught, he is stealing the glory of the guru without knowing the illumination of the blessed one. This is the kind of stealing spoken of here.

Jesus was dragged in the muddy roads with a heavy wooden cross on his shoulders. On the Mount of Calvary he was crucified on the very cross he had been carrying. It was with agony, pain, and death that he earned his Christ-hood for himself and the world. How ridiculous to see a well-fed man who knows only the enjoyment of a pampered rich man's comforts donning a religious robe and decorating himself with jewels and a golden cross suspended on a golden chain. Is that not stealing of the worst order?

This stealing is more subtle and more prevalent in other fields such as poetry, music, and other creative arts. As long as a person only wants to steal the designs or ideas of others, he will never find original inspiration in his own heart. Great treasures are hidden deep in the unconscious. When we look within for original ideas with absolute sincerity, we will find the *ratnagarbha,* mine of precious stones, in our own intuitive world.

Patañjali says that a person well-established in asteya, honesty, will be amply rewarded with the power to detect the great treasures of the world right where he or she is. It is to this end that the honest endeavor of a person is to be expended. Unfortunately, most commentators have taken this in the very vulgar sense that the yogi will find hidden precious stones. You are a treasure unto yourself: seek and find.

Sūtra II:38

brahmacarya pratiṣṭhāyāṃ vīrya lābhaḥ

brahmacarya: adhering to uprightness in life, walking in the path of the Absolute (*brahman*)
pratiṣṭhāyāṃ: [one] firmly established
vīrya: energy, strength
lābhaḥ: gains

One firmly established in walking the path of the Absolute gains energy.

Spiritual life is considered to have four aspects, each with its own identity. They are: the *brahmacari*, the seeker and student who is learning to recognize the path of the Absolute; the householder or *dharmacari* who walks in the path of dharma and fulfills several roles that come as a consequence of the dharma that is being unfolded; the *mumukṣu*, one who is intensely desiring to be liberated from the entanglements of karma that have ensued from acceding to the demands of dharma; and the *brahmaniṣṭha*, one who is fully established in the identity of the Absolute.

Although one's entire life is to be an incessant flow in the path of the Absolute, embodied life requires people who happen to have intense proximity with nature (prakṛti) to set apart at least a quarter of a century to participate in the fulfillment of their nature that stems from the body/mind complex, from what they have inherited, and from the personality traits that have been pursuing them through several lives.

With the conjunction of nature, your mind deviates from identity with the Absolute and you assume many specific roles within your world of interests. You see yourself as an individual belonging to a family or clan, a certain community of parochial coloration. When such specificity enters into your consciousness, collective dharma dissipates into several relativistic identities. Then you look for the norms that guide the particular role that is congruent with whatever you have imbibed from your position. The dharma that you seek is that of a specific person with a unique personality. The consequences of this are roles such as that of a lover, a husband or wife, a father or mother, and a responsible member of the community. Many pragmatic, utilitarian considerations are to be compromised with. Endless obligations and compulsive actions come in the course of life, for which you have to expend your physical, vital, mental, and spiritual energy.

When you wean away from family and social obligations and again assume the role of a seeker of the Absolute, you return to the mainstream of brahmacarya. The dissipation of energy ceases. Once again there is a channeling of all energy with a single-minded concentration on the final search. The inner reservoir of energy for the final attainment of the Absolute is amply gained by one whose only interest is to walk in the path of the Absolute.

Sūtra II:39

aparigraha sthairye janma kathamtā sambodhaḥ

aparigraha: non-acquisitiveness, non-possessiveness
sthairye: being confirmed, becoming steady
janma: [of] existence, birth
kathamtā: the "how" and "wherefore"
sambodhaḥ: knowledge of [arises]

Non-possessiveness being confirmed, knowledge of the

"how" and "wherefore" of existence arises.

In the world of transactions you become a possessor or an owner only when you buy something for yourself or when a thing comes to your possession by chance or choice or as a gift from someone. This is how we understand possessiveness in our daily transactions. But this is not the order of nature. A child comes to have a consciousness of "I am" or "mine" only when it reaches the age of one or two. Much before that, the child that was to be was a sperm in some man and an ovum in some woman. The sperm and ovum come together, become a fetus, and grow to maturity in the mother's womb. When it comes from the mother as a child, it already has all the faculties of a living body, the ability to perceive and to cogitate. None of these are taken into possession by the child. Everything is given. Thus, in nature, one who possesses does so without his or her desire or will.

From a worm that is wriggling in the dirt to the proud person with many possessions—all have come from nature, all are sustained by nature, and all will return to nature. When the time to leave comes, it cannot be delayed. In between, only human beings come under the delusion of thinking that they are the owners of things. The sense of possession makes them so infatuated that they try to hold on to things.

Sri Ramakrishna said that God has laughed twice. Once, two people divided land and put up a fence to separate the two pieces. When they said, "This is mine and that is yours," God laughed. When a self-confident doctor assured a patient that he would take care of the patient's life, then also God laughed. Many who have claimed this Earth have become the dust under our feet. These physical organisms of ours are only temporary arrangements. When the time comes, they will disintegrate. Many plays, novels, and stories have been written on this theme of a person's illusory identity as a possessor. Omar Khayyam's *Rubaiyat* contains many beautiful couplets on this idea. In the *Mahabharata* it is written that the greatest miracle in this world is people's forgetfulness about their imminent death.

A knower of the "wherefrom" and "how" of things cannot entertain the thought of possessing something at all. When such is our state it is ridiculous that people go so far as to think of another person as theirs: "my daughter," "my son," "my wife," "my husband." Until recently, men in all countries thought that women were chattels that they possessed. In this sūtra, non-possessiveness is given as the cause for the knowledge of the "how" and "wherefore" of things but non-possessiveness actually becomes a reality only when this wisdom becomes known.

Sūtra II:40

śaucāt svāṅga jugupsā parair asamsargaḥ

śaucāt: from purity
svāṅga: with one's own limbs or body
jugupsā: disgust, aversion
paraiḥ: with others
asamsargaḥ: [and] avoidance of contact

From purity: disgust with one's own limbs and avoidance of contact with others.

In the Taoist culture a dichotomy is made between yin and yang. A similar dichotomy is in almost all spiritual disciplines. The Vedāntins call it *cit* and *jada,* the Jains, *cit* and *acit.* The Christians speak of the godly and the worldly. When two pure elements are combined as a mixture or compound, the purity of each is replaced by an amalgam. Everything in this world is devoid of its primeval purity: we cannot see pure spirit anywhere nor pure matter anywhere.

Spirit interpenetrates into matter and matter articulates the spirit. If the animating spirit leaves a body, it becomes a corpse. It has no sensation or knowledge, neither pain nor pleasure. Spirit cannot manifest itself and become a percipient or cognizer to perceive, to cogitate, and to evaluate. Spirit has to shine through physical entities such as the various faculties of our body. As the body is constituted of material or physical elements, it is governed by physical laws from which it cannot deviate. The biologic aspect is a meeting ground of spirit and matter. The very basic function of biochemistry is a variety of modes of absorption and secretion. When physical and chemical energies come together to form biologic organisms, a given state transforms into another through a continuous process of organization and disorganization.

If you watch your mouth for a little while, you can notice the ceaseless emitting of saliva from the salivary glands. Anything that is thrown out of any part of our bodies is an excretion. We know it to be dirt. That is why we do not allow secretions from our nose, mouth, and so on to come into contact with other parts of our body, our clothes, or other persons. Considering all this, people are very dirty.

From the pores of the skin perspiration is always coming, as gas or in beads, which contains chemicals like sulfur that have strong odors. If people do not wipe and wash themselves and change into fresh clothes (in tropical countries, as much as several times a day), they can stink more than pigs do. And yet out of vanity people spend hours before mirrors looking at their own faces, combing their hair, adjusting collars and ties, or what not. Those who are endowed with the brightest light of the spirit lose their track and fall into the filth of their physical secretions.

But if you see the worth of the thoughts that can shine in your mind, the ideas that can bring beauty and happiness to all around, you will find the same body a helpful tool to focus on the great and forget about the non-essential. Many people spoil nature's purity by painting themselves with chemical substances of various kinds. In their vanity they think they are beautifying their bodies. In this respect the tribal people of Africa who paint themselves with mud are far better than those who support multinational enterprises that create needs in people to dirty themselves every day with chemical substances. It is a pity that people take dirt for purity and the purity of nature for unattractiveness.

If people only had the wisdom to know that it is not painted lips that speak truth but the sincerity of one's heart; it is not painted eyes that are attractive but an honest look; it is not a cultivated voice culture that holds people spellbound but the irrefutability of the truth that a person speaks.

Śauca thus implies a discipline by which the essential is discriminated from the non-essential, the precious from the worthless, the spirit from outward appearance. Those who have come to appreciate the essence will cast away the chaff. Those who discriminate in this way have only disgust for all the pretensions of the world. They treasure the pearl of priceless worth that is at the core of every one's being.

Sūtra II:41

sattvaśuddhi saumanasya ekāgra indriyajaya ātmadarśana yogyatvāni ca

sattvaśuddhi: [from] inner purity, purity of the inner organ

saumanasya: cheerfulness, gladness

ekāgra: one-pointedness
indriyajaya: control or mastery of the senses
ātmadarśana: the vision of the Self
yogyatvāni: fitness for
ca: and

From inner purity: cheerfulness, one-pointedness, control of the senses, and fitness for the vision of the Self.

The verity of science is derived from the belief that truth is one. Physical sciences attempt to unify everything on the basis that matter is one and from it all forms of energy manifest. In chemistry all elements are considered to be only arrangements of primordial energy. However different the pure elements and their compounds and mixtures appear to be, the chemist is a monist. The biologist is also a monist who believes in the unity of life and is not confused because of the size or behavior of any species seen in the biologic world. The religious person thinks of God as one and of God manifesting as all this.

An analogy will be helpful in understanding the dialectics of the one and the many. If a certain area has a powerhouse, the power generated there goes to many individual units such as homes, public institutions, factories, theaters, and so on. Each unit has its own power control but the supply for all is controlled by the powerhouse. We can understand the powerhouse as representing the supreme Self, the nature of which is sat-cit-ānanda. The individual units are very much like people, each of whom has an inner organ that controls their wakeful, dream, and deep sleep hours.

Although the power in the powerhouse and the individual units is the same, at each individual unit it can be stepped up or down as required. When power is transmitted through a stove, it gives heat; transmitted through a fan, it makes a current of air; through a refrigerator, it freezes, and so on. Similarly, when the pure aspect of Self (pratyaṅg caitanya) is directed into the individual, it is only a reflected reality or self (abhāsa caitanya).

The pure light that comes into the individual has the same quality as its absolute source. But the individuated person experiences only the reflected image of the Self. The medium through which the reflection comes is nature. That aspect of nature that gives a pure, clear replication is sattva. When it is not contaminated it is *sattva śuddhi*. The two impurities that can cloud or pollute the mirror are rajas and tamas. Rajas brings exaggeration and perversion. Tamas brings blackout, concealment, veiling, depression. The present sūtra gives the characteristics of a personality that is stabilized by pure clear sattva alone.

Through physical, biological, psychological, and sociological evolution, a personality assumes its long-standing peculiarities, like the cactus plant that is seen in the desert. Nature is hostile to it. It gets very little water. Wandering camels may come and eat it. So for defense it has sharp thorns pointed in all directions. When the same cactus is removed and made to live in an environment where it is not threatened for a considerably long time, it undergoes so much change that we get thornless cacti. In the same manner, even if a person has developed a grotesque personality under the influence of genetics and by adverse circumstances in childhood and adolescence, it can be changed into something beautiful.

When the inner organ is clouded with rajas it immediately becomes egoistic and we become aggressive. On the other hand, if the purity of sattva is maintained, we will forego ourselves and give preference to the well-being of the other. We will say, "Go ahead and be happy. If you smile, I feel contented." We build bridges between us with love and understanding. On such bridges we can walk to and fro and rejoice every time we meet. Such an attitude is called *saumanasya,* cheerfulness. When there is no distraction of fear or confusion, the mind automatically becomes concentered, ekāgra. In that state, the sense faculties are active only when they are commissioned to carry out their duties. That means a person of pure, clear inner organ has control of the senses, *indriyajaya.* When all these qualities are developed one is endowed with the competence and excellence to be a seer of the Self, *ātmadraṣṭa.*

Sūtra II:42

santoṣād anuttamaḥ sukha lābhaḥ

santoṣād: from contentment
anuttamaḥ: unsurpassed, unexcelled
sukha: happiness, comfort, pleasure-giving, pleasurable
lābhaḥ: comes from

Unsurpassed happiness comes from contentment.

From the time of birth to the ultimate termination of the psychophysical organism, life is both polarized and torn between two values that are like two sides of the same coin. They are necessity and freedom. If necessity can be marked at the negative pole of a vertical parameter, freedom comes on the plus side at the omega point. Necessity binds us to the body and the physical basis of life whereas freedom allows us to soar very high into the sublime. Life is a perpetual theme of ascending and descending dialectics.

In the explanation of the previous sūtra we spoke of the pure state of the Self and how it reflects in the mirror of nature and makes us identify ourselves with an image or shadow cast by the light of the Self. The mirror on which this image falls can be likened to a magic mirror where, instead of a single replica being shown, there can be a proliferation of images, each of which looks different with a uniqueness that holds good only for a very short time. It is as if the jīva in us is exposed to a kaleidoscopic dance of dark and bright images that can confuse the cognizing principle in the individual.

The magic mirror can be compared to a fast-running mountain river making a frothy cascade on which the Moon is shining. Although there is only a single Moon in the sky, it looks as if the one Moon has become fragmented into a million Moons, all appearing and disappearing in the ripples of water. In each of the countless bubbles of the froth a different Moon is seen. Like that, our stream of consciousness, although it is one and the same—not only in an individual but in all—is seen as many because of the mirroring capacity of the psychosomatic system. The identification of the cognizing agent is rapidly shifted from one format to another and one value infatuation to another.

The more necessities we feel, the greater the fragmentation of life. Unfortunately, the greedy among us take full advantage of this weakness and an enormous system has been built up all around the world to exaggerate our needs. As we grow from childhood to adolescence and adolescence to youth, the spectrum of necessity multiplies by millions. Our individuated selves become like unsatiated gaping mouths wanting to devour more and more.

Want is called *kāma*, desire. Where there is desire there is a programming of action. A program of action necessarily brings in the need to expend more and more energy. Thus life becomes a burning conflagration of desires. Every desire that is fulfilled is only a stepping stone to another desire, so each fulfillment seems meager, a trifle.

The world of necessity holds before us the need to

nourish and sustain the body, to tickle the senses, to over-awe the mind. These all belong to the negative pole of the vertical parameter. There is a noble desire that transcends all these: the desire to free oneself from the dictates of the transient, to gain absolute freedom. This is the desire for emancipation or realization. Emancipation comes with the recognition of the homogeneity of the worthwhileness of every passing moment. It is a peak experience, not a transitory peak but a continuous one in which the fluctuating differences in the environmental factors that envelop each situation are glorified for whatever merit is outstanding in that given situation.

For example, if you have the prowess, physical stamina, and dynamism to be a fast runner engaged in a marathon or an Olympic race, you can rejoice that you have a been given such facilities. If, however, you happen to lose your vigor and be confined to a wheelchair, unable to move except in a small room, you can accept that position as having the advantage of not having to leave your place any time. Without using physical limbs, you can explore the furthest regions where thoughts can go. You continue to be happy by changing the format of your value vision.

If you sit tongue-tied while another excels as a great musician, you can be happy that your brother can bring such joy to thousands of people with his music. You can be relieved that you don't have to exert yourself in trials and tribulations to train your voice and can instead appreciate hearing the beautiful music. Nothing prevents any of us from making every passing moment the highest and the grandest. This requires the sensibility to appreciate a higher value and a realistic attitude of knowing exactly where you stand and how, from that vantage point, you can have the clearest vision of the most magnificent gift of life. Then you are always happy.

The *Bhagavad Gita* gives two classical analogies of a yogi

who is in a state of contentment. In a room where there is no wind, the steady flame of a lamp is burning with a pearl-like brilliance—even so is the mind of a yogi that is always shining forth and is not swayed by the horizontal winds of necessity. Another example is that of a tortoise. On finding the environment conducive, it puts forth its head, legs, and tail; when the environment is not conducive, it withholds them. A yogi of contentment enjoys what comes naturally and does not stretch forth his or her hand in need for whatever is not given. Such a person is truly free.

Sūtra II:43

kāyendriya siddhir aśuddhi kṣayāt tapasaḥ

kāya: [of] the body
indriya: [and] sense organs
siddhiḥ: perfection, accomplishment, attainment
aśuddhi: [of] impurity
kṣayāt: through destruction
tapasaḥ: [by] self-purification, austerity

Perfection of the body and sense organs through destruction of impurity by self-purification.

You are an individual because you have a body. Your body is maintained by the nourishment given to it. It has a structure that enables it to function as an excellent instrument for you to seek and find perfection. For the performance of anything there has to be a performer and a well-designed device that is maintained in excellent condition. The jīva or individual person is the performer; the body/mind complex is the instrumental device. Maintaining it in perfect condition is the duty of the performer.

The human body is not built with heavy metals like steel, copper, or gold. But it is capable of maintaining its functional excellence for a long time without much wear and tear if proper attention is given to it. Three main components of this physical system are: the precipitation of energy and control of the vital system; plasticity maintained through lubrication and adhesiveness; and thermal stabilization of the organism to keep the body functioning normally irrespective of external temperature. These three principles are known to traditional Indian physicians as *vāta, kapha,* and *pitta*. When these three principles are in harmonious reciprocation, bodily function goes on unhampered. When they are in disarray, diseases come. As these three principles of physical organization are asymmetric in their functioning, they are called "the three evils."

Sattva, rajas, and tamas, the psychic counterparts of vāta, pitta, and kapha, are also asymmetric. When these six elements function harmoniously, we are healthy. When they are confused, we become unhealthy in both body and mind. It is very difficult to maintain perfect health because the malfunction of any of the six can throw the other five into disarray as well.

This sūtra enjoins us with the responsibility to give attention to the body/mind organization so that the whole complex can always work efficiently. For this purpose, the great treatise of Caraka on Āyurveda, the science of life, begins with an introductory chapter on preventative medicine. It gives full suggestions on how to maintain the body/mind in good health by programming each day and includes warnings about the bodily changes that come according to seasonal changes. Instructions are given on what is to be avoided and what is to be accepted so that the body/mind will fit into each particular season.

Detailed instructions are also given both for diagnosis and prognosis of the imbalances that can come from vāta, pitta, and kapha and sattva, rajas, and tamas. All food items are classified so that nutritional food of the right kind can be programmed for a balanced diet. In India the main divisions are of *śīta* and *uṣṇa*. Śīta is "tending to become cold;" uṣṇa is "tending to become hot." In China the divisions are yin and yang. This particular section of the science of life, called *āyuśkāmiyam,* if conscientiously adhered to, can be the discipline to maintain the firmness, agility, vigor, and the formal as well as internal good shape of all the constituent parts and the body in general.

Maintaining the body to be clean and pure is a major aspect of the discipline. It has a counterpart that relates mainly to our dispositions. The emotional propensities of a person are very value oriented. All five senses are attuned to values that can be of a lower nature such as animal instincts or they can be of the cultivated value vision of a noble person. Aesthetic qualities that do not lead to transcendence are of a vulgar nature. There should always be an ennobling and elevating aspiration guiding us to the higher, more sublime aspects of life. That will give our minds an efficiency that is maintained by purity.

We have seen how both the body and mind can be prevented from being soiled and how the impurities that have seeped in can be eradicated. This is the discipline of tapas that, in the course of time, will give us the perfection that we seek.

Sūtra II:44

svādhyāyād iṣṭa devatā samprayogaḥ
svādhyāyāt: by self-study
iṣṭa devatā: the worshipped or beloved deity

samprayogaḥ: union with, communion

By self-study, union with the worshipped deity.

We see two paths being adopted by people who are aiming at perfection. One is the path of worship *(upāsana)* and the other is the path of contemplation (dhyāna). In this sūtra the difference between the two is effaced. A thorough examination of the idea of worship and the idea of contemplation will lead to the conclusion that they are complementary.

Upāsana is ritualistic, stemming from an attitude of duality in which the worshipper and worshipped are seen as distinct entities. The worshipper looks upon himself or herself as a creature and the deity being worshiped as the creator. The finite, imperfect, and helpless individual is turning to the infinite, omniscient, and almighty. Very often, the deity is personalized. The worshipper conceives of four stages in the path of devotion: first, gaining a physical comprehension of the form of the deity *(salokya);* then advancing and placing oneself closer *(samīpya);* then seeing many qualities of the deity in oneself and identifying the sameness *(sarūpya);* and finally, merging with the deity *(sayujya).*

The way of the contemplative is different from that of the worshipper. The contemplative throws away all crutches and looks for the validity of the Absolute by systematically refuting everything that is of a relativistic order. The method adopted is that of a deeper familiarization with one's Self. All dualities of existence and non-existence, knowledge and non-knowledge, pain and pleasure are discarded until the contemplative comes to pure transcendence. Self-study, a critical examination of the body concept and the mind concept, ultimately leads to a dismissal of all conceptual picturing. That leads to what the Buddhists call "no-mindedness" or "thatness." As no value is dearer than the value of Self-realization, the contemplative also arrives at the realization of the adorable Absolute.

The way of the worshipper is that of the religious pilgrim to truth and the way of the contemplative is that of the uncompromising path of the philosopher. Both ultimately arrive at the Adorable in which both the worshipper and the contemplative vanish.

Sūtra II:45

samādhi siddhir īśvara praṇidhānāt

samādhi: [of] absorption, equipoise in consciousness
siddhiḥ: accomplishment, perfection, attainment
īśvara praṇidhānāt: [comes from] continuous contemplation on īśvara

Accomplishment of absorption comes from continuous contemplation on īśvara.

In the previous sūtra there was a reference to the deity whom one loves intensely. The reference to a deity in Yoga is to be understood in the light of the Sāṅkhyan epistemology to which the discipline of Yoga adheres. Īśvara is the crowning interest of all dispositions. As an individual, each person has a unique way of formulating ideas, moving in a certain stream of consciousness, and engaging in a series of actions. The prime mover in all the causal, subtle, and gross applications of the I-consciousness, the mind, and the body is īśvara.

The īśvara referred to here is not like the Allah of Islam or the Yahweh of the Jewish and Christian notions. It has more resemblance to an over-soul supervising the entire life of an individual than to a theistic godhead. The *iṣṭa devata* spoken of in the previous sūtra and the īśvara spoken of here both have reference to the ruling passion of one's life. Each person has their own *svadharma* to live. Svadharma is based on whatever disposition is most natural to a person. One's disposition comes from the crowning interest of one's life. That is īśvara. For the musician, it is music; for the creative artist, it is aesthetic creation. For a social worker, the welfare of her fellow humans is what inspires her all the time. For a philosopher, envisioning truth is the supreme interest. Thus the interest that governs life each day leads one in a certain path.

In an earlier definition of īśvara, that principle was described both as praṇava, AUM, and as *paramācārya* (supreme teacher). Sitting, walking, lying down, speaking, acting, reacting—all these come under the term *cārya*. One who manifests as the goal, provides a path, and illuminates that path is called *ācārya*. Jesus said, "I am the goal, the way, and the light." For Christians, Jesus is the paramācārya and ācārya is understood in a theistic and personalized manner.

But in Yoga it is not necessary to think of a personal God. For example, all the dictates and implications of pure music can be the ācārya for a musician. If you are not obsessed with an egoistic pride of being the performer, then the most natural thing is to resign yourself to the ruling passion within and to the environmental factors that are always coming into resonance with your svadharma. That naturally brings a great inner harmony and you do not again and again stumble on the contradictions of life.

A fast-running river that has a wide space in which to flow and a bottom that is flat and even will appear as if it is not flowing at all. If your life is well harmonized with your supreme interest you will conduct yourself as if lost in it, having a natural absorption known as *sahaja samādhi*. You do not become any less than yourself by effacing your ego and allowing yourself to be prevailed upon by the dictates of the Supreme that govern you from within. That is how samādhi is attained through continuous contemplation on īśvara.

Sūtra II:46

sthira sukham āsanam

sthira: [should be] steady, firm
sukham: happiness, comfort, pleasure-giving, pleasurable
āsanam: posture, seat, foundation, steady position

Posture should be steady and comfortable.

The mind is mercurial. Even when the physical limbs remain quiet, the mind can go far and near, to the past and to the future. When it becomes concentered it comes to a steady state. Bringing the body and mind to remain concentered in the here and now is finding your own foundation, āsana. Living in the here and now is living in the present. Everything in the present falls together to make a meaningful ensemble that leaves out anything irrelevant. Thus the present is an overt recognition of the factors of your life interests manifested at a certain time and place.

Life becomes meaningful only if you can hold onto an adorable value. When you find a consistent value to live for, you strike a root in the reality of life. Jesus speaks of it as the wise man who builds his house on the foundation of a rock, unlike the unwise man who builds his house on sand dunes. A house built on shifting sands is sure to crash. This image is very significant. Most people live in the fleeting present. Only the wise one lives in the eternal present. It is the continuity of perceiving a value and giving perfection to it that makes life worthwhile.

There are many foundations of human culture that have been nourishing the life interests of people all over the world. According to the *Upaniṣads*, brahmavidyā (science of the Absolute) is the fountain source of all sciences. What is basic to brahmavidyā is the unitive vision of the One to which the many belong. The Jewish people developed their culture by putting their faith in a law-initiating God whose law is at once powerful and binding. They conceive beauty as the central hub to which all the spokes of law converge. The Christians restated the Jewish concept of law by conceiving of God as love. They put their faith in a God whose loveful sharing is similar to human love. Loving God and serving humanity are the two wings of Christian dedication.

Muslims look upon the Absolute as incomparable and yet complemented by the attributes of Allah that comprise all the essential values that can make life on Earth graceful and caring. The leveling of all differences to the impartial love of Allah is the model for humanity.

There are many well-established roots to which people give themselves with unflinching trust. In the wisdom context of a guru and disciple, the guru is the foundation and root of the disciple. In the family context, for sexual ethics and loyalty, the husband is the root of the wife and the wife is the root of the husband. In a constitutional government, the preservation of law and the maintenance of equal opportunity is the root of the government. In creative art the noble envisioning of truth that can enhance the dignity of human life is the root of the artist and writer. Latter day scientists adhere to the reliability of a mathematical logic that gives relevance to valid reasoning.

There is no field in which you cannot find a stable seat on which you can be established to make the pursuit of your life, growing richer and richer. Then you can say your seat is firm and comfortable. The āsana to which a yogi should aspire is certainly not the physical posture of an acrobat. Unfortunately, many protagonists of Yoga have taken such a low and almost worthless view of this very profound sūtra on which the entire practice (sādhana) of Yoga is based. The truth that surpasses all wisdom and, on being found, becomes a light forever is indicated here as the seat on which you have to establish yourself. That will be firm. That will be comfortable.

Sūtra II:47

prayatna śaithilyānanta samāpattibhyām

prayatna: the effort
śaithilya: apportioning
ananta: [on the] endless (nature of perfection)
samāpattibhyām: continuous meditation

Apportioning the effort with continuous meditation on the endless nature of perfection.

Nature's program can be looked upon as a good model for the perfection of a yogi's attainment. Nature arranges things as if it has all of time at its disposal. If you watch a cycle of life, beginning with a seed and culminating in a seed, you will see that nature does not throw out its effort like a volcanic eruption. Like a steady quantum pulsation, there are many piecemeal programs arranged within a long term holistic program.

The seed waits until it is laid in the proper soil with enough moisture. First it swells up. Cracks come on the shell of the seed. It breaks. Slowly the sprout comes. The root goes down and secures a firm position for the germinating seed.

The first leaves begin to show. In between two phases a pause comes. For some time the sapling shows nothing but the sprouting of new leaves. Then a new program begins and branches go off in all directions. More leaves come. The leaves become smaller and smaller. Then like a surprise the flower comes. The bud takes its own time to become a fully bloomed colorful flower and get pollinated. Again a pause. Then comes a tiny fruit. The petals of the flower wither away. The fruit becomes mature and colorful. The seeds in it grow hard. There is no hurry. There is no excitement. Such is the way that nature points out.

At Kanjeevaram near Madras there is an ancient temple called Ekamreśvara, dedicated to a single mango tree. According to scientists, that mango tree has been bearing fruit for more than four thousand years. The tree is not excited; it does not bring all its fruit at once. Year after year when the season comes, it puts forth its flowers. After blossoming it takes two to three months to bring tiny little mangos. After the appearance of the fruit, it takes another couple of months for the mangos to become fragrant, sweet, and edible. Comparatively we can say that mango tree has an endless program, *anantam*.

If we believe the evolutionary theories put forward by biologists, we have come a long way from our bacterial ancestors to become bipeds with nervous systems and organized brains that discern right from wrong. Now we have discovered that we have before us a way to perfection. It will not bring the desired fruit miraculously. Some effort is to be applied, but it does not bring results by quantitative pressurization. Our effort should have the quality of quantum pulsation. It has to be regular, repetitive, and consistent.

The word used in the sūtra for apportioning the effort is *śaithilya*, which literally means "broken up into small bits." A yogi should perform action thinking of the whole cycle the universe goes through to complete one round, only to repeat it again. After the maturation of wisdom, the organs of action are regulated in such a manner that only minimum effort is expended. The yogi speaks in sweet and gentle words that come from a depth of serenity.

We cannot speak without inspiring and expiring. When we come to the study of *prāṇāyāma* we will be told that vital energy (prāṇa) is to be conserved. Silence *(mauna)* is a natural way of conserving prāṇa. The yogi does not run around with any wanderlust or pursue ambitious projects that involve unnecessary hard work that can wear out his or her stamina. Thus there is an apportioning of effort.

In each pause you bring composure to yourself. Thus being mindful of the eternal quality of perfection for which you are aspiring and toward which you are moving all the time, you accomplish everything by not doing anything. (The entire text of Lao Tzu's *Tao Te Ching* can be read as a beautiful elucidation of this sūtra of Patañjali.) The yogi's goal is to ultimately become an unmoved mover whose seat is stabilized and yet who moves everything and everyone. Such is the beauty of the concept of āsana.

Sūtra II:48

tato dvandvānabhighātaḥ

tataḥ: then
dvandva: pairs of opposites
anabhigātaḥ: no disturbance from

Then no disturbance from pairs of opposites.

Stabilization in one's own seat is the beginning of

samādhi, union with the Self. In the *Bhagavad Gita*, Yoga is defined as *samatvam*, "sameness" or "the harmonization of opposites." The plenum is such that it allows additions and expansions without being disturbed in its fullness or perfection. No act of reduction makes the Absolute less than the Absolute. Resolving this paradox is not accomplished by reducing contradictories into uniformity. It is resolved by the transcendence of pairs of opposites. The glaring contradictions are: birth and death, commencement and termination, coming together and splitting apart. The world is continuously tormented by these dualities. A yogi develops a neutrality in which the plus and minus do not cause attraction or repulsion. Leaving the fluctuations of becoming, one remains in a state of being.

If we look at any part of the body or mind, glaring contradictions can be seen. With our eyes we can lovingly caress those whom we care for. With the same eyes we can suspiciously watch those whom we suspect. With our lips we can give a bewitching smile. Just behind the lips are shining pearl-like teeth with their flashing brilliance. The same teeth are hard as diamonds. We can bite and tear another into pieces. The eyes can shed tears of sorrow or tears of joy. Hands that embrace in love can also stab to death. The legs that help us to move to those whom we love can also be used to flee from those whom we fear or conduct us away from those whom we hate. In the upper portion of the body is the head in which many brilliant thoughts and loveful intentions can shine, while at the other end of the body feces and urine are stored. The heart that entertains hope and love can also broil with hatred and an unquenchable sense of revenge.

In spite of all these contradictions, the yogi excels in transcending all pairs of opposites. Narayana Guru, in his *Ātmopadeśa Śatakam*, says: "Do not wake up again and remain without sleeping." A person who seems to be engaged in ceaseless activities can do so without any sense of agency of action. We can thus see action in inaction and inaction in action. A contemplative sitting apparently quiet can have inner activity that both centripetally and centrifugally affects the cosmos to which he or she belongs. In such a yogi, becoming and being are reciprocal functions of a truth that cannot be adequately explained with words.

The entire theme of Yoga is conceived in the discipline of āsana as a mystical state of being. From this glorifying of āsana in the sūtras, we can easily see it is not one of those postures that is said to be the most appropriate posture for this or that kind of healing. The word *āsana* is used in a very comprehensive sense; being established in āsana corresponds to terms like *guṇātīta* (one who has transcended the effects of the three nature modalities), *brahmavidvariṣṭha* (one who is totally merged with the Absolute), and *yogarūḍha* (one who is fully established in the state of aloneness).

Sūtra II:49

tasmin sati śvāsa praśvāsayor gati vicchedaḥ prāṇāyāmaḥ

tasmin: upon this [perfection of āsana]
sati: being accomplished
śvāsa praśvāsayoḥ: of inspiration and expiration
gati: [of the] movement
vicchedaḥ: the regulation
prāṇāyāmaḥ: the regulation of vital forces, regulation of breath

Upon this (perfection of āsana) being accomplished: prāṇāyāma, the regulation of the movement of inspiration and expiration.

In the elucidation of the previous sūtras we have seen that āsana is a comprehensive concept that includes the preliminaries of discipline leading to the perfecting of one's Yoga, which brings samādhi. The present sūtra focuses on the most dynamic principle, prāṇa, which on one side relates the manifested individual to the cosmos and, on the other, relates the psychophysical system to the Self. As the present study implies many subtle principles and their correlations, the student needs to diligently apply his or her mind to get a comprehensive idea of what is going to be said. We will proceed in a systematic manner.

First, think of the pure source of everything that can be identified either with īśvara, the inner regulating, governing and manifesting principle, or with pratyak ātma, the homogenous state of the Self that is unconditioned. Then picture a phenomenal principle in which the īśvara or pratyak ātma mirrors itself. That is the phenomenal self, jīva. The nature of the Absolute is unalloyed bliss, hence the phenomenal self also is basically blissful. For that reason, Indian philosophers think of the individuated self as a phenomenon woven out of the blissful principle. They call it *ānandamaya* (bliss through and through) or *ānandamaya koṣa* (enveloped in bliss). *Maya* means "through and through" and *koṣa* means "sheath."

As the individuated person has five sense organs, five organs of action, and the capacities to cognize, cogitate, evaluate, and be affected, experiencing bliss comes through the bringing together of a specified existential factor (sat) with an imperiential recognition of bliss (ānanda), where the conjunction happens in knowledge (cit). Such a specifically structured knowledge is like an accomplished talent. It is called *vijñāna*. The specific knowledge that has become part and parcel of the personality corresponds to the mutations that are effected in the genes in which, according to modern genetics, the RNA acts both as informant and conveyor. The specific talents that one has achieved are deep-seated aspects of personality that are obscured by the unconscious. When an artist is about to accomplish a creative work, ideation comes from the unconscious and all previous experiences line up to give the execution a certain amount of perfection. The artist consciously manipulates the in-built coordination to achieve the desired results. Hence it is said that *vijñānamaya koṣa* is enveloped by *manomaya koṣa,* the sheath of the mind.

For mentation, words are structured in the mind and there has to be a direct channeling of the electrical energy that is stored up in the body. Prāṇa is the vital principle that supplies energy for both the conscious and unconscious functioning of the organism. Therefore, *prāṇamaya koṣa* is said to be enveloping manomaya. For the flames of prāṇa to burn, it uses the physical world as its fuel. So it is said that *annamaya koṣa* (the sheath of food) envelops prāṇamaya.

Thus we come to the most important concept of a great energy functioning in us from the periphery to the core. Most people think of prāṇa as the air that is breathed in and the air

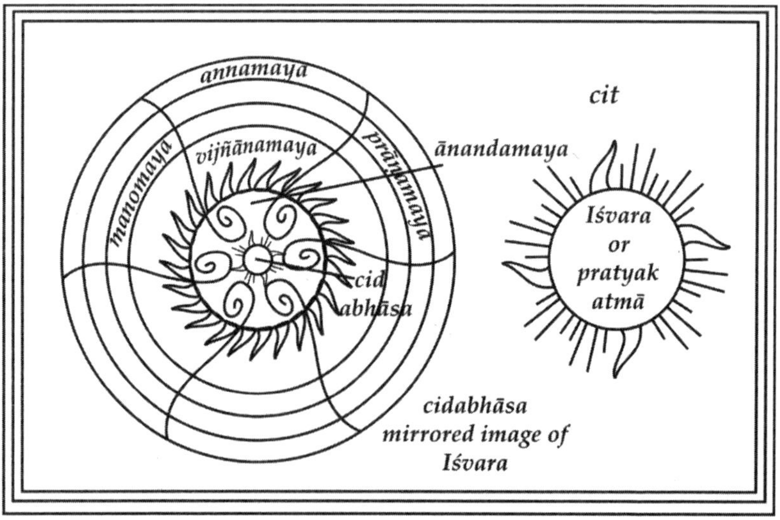

that is breathed out. But it is incidental that such a bodily function is happening. A yogi is expected to retain the circulating energy provided by prāṇa within the individuated organism. The prāṇa that is to be circulated is the main bulk of the electrical flow and consolidation within a person. Hence yogis have developed a mode of directing prāṇa in resonance with āsana or the state of being in which nothing is expended.

Practical guidance is to be received to coordinate the physical body and the mind in regulating the prāṇa. The meditation of *Gāyatri* at eight points within the body and two points outside it is recommended as one device. Such a device is given with the intention of circulating even the grossest aspect of prāṇa in an ascending and descending manner. Our common experience is bringing the breath upward and then expiring, then bringing the breath inward, taking it down to fill the lungs. In the yogic discipline, prāṇa (the ascending vital breath) is taken upward all the way from the toes to the crown and the apāna (the descending vital breath) is taken downward from the crown to the toes. This and similar practices are to be directly learned from a preceptor.

Sūtra II:50

bāhyābhyantara stambha vṛttir deśakāla sankhyābhiḥ paridṛṣṭo dīrghasūkṣmaḥ

bāhya: external
ābhyantara: internal
stambha: [or] suspended
vṛttiḥ: [its] modifications, modulations, oscillations, functions [are]
deśa: [by] place
kāla: time

sankhyābhiḥ: number
paridṛṣṭaḥ: regulated, measured
dīrgha: prolonged
sūkṣmaḥ: [and] subtle

Its modifications are external, internal, or suspended, regulated by place, time, and number, prolonged and subtle.

Just as a certain physical posture is not āsana, the gross form of breathing exercises is not prāṇāyāma. The aspiring yogi (sādhaka) belongs at once to the cosmos and to the spirit center of the universe. Whatever a person does, it is done to achieve a certain result. An aspiring yogi undergoes self-discipline to ultimately come to a state of aloneness (kaivalya). Aloneness has no social significance. The action that is implied in dissolving oneself in aloneness is an action that cancels out all other actions. Hence it is called *nirvṛtti.*

Humans are active in the daytime and replenish their energy at night with sleep. As the physical and mental states of day and night are different, the discipline you pursue in the daytime and night cannot be the same. For this reason the time factor is reckoned with in this sūtra. Just as the time of day is significant, the place where you do sādhana is important. A person sitting in a dingy room with doors and windows shut is different from a person sitting outside who is aware of the vast expanse surrounding him. Time and space both have an impact on your sādhana (practice).

In ordinary breathing you are not very conscious of how much air you are taking in or breathing out. But when you start watching your prāṇa and apāna, it is only natural to count the duration of each phase of breathing in, keeping the breath inside, breathing out, and keeping the breath outside. The counting of the time familiarizes you with the pattern of your respiration. One who is aspiring for nothing but aloneness gradually reduces his or her dependence on external air. Just as you withdraw from the five senses of perception and the five organs of action, and withhold from external aids, you should naturally not be dependent on external air. As in hibernation, a suspended animation is gained by not breathing in.

Consequently, the multitudinous impressions of the mind become quiet and the time that the yogi can sit in the deep serenity of inner aloneness is slowly prolonged. In the prolongation of the restraint of the breath outside, serenity increases until one finds that the sublimity of samādhi brings aloneness.

Sūtra II:51

bāhyābhyantara viṣayākṣepī caturthaḥ

bāhya: external
abhyantara: internal
viṣaya: objects of interest
ākṣepī: going beyond
caturthah: the fourth [variety of prāṇāyāma]

That fourth variety of prāṇāyāma goes beyond external and internal objects of interest.

For both stimulus and response there has to be the channeling of energy. Any energy that is evoked, channeled, and expended is of the prāṇa. Savitarka and savicāra are the two occasions of stimulus affecting the mind. When provocation comes from the external world such as in savitarka, the stimulus originates from an object of interest that is outside oneself. The recall of a memory or the maturation of a latent instinct that comes in the form of an ideation is savicāra in which the stimulus comes from within. In either case, a reaction is imminent. So there can be two sources of demand upon the energy of the mind-stuff, which can also be identical with the libidinal energy.

The breath connected with the evoking of energy and its canalization is like a mechanical device. Before it is turned on, there has to be the registry of an interest in the unconscious or preconscious. Without the rousing of an interest, there is no demand for the expending of energy. A person who is internalized—first with āsana and then with prāṇāyāma—is cut off from all external interests. That naturally develops into the abandoning of catering to inner urges. Thus the demand on the body/mind to rush energy to any part of the body is negligible. That means the inner movement of energy comes to a standstill.

Before we come to the sūtra on *dhāraṇā* (holding a focus) Patañjali wants to distinguish it from the inner preparedness for total composure that comes at the end of the discipline of prāṇāyāma as the most gentle acceptance. This Patañjali recognizes as the fourth kind of prāṇāyāma. The triple modalities of sattva, rajas, and tamas, and the three states of consciousness (wakeful, dream, and deep sleep), are transcended by the fourth state, turīya. Similarly, the fourth aspect of prāṇāyāma has no reference to any stimulation whatsoever, either from perceptual objects or subjective transformations of the mind-stuff.

Sūtra II:52

tataḥ kṣīyate prakāśāvaraṇam

tataḥ: then

kṣīyate: is dissolved
prakāśa: [of] light
āvaraṇam: [the] covering, veiling principle

Then the covering of light is dissolved.

Sūtra II:53

dhāraṇāsu ca yogyatā manasaḥ

dhāraṇāsu: for holding a focus, for consistent focus, for retaining or sustaining an idea or principle
ca: and
yogyatā: is fit
manasaḥ: the mind

And the mind is fit for holding a focus.

The five sense organs are five howlers, always bringing provocation by spotlighting objects of interest. An interest can be conditioned with pain or pleasure. When the prāṇāyāma is in the fourth state where the only interest is unbroken ānanda, the sense organs are all withdrawn from annamaya koṣa, vijñānamaya koṣa, and manomaya koṣa; then prāṇa is in perfect unition with ānandamaya.

This is the opposite of someone in suṣupti, deep sleep. In suṣupti, tamas envelops rajas and sattva, and therefore sattva has no chance to mirror individual things. When prāṇāyāma restrains all channels of the manifestation of prāṇa except its resonance with cit, then—instead of tamas shrouding the individuated self—the supreme light of the Self obliviates the impact of physical light, that is, the physical energy that is directly responsible for creating perceptual discrimination.

The mind is usually very busy generating images or

inferring them out of partial illumination and creating a big commotion based on each such provocation. In the transactional wakeful experience and the dream state, a lot of energy is expended in the act of perception and the act of imagination. In the fourth aspect of prāṇāyāma, these two out-going flows of energy are neglected and the concentration is only on the nature of the Self, which is ānanda. This is conducive to the mind going into the steady state of dhāraṇā.

As the three aids for dhāraṇā suggested earlier—maitrī (friendliness), karuṇā (compassion), and muditā (gladness)—are based on the imperiential unity of seeing all in oneself, there is no verbalizing of any mantra or any creative auto-suggestion of the purport of maitrī, karuṇā, and muditā. Dhāraṇā strongly manifests as pure ānanda when all specific modulations are automatically negated. Hence these two sūtras are complementary and are to be taken together as a consequence of the highest achievement of prāṇāyāma.

Sūtra II:54

sva viṣayāsamprayoge citta svarūpānukāra ivendriyāṇām pratyāhāraḥ

sva: their own
viṣaya: objects of interest
asamprayoge: do not come into contact with
citta: of the mind
svarūpa: the essential nature or form
anukāraḥ: follow
iva: and, as it were, as if
indiryāṇām: when the senses
pratyāhāraḥ: [that is] withdrawal from distraction, withdrawal from the instrumentality of the mind and senses

When the senses do not come into contact with their own objects of interest and, as it were, follow the essential nature of the mind, that is withdrawal from distraction, *pratyāhāra*.

Yoga teaches us to have an attitude of disadoption to the natural promptings of the sensory system. Although the external energy coming through the sensory organs has within it rational as well as irrational promptings, the main device to interrelate the physiological part with the psychological is the use of words. Every word links personal consciousness with an item of consciousness. Words are revealers of meaning. Meaning always points towards an affective purpose. Affection comes by relating the tonal aspect of a word and the psychic image it is projecting.

These two parts of the function of a name or noun, when taken together, are called *pratyāya*. *Prati* means "functioning as a counterpoint;" *aya* refers to the immediate presence of an existential factor that is recognized as "this." The stream of consciousness is going from one "thisness" to another "thisness." One item of cognition is distinguished from another item because of the specifying quality towards which the question "What is this?" is always directed. Thus pratyāya is the unique or novel presentation of a new monad of consciousness that is given primacy of attention.

What Patañjali suggests is not allowing any new "this" or pratyāya to initiate any function in consciousness. So he says, "Have pratyāhāra." *Hara* means "withdrawal" or "dismissal." When a number of promptings to accept a memory by relating it to previous images of pain/pleasure interaction are dismissed, the prompting of consciousness becomes less and less. This is what Patañjali is advising the yogi to do in order to move bit by bit to the cherishing of unmodulated consciousness.

One thing to notice in this sūtra is that pratyāhāra is

interposed between the first mention of dhāraṇā and the more serious mention of dhāraṇā with which the third chapter commences. We have to understand the entire mechanism of attraction/repulsion in the organism that has the pure Self (pratyak ātma) at its extreme plus point of verticality and the object of interest at the extreme plus pole of the horizontal. Unless we know how the whole matrix of the psychophysical system is arranged, it is very difficult to make heads or tails of this sūtra.

After the detailed discussion of the disciplines of yama and niyama, we were given the unusual way in which āsana and prāṇāyāma are used by Patañjali. With āsana alone, one comes almost to the brink of samādhi. Then we were told how prāṇāyāma takes a person to the farthest point in discipline by which one can at least vaguely sense pratyak ātma, the reflected image of which is to be transcended to arrive at the blissful state of the Self. Thus both āsana and prāṇāyāma are placed on a very high pedestal before the mention of dhāraṇā. Dhāraṇā comes first as a premonition of how one is going to be stabilized in āsana and be purified by the three screening disciplines by which one arrives at the fourth stage of prāṇāyāma.

Now let us have a schematic look at the arrangement of the several layers ranging from the noumenon to the phenomenon. We begin with the pure bright spirit center, pratyak ātma. The unaffected, unpolluted light of the pratyak ātma is borrowed by the individuated self for its own phenomenal basis. Once the phenomenon is structured, it becomes magical. For its psychic stuff it has what the *Aitareya Upaniṣad* calls *marīci* (light rays creating illusions like the dome of the sky). In this realm the individual carries with it the essence of its psychobiologic life up to that point. The *kāraṇa śarīra* (causal body) contains the essence of all the previous lives and the conditioning achieved in the present life.

The causal body is constituted of four main factors. First, it has the light of the Self as its ground. Then it has the dynamic of the blissful Self to push consciousness to a new level where its inherent value essence and an existential factor can be brought in conjunction with an experience. The third factor is an archetypal impact that can propel unconscious energy into the preconscious field of the subtle. Finally, it has the magical power to make the archetypal thrust change into the establishment of an interest with a certain identity.

A person who is infatuated with love identifies with the archetype of a lover. A person who is soaked with fear identifies herself as a fugitive. An angry man shaking with hatred identifies himself as an enemy. Thus the archetypes we speak of are not identical with Jung's archetypes of Mother, Father, Trickster, and Magician. There is a much richer literature of archetypes to be found in the *Mahabharata* and similar books. In any case, when an archetype dominates, it uses causal energy to become a manipulator of dreams, then the dream percolates into the wakeful, giving it both the status of a daydream and of an action program.

When an interest is evoked there is a two-pronged activity going on. One is the conscious mind choosing to apply external senses, with deliberation, and the other is a value-discernment operating in the unconscious, regulating the out-flowing energy of the desire to actualize. Hence it is necessary to rectify value-norms so that the external world will not have an undue impact on the mind. At the same time, the deliberating mind is to be trained to withdraw the external senses from objects of interest.

It is said that just as the mind—when enlightened about right and wrong values—decides not to feed a stimulus with associated memories, the external senses also, as if they were imitating the mind, withdraw themselves from objects of distraction. We will get a more detailed picture as we examine the presentation of dhāraṇā in the opening sūtra of *Vibhūti Pāda*.

Sūtra II:55

tataḥ paramā vaśyatendriyāṇām

tataḥ: then
parama: the greatest, the highest
vasyatā: mastery
indriyāṇām: over the senses

Then the greatest mastery over the senses.

In the evolution of life, the first sign noticed in a sentient being is its ability to react on the basis of a sensation. A primal form of life such as a protozoa has no eyes or ears; it has no brain. It has the nucleus of a sensory organ that cannot be discerned from its body. It is almost a limbless being and yet it can differentiate between light and darkness and has a tendency to jerk and deflect away from light. What is primary will stay with a being even through many phases of evolution and cannot be dismissed as of no consequence. Further, all the elaborations of physical evolution stem from the primary phase, that is, sensation. Mastery over sensation is, therefore, mastery over all parts of the body/mind complex. Āsana, which is given immediately after yama and niyama, is not the beginning of Yoga. It marks, so to say, the ascent from a base camp toward the peak in a pilgrim's progress. All the preparations for the start are given in yama and niyama.

An analysis of sensation noticeable in the primary forms of life will show the external world of the cosmos confronting the manifestation of a conscient being. No living being is immune to the challenge of its external environment. If a pebble is thrown on the surface of a lake, it is immediately followed by a formation of wavelets at the place where the stone is dropped. Then the ripples recede to farther and farther reaches. Each living being is like a highly sensitive pond or lake of a chemical reservoir. Like the hitting of one billiard ball by another, any chemical molecule colliding with another creates chain reactions. The original Sanskrit word for sensation is *vedana,* which means "being hurt." This world is an arena where everyone hurts everyone else. At the zero point, sensation begins as a hurting of the equilibrium of the constituents that are put together to make individuation. As an organism grows, new devices are developed to meet inevitable offenses that come from all around. Ultimately, when the organism grows to the magnitude of a mature human being, one is like a martyr thrown into the jaws of hungry lions in a Roman arena.

To restore the spark of consciousness that originated in the spirit back to the spirit is the theme of Yoga. With yama and niyama the individual has already undergone a rigorous discipline. In the combat of life the ego—aided by intelligence and memory—equips itself to return again and again to the center of neutrality. The first establishment of stable tranquility is designated as āsana and the retention of that tranquility all through life is vouchsafed by prāṇāyāma.

At this point the aspiring yogi has a choice. You can prefer to remain in this world as a comrade and friend of your fellow beings and dedicate yourself, or you can bring an ultimate termination to your individuation by returning to the plenum of the spirit and becoming one with it. If the second is your choice, you have to go beyond āsana and prāṇāyāma by developing the ideology of transcendence, that is, a new dhāraṇā.

Dhāraṇā is an understanding that retains a certain state

of being. In the maturation of dhāraṇā both the prospective and retrospective sprouting of imagination and memories are abandoned. That is a very drastic step to take for those who retain their love for this world. Hence the triple steps of dhāraṇā, dhyāna, and samādhi are given only in the third chapter, *Vibhūti Pāda.* Although the second chapter terminates with this sūtra, to give a finish to the theme, we need to incorporate a few sūtras of the third chapter. For people preferring to live the normal lifestyle of an individuated person, the instruction in the discipline of Yoga is now complete. It is optional whether to go beyond this or not.

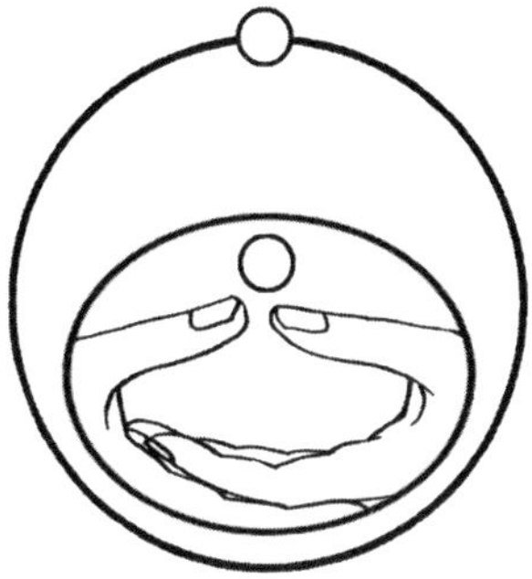

Conclusion

Like the extension of topic from the first chapter into the second, there is a spilling over of the subject that was under discussion in *Sādhana Pāda* to *Vibhūti Pāda*. After the explication of the psychophysical disciplines recommended to an aspirant yogi in the *Sādhana Pāda,* Patañjali continues with the culminating aspects of the eight constituent parts of Yoga: dhāraṇā, dhyāna, and samādhi.

Vibhūti Pāda deals with the emergence of specific qualities from the maturing consciousness of a yogi. The emergence of anything from the unknown to the known is *bhūti.* When such an emergence can be closely observed and its qualities can be described to others, it is a specific emergence, *vibhūti.* Here the emergence (bhūti) is not of an object out of a previously known object. It is a new dimension of the subject being revealed to the subject itself.

All states of awareness manifest from the causal consciousness. What is called the conscious, the preconscious, and the unconscious all pertain to the individuated mind of the embodied being. When mentation is completely obscured by the causal status, it is called the unconscious in Western psychology. Even though it is called the unconscious, it is not the absence of consciousness, but the natural depth in the psyche of a person where all potential urges and drives are lying ready to operate and percolate into states of awareness.

From the depth the potential awareness changes into the preconscious, giving incentive for the mentation to channel energies into the relevant sense organ or organs. This can be equated to a seed lying buried in the moist earth, becoming stirred within, and putting forward a sprout, thus breaking the shell, which until then has been safeguarding the sperm of the seed. Similarly, hidden drives, urges, and motivations enter into the threshold of consciousness and the preconscious creates the semblance of an awareness that can reach out into attentive awareness by becoming fully modulated. Thus every manifestation of vibhūti involves the three states of consciousness: deep sleep, dream, and wakeful awareness.

Sūtra III:1

deśa bandhaś cittasya dhāraṇā

deśaḥ: the focus, locus, place, point
bandhaḥ: holding, binding, confining
cittasya: of the mind, of the faculty of memory and recall
dhāraṇā: [is] holding the focus of the mind, the consistent focusing of consciousness

Holding the focus of the mind is *dhāraṇā.*

In the present sūtra, dhāraṇā—which was casually mentioned even before the discussion of pratyāhāra—is presented and defined. All perceptions are supported by corresponding conceptions, the formulated impressions we have within us of everything with which we are familiar in some manner. They are based on the conviction of the verity of whatever impressions we have of the things we deal with. The yogi also has basic postulates and conceptions. They are his or her dhāraṇā.

A dhāraṇā can be real or unreal. Whether we are able to act efficiently or clumsily depends on the amount of discrepancy between the world "out there" and our conceptualization of things, ideas, and theories. The more definite and valid our concepts are, the greater is our chance of applying our knowledge in any field. In other words, we live on our dhāraṇā.

We can compare ourselves to dewdrops in which the entire world is reflected. The world is very big, extensive on all sides, and contains countless millions of things. However vast and varied is the outside world, no detail of it is left out of its reflection on a dewdrop. We are also like that, reflecting the world on small, specifically qualified areas of the skin that covers our body, such as the two transparent and sensitive spots on the skin that covers the eyes. Although the physical area where visual perception is registered is very restricted, its counterpart is the unrestricted cosmos outside.

All that we see—from the farthest star to the tip of our nose—can be traced to one point of convergence in the body, to some area of the brain where an electrical consolidation changes into a chemical consolidation. It is as if the entire world is held in its position of visibility by this point. It is very enigmatic or paradoxical that the infinitude of space that we all experience has only a single point of view for each person and that point is within oneself.

How big is this area from where we are looking into infinite space crowded with numerous forms? Both for time and space we think in terms of a here and now. Once a philosopher asked this question, "This place where we exist, this moment where we experience, how big is it? Is it only of the size of the head of a pin, or is it as big as a saddle on which the individual can comfortably sit?" The localizing of the point from where awareness centrifugally radiates itself to register its horizon and the point at which all experiences centripetally converge to become an imperiential transcendence defies all our concepts of dimensions. It is not to be understood as a physical point at all. It is the very center of awareness.

We have two options. One is going out from our eyes into the details of every form and color spread out within the ambit of the horizon. The other is leaving the vision of all forms and colors and coming to one center, the central locus of vision. It is this centripetal convergence with which we achieve our āsana and carry out our prāṇāyāma. If consciousness is held in absolute focus at that center without any need to fluctuate, then the yogi can be said to have come to dhāraṇā.

This center is right at the point of conjunction of the binary principles—inertial matter (prakṛti) and the luminous spark of consciousness (puruṣa)—that are the starting point for the Sāṅkhyan epistemology, which forms the basis for the Yoga philosophy. Although puruṣa and the modalities of the elemental world are contradistinctive, nature provides the material basis for spirit to express its luminosity.

Between appearance and reality there is an enigmatic or paradoxical middle ground. We cannot conceive of appearance without an experiencer to whom a certain phenomenon occurs. We can view the ground from a physical point of view or from a metaphysical point of view. When we try to examine the phenomena of the world, we have to make many reductions and abstractions to delimit the field of cognition. Spatially we limit the field to that which we can measure in terms of physical dimensions such as length, breadth, height, and weight. We detach ourselves from the bodies in question and limit ourselves to certain qualities that can be rationally conceived and formulated.

The result is that we come to a notion of measurement that is far different from the original stuff that we were assessing. Instead of arriving at reality we only arrive at approximate measures of quantifiable entities. Hence the physical view of things alienates the subjective agent of knowledge from what is being assessed in terms of objectivity. Then the aloneness arrived at is a fictitious notion generated in the world of fluctuating energies. To hold on to this is even worse than being deluded by appearance. In a world where both the subjective cognition and the objective matter to be cognized are in a state of flux, what good is it to concentrate?

There is another way of making an assessment of reality. That is to seek from within the truth of the perceiving stuff that is derived from the subject. If we go into cerebration about the physical nature of appearances, we will not arrive at any better angle of vision than that of the physicist or physiologist. In the pure idea that is made to bear upon the methodology of practical reasoning, we will stumble on the aesthetic idea of the fixation of psychological apperception. That is a solipsistic way of begging the question. If all sensory elements are removed from pure knowledge, the subject is so alienated from itself that there cannot be the tribasic occurrence of the knower, known, and knowledge. In this enigmatic coming together of the spirit and matter we have to locate the basis of the retention that can be attributed both to the subject as well as the object.

The impossibility of discerning it made philosophers like Nagarjuna speak of nothingness *(śūnyatā)*. Patañjali presents it as kevalam, the unconditioned indescribable unity of all the complexes spoken of as the indistinguishable union of prakṛti and puruṣa. The *Upaniṣads* describe it as that from which both word and mind recoil. Sri Ramakrishna speaks of it as the fate of a salt doll that goes into the ocean to assess its nature. Thus the starting point of *Vibhūti Pāda* is unknowable. This paradox cannot be solved by any rational method. In the fourth verse of his *Ātmopadeśa Śatakam* Narayana Guru gives an integrated vision of the Vedāntic and the Yogic position:

> Knowledge, the objectivization of the value of the known,
> and one's personal knowledge are nothing other than *mahas;*
> merging into that infinite supreme
> knowledge, become that alone.

This is the closest understanding we can gain of dhāraṇā: to return to the very foundation of our self and to remain in it in a state of beatitude. Before we go into this subtle aspect, which is limited to the intuitional insight of a very few yogis, we should make ourselves familiar with the norms of concentration as understood in the day to day conjectures of an ordinary person.

From the simple law of pulsation to the cosmic law of an expanding and contracting universe, all laws have a functional similarity, whether the law belongs to the microcosm or the macrocosm. This law is evident in our experiencing of dhāraṇā. Dhāraṇā is derived from the fact that something is held and retained in a purposive manner by a container such as the outer cover of a single cell or the insulation of a living body. The retention can be within the spatial limit of an outer skin, so far as mass is concerned, or of a time span, the duration from the organism's primal organization to its ultimate disintegration. Spatial retentions and temporal retentions are all dhāraṇās.

There is another way to understand dhāraṇā. From the very start, human beings have a purposive consciousness wanting to direct their lives, consciously as well as unconsciously, to arrive at a steady situation in which inner calm can be maintained for short durations or even longer durations. Thus the dhāraṇā that is seeded in consciousness is a program for the whole life. However, to bring consciousness to its aloneness or to an absolute steady state is totally opposed to nature. Nature is a continuously proliferating phenomenon. This world in Sanskrit is called jagat, a cosmic flux that does not permit any reversibility or any holiday. In this continuous automation of motion, the consciousness implied in it needs to be taught or organized to keep to a certain rhythm in which the motion is annealed by the rhythmic pattern in which the motion occurs.

A confused mind is like the flooding turmoil of a river with many rapids. By plunging into the middle of it, no one can generate any harmony in it. Each individual needs to chart a course whereby the navigation of life can be made a smooth sailing. The challenge is to live through the misery and joy of life in which we are exposed to a million encounters, continuously recognizing the imagery and returning again and again to the essential. Patañjali responds to that challenge by showing us how to become one with the essence. Between a hearty laughter and a heart-rending primal cry, there is a meeting point that cannot be adequately expressed in words. If we do not get to its essence, every hour can be an hour of turbulence, uneasiness, and anguish. Yet an unexplainable order of beauty and goodness enters into the mainstream of life.

From the first formation of cause, a future harmony is to be envisaged. This is where our parents, society, and governments all fail. Effects cannot be corrected without conceiving a cause that will harmoniously elaborate itself, with bright reasoning prevailing between a volatile will and a frenzied action program.

Patañjali forewarns us that only with a continuous and consistent vision of the purpose of life maintained for a long time, with several inner corrections carried out from day to day, sometimes from moment to moment, can the inner and outer match in their beauty, meaning, and goodness. We should begin from the least illumination of consciousness and go through its evolution in life up to this day; then we will have a transparency of vision of ourselves through time and space, and through all the interactions that we have come through.

Even in repairing a machine—a watch, an automobile, or an airplane—hours of concentration are needed to understand all the correlations that go into its smooth functioning. Compared to that, the human system is far more elaborate. But we can direct the little spark of consciousness in us to go on a meaningful reconnoitering. Then the inside design of the entire structure will reveal to us the functional purpose for which every bit of us is put together. Then alone does dhāraṇā become an accomplished reality.

Sūtra III:2

tatra pratyayaikatānatā dhyānam

tatra: in that
pratyaya: consciousness, cognition, content
eka: in unitiveness
tānatā: the continuous flow, unbroken flow
dhyānam: [is] contemplation

In that, the continuous flow of consciousness in unitiveness is *dhyānam.*

The epistemological relationship of the higher or pure Self, the individuated self, and their final union represents the same scheme held by theistic religions like Judaism, Christianity, and Islam and non-theistic religions like Buddhism. Three stages are conceived: an original state, a state of transformation, and a state of final union. In Semitic religions the original state is considered divine, the second state as the egoistic phase of rebellion, fall, and regret, and the third state as the return to the source. In Buddhism it is the mindless state, the conditioned state of habit formation making many cascades of turbulent karma, then coming to the state of *nibbāna*, the cessation of streaming. In Sāṅkhya and Yoga, the original state is the equipoise of the triple modalities of nature in which the association of puruṣa with prakṛti cannot be discerned. The second state is the impact of the three modalities and three states of consciousness affecting the puruṣa through wrong identity, and the final is the release of puruṣa into the state of aloneness through the discipline of *pratiprasava*, regressive remergence.

We do not know, except through speculation, what was before the origin of our bodies and what will be after their cessation. Only the middle region is known. When the mind enters into the wakeful consciousness of a gross, transactional world, awareness flows like a stream (kṣipta). The streaming of consciousness is confronted by five kinds of sensory provocations. It is as if there are five rocky blockages in a river. Then the water of the river cascades with great turbulence and the mind is fragmented into multitudes of names, forms, and relationships of values. The mind is in a state of vikṣipta. However, there is a common element running through the transient sensory experiences. In the final analysis the affectivity can be attributed to ānanda, the blissful state of the Self.

Even in our daily experiences the data brought by the five senses is empirically tied together to give orientation and meaning to every gestalt. Thus the turbulent state of the mind flows into a more unified stuff of consciousness. If the yogi does not aggravate the situation with the associations of ideas and previously formed habits, consciousness once again becomes transparent and void of both memories and imaginations at the point of focus or ekāgrata. A state of pure duration is established. Then the mind has come to its spontaneous culmination in contemplation, dhyāna. One can meditate but one cannot contemplate. Contemplation is not a causal factor; it is a consequence. The ground on which concentered consciousness flows is of pure existence, subsistence, and the basis of all values (sat, cit, and ānanda). Therefore the accompanying consciousness also participates in the triads of sat, cit, and ānanda.

Sūtra III:3

tad evārthamātra nirbhāsam svarūpa śūnyam iva samādhiḥ

tat eva: in that
artha: [when] the object, meaning
mātra: alone, only
nirbhāsam: shines
svarūpa: [of] one's own form
śūnyam: [there is] a void, emptiness
iva: as if
samādhiḥ: [that is] absorption, equipoise in consciousness

In that, when the object alone shines, as if there is a void of one's form, that is *samādhi.*

Dhāraṇā leads to dhyāna and dhyāna to samādhi. For dhāraṇā, the inner organs are to be trained in a certain way, which consists of two withdrawals. One is the withdrawal of the senses from objects of interest. The other is the withdrawal of one's identity from the ego. Until Self-realization comes, the ego is wrongly identified as the Self. So if the mind is withdrawn from objects of interest, its immediate reaction is to concenter around the ego. In the case of perceiving external objects, there are certain empirical limitations that prevent a person from seeing what the sense organ does not permit. But in the case of visualizing one's ego, the stuff of the ego itself is imagination, so egotistic imagination can go wild. Thus it is far safer to perceive an external object than to dwell on one's ego.

The alternative is offered by dhāraṇā: dwelling on one of several spiritually rich imaginations such as an ideal like maitrī, karuṇā, or muditā. Suppose you take fellowship with others for continuous actualization. Significance is not assigned to any particular item to which fellowship is extended. What is important is the unitive vision of seeing all as points of contact in a network of fellowship. In that total abandonment of oneself into the vision of fellowship, the idea "I am" never occurs at all. The intelligence stands unassailed by the data brought in by the senses or by egotistic thrust of wanting to possess anything or anyone. This unflagging steadiness of the intellect between the world outside and the ego inside brings samādhi (absorption).

In the great dictum, *aham brahma asmi* (I am that Absolute), a radical transformation comes to the ego identified with the functional dynamics of the living organism, whereby the finite ego is changed into the infinite, which thereafter cannot have any specific name or form. Knowing oneself to be *brahman* (the Absolute) is *svarūpajñāna*. Instead of brahman, if there is only identification with the ego, one might mistakenly think that is svarūpajñāna. In contemplative life, such identification with the ego is a pitfall to be avoided. Hence the entire stress is on making your dhāraṇā as vivid as possible. That will automatically help you to withdraw yourself from objects of the senses outside and fanciful identifications of the ego within.

Sūtra III:4

trayam ekatra samyamaḥ

trayam: the three (dhāraṇā, dhyāna, samādhi)
ekatra: taken together, as one
samyamaḥ: [are] samyam

The three (dhāraṇā, dhyāna, samādhi) taken together as one are *samyam*.

In Sāṅkhyan philosophy, which provides the epistemology of Yoga, the primeval principle that cannot be discerned with word and mind is the great principle of plenum *(mahātattva)*. In it two binary principles are interlocked as the indispensable basis of the supreme law that is at once being and becoming. The common term for being and becoming as one inseparable reality is sat. This is relevant to the primary atomic structural substantiation of the world ground as well as to the galactic cosmic phenomena. All through it the two opposite principles are canceled out. These two mutually opposing and supporting principles are recognized in modern science as the positive charge and the negative charge. When they cancel out, a neutral stabilization of the polarities arises. It appears to be non-functional. Hence, if a fully accomplished physicist is asked, "What is energy?" the answer we get is that energy equals inertia. If energy is inertia, why is it spoken of as a force? When the inertia is roused to its characteristics of explosion and implosion, it is a force ranging from a pulsating dynamics to a Big Bang.

In the ancient teaching of *Mahānirvāṇa Tantra*, the state of the supreme ground in which opposites reside without contradiction is called *śakta*. The implosive/explosive interaction of forces is characterized as *śakti*. In other religions also we see the same formula clothed in different linguistic or ethnic nomenclature. There is no description given of the Absolute in any religion that does not include the pairing of opposites. The *Upaniṣads* use monomarks like *sat* or *tat*. In the Jewish religion, the Absolute is the unnamable, translated in the Old Testament as *Elohim*. The Jewish people use the word *Adonai*. The closest to it is the Absolute. In the Kabbalistic tradition, the term *Elohim* comes from *ALHIM*, standing for the sum total of the aspects of the Great Mother through whom can be realized the Father or first principle, *Ab*. In Christianity, *Elohim* is equated with the Trinity. Allah, by definition, is "That which is not." Euripides puts it "Who knows but life may after all be death and death be life?"

In the final phase of transforming dhāraṇā into samādhi, there necessarily has to be an initial binary duality to neutralize the ever-explosive and ever-implosive energies into a pacified state of beatitude. Therefore, two realms of inquiry are to be closely looked into. One is *dharma*, which pertains to the world of becoming. The other is *brahma*, the world of being. When these opposites are in a state of equipoise, sameness, there is no separate spirit or matter, Śiva or Śakti, immanence or transcendence. Just as in quantum pulsation, there necessarily has to be a "constant h," a pause has to mark a punctuation in the eternal flow or motion.

In the state of the most acute kind of contemplation, the contemplative may become intoxicated, identifying himself or herself with God, Buddha, Christ, or Allah. This we see in the example of Jesus considering himself, "I am that I am," or Siddartha forgetting his personal identity in a state of enlightenment, or Mansūr Hallāj fearlessly declaring *"an al haq,"* even though he had to pay for his pronouncement with his life. In the highest state of ecstasy, life and death are the same. There is no question of courage in martyrdom. It becomes an implicit abandonment to the compulsion of the situation.

It is from there on that a vibhūti or mystical experience parts company with esoteric fantasies. One gives up oneself absolutely to the all-absorbing spirit that converts both explosion and implosion to a neutral state. Unless we decipher the secret of life and death, the totality of functional energy (śakti), and the total silence of functional energy, (śakta) we do not qualify ourselves to understand the highest vibhūti, which is none other than total aloneness bereft of the alternation between dialectical polarities.

The five factors of citta vṛtti (kṣipta, vikṣipta, mūḍha, nirodha, and ekāgra) provide us with a familiarization with the whole path. Although Yoga aims at samādhi and kaivalya, a peaceful steady state of silence, the very nature of kṣipta is continuous motion. The fact that a yogi is advised to have a posture, āsana, which is stable and comfortable, is like negating all tendencies to move. Turning kṣipta into samādhi may seem like a contradiction of one's own reality. However, when this dialectical interplay is properly understood, kṣipta is understood as the life force. Physiologically, the normal function of a living body is arrived at through the complementarity of two contradictory forces, which are continuously controlling and regulating all flow of energy.

Aloneness does not actually mean an alienation from anything. It is arriving at a neutral zero by finding out the law of contradiction, which, in modern days, is spoken of as finding a homeostasis. In our daily practice we should again and again come to the neutral zero, where the ekāgra, one-pointedness, of consciousness comes without effort. Only through a relaxation of all compulsions acting in the body does one come to the supreme silencing of the plurality of function. That is real ekāgra, and not taxing one's sensory system or lifting oneself out of all awareness. An ideal state, which is close to this establishing of neutral vision, is what happens every day in suṣupti, at least for a few minutes. Thus Patañjali's choice of citta as the starting point, and vṛtti nirodha as the means of the fulfillment of life, is a very ingenious theory.

The general energy source, energy release, and energy organization of an individual's total life is very similar to the process of word dynamics assuming the capability of a spoken word. Before a word is attempted for articulation, its purport and the nature of the effect that it will convey to a listener have to manifest in the threshold of consciousness. Only when an idea gathers into the nucleus of a word formation does a person get an instrument to work with. This facilitates the conjoining of the latent or potential devices in the sensory and motor system into a word dynamic.

When a word is articulated to another, the same word dynamic helps the listener to gather all the relevant potentials to interpret the word that is heard. This is the origin of samyam. Through millennia, ideas have been coming to disciplined seekers in an intuitive way, like a flash of lightning. These ideas have then been passed on from the seers to their disciples, and on to their disciples, for the well-being of the listeners. Samyam is like a creeper originating from a seed, then branching off in different directions and threading through the perceptive consciousness of all those who are ready to be spiritually evolved. The instructions from a teacher to a student, through a hierarchy of such teachers and students, have been transforming humankind through millennia with the suggestive power of samyam.

In samyam, the word of the preceptor is the main instrument by which the disciple's persona is carved out or orchestrated. In every person there are resonating ideas as well as dissonant ideas. When all the possible resonances adhere to each other, a nucleus emerges as a persona. The dhāraṇā that is put into a Yoga aspirant's consideration can be as minimal as a mustard seed. But when it resonates with several potentials, the inner organs of consciousness jointly assume responsibility to choose the right model for evolution and the personality of a yogi comes into being. This is like the organic growth of a sperm in an egg becoming a chick, the chick coming out as either a hen or a cock, which grows into maturity and breeds its species. Similarly, the Yoga student goes from listening to instructions, to meditating on instructions, to finding in all external environments appropriate challenges to be accepted and converted into one's own natural counterparts in the process of evolution.

We have to keep in mind the three prospective states of mind, dhāraṇā, dhyana, and samādhi. At each level you need to have conscious participation to make sure that the word dynamics taken for samyam will yield the correct result. When you are at the dhāraṇā level it has to resonate with your own inner dharma. You should not try to change yourself so much as to alienate yourself from your svadharma. A test of whether your dhāraṇā is congruent with your svadharma is the continuous experience of the growth of an inner joy.

Thus the very first consideration in actualizing dhāraṇā is to look introspectively at the quantitative and qualitative growth of joy within yourself. When that flourishes, dhāraṇā is both the foundation of Yoga and the pointer to the goal of achieving perfection. Then you will be ready to go into dhyāna. Actually, the samyam that is used to clarify the nature of dhāraṇā itself has the contemplative quality of dhyāna. It is in this sense that meditation is a mediation. The oscillating inner light of consciousness has to weave between the objective and subjective banks of the river of consciousness, like a big fish moving in a stream, alternately touching one side and then the other. Dhāraṇā becomes a habitual measuring of the joy that you feel, and the joy that you are able to share with all with whom you resonate outside.

In contemplation (dhyāna), you have to assure that your ego does not transform into a parasite privately feeding upon your spiritual exercise, gloating on the importance of your relativistic position in integrating the external and the internal. To grow into the unlimited dimensions of the Absolute, you should be on the lookout for any relativistic factor becoming negatively conditioned in your transactional consciousness. A yogi par excellence is described as one who transcends the localization of his or her spiritual or moral enterprise.

The locus spoken of here is called *bindu*. If a bindu fixation comes from one's personal preference, that will soon grow into a mark of self-appreciation in its narrowest sense. Such a mark is called *kala*. Laying marks or *kala* is called *kalpana*. When a kalpana is socially oriented and prompted by altruistic ideals, it is called saṅkalpa. In social circles, such socially attainable efforts are very much appreciated. That may encourage a person to be a social reformer or a philanthropist. But those efforts will not bring a person to liberation. There has to be a self-releasing awareness that prevents the identification with socially accepted titles from imposing on the consciousness of an aspiring yogi.

This implies the necessity to normalize and naturalize one's life from moment to moment with continuous discipline. The contemplative has to be super-conscious of the innate factors that prompt consciousness and the outside factors that color consciousness. The yogi has to go beyond the binding of localization and of any special mode into which the personality gets bonded. Then alone does the yogi become a transcendent being *(bindu-nāda-kalātita)*.

Dhyāna ultimately brings the yogi to a unity or unified state of consciousness in which there is no borderline between the conscious, preconscious, or unconscious states of awareness. When one comes to such a maturation, that which is called "innate" and that which is called "environmental" lose their specific meaning. It is as if all dualities wither away. From that time on, samādhi sets into one's nature. Thus with samyam, one can free oneself almost entirely from the compulsions of phenomenal impressions and biological and sensory adhesiveness to the wakeful symbols of external life.

Samādhi is the culmination of the eight steps of discipline enjoined by Patañjali's *Yoga Śāstra:* 1) restraint (yama); 2) commitment to a behavioral pattern (niyama); 3) entering into a psychophysical state or condition that provides a comfortable and stable posture for directing one's attention to observe one's changing inner environment (āsana); 4) slowly and gradually translating the involuntary function of respiration into the conscious deliberation of an observing consciousness (prāṇāyāma); 5) consciously disciplining one's awareness to delimit the choices of interest within a frame of reference from which extraneous interests are dropped and a basic interest is again and again promoted (pratyāhāra); 6) the consequent stabilization of a well scrutinized and emphasized idea of direction (dhāraṇā); 7) expansion of the boundaries of awareness in which the conscious observer and his or her consciousness become mutually merged to give the effect of an unmodulated state of pure consciousness, a state of at-one-ment or beatitude (dhyāna); and 8) the equipoise of the state of aloneness (samādhi).

In all these what is consistently operating in consciousness is a disciplined modulation with a programmed direction. The modulation is directed in ways that raise consciousness from a specific mode of time, space, and physical involvement to the final stage in which awareness returns to its source and merges with the spirit that originally initiates consciousness into an organism for the primary animation of every embodied being.

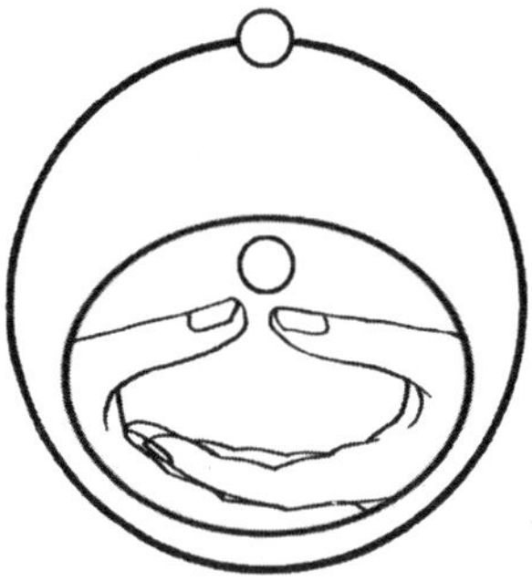

Appendix I:
Letters to an Aspiring Yogi

Letter One

AUM namo bhagavate vāsudevāya AUM
Obeisance to the supreme light that dwells in all hearts.

There is an implied benevolence in this universe. It comes to each living being in a million forms of grace. By cultivating a consciousness of such grace, you can enter into a reciprocal dialogue with the unknown from which the known is being presented from moment to moment. This dialogue is a path to growth, to understanding, and to the meaning of your ultimate fulfillment.

Just as there is an implied benevolence present everywhere, there is also a challenging and obstructing counter force on which you stumble almost every day. This comes in the form of confusion, doubt, lethargy, frustration, a sense of being deceived or rejected, blocks, self-pity, or the need to wait in anxiety and impatience. A gentle, constant, and faithful dialogue with grace has the miraculous power to wear away or dispel the dark forebodings of negativity.

To be happy is the birthright of all beings. The world is so structured that happiness comes from your own core and it can be communicated and shared with whomever you choose. Flowers, birds, pet animals, and children share this joy abundantly without anyone asking for it. With a little insight into human nature, such as in our own nature and that of others, you can widen your horizon to share your love and happiness with many. However, love without self-illumination and happiness without understanding can become deceptive traps. It is important to know.

When you love, you are a lover, and when you are loved you are the beloved. You should know what it is and who it is that you love. Also you should know what is in you that becomes a precious value to attract someone else. In fact, what is in the lover and in the beloved are the reciprocal, complementary halves of the same reality called the Self. Desire to know it in full for your own good and the good of all.

Now the science of union. By union we mean the union of the discerning and judging faculty of the mind with the universal law that governs the physical world and the realms of consciousness. Such a union brings clarity of vision, certitude of meaning, decisiveness of action, and stabilization of emotions. When you progressively achieve it you will experience great inner calm, serenity, a natural warmth of life that is ever glowing in your mind, and an easy flow of compassion from you to all around you.

Turn your attention first to your mind. Watch it. Your mind wanders. It is the same with all. The flow of the mind and the passage of time are not two. This flow began at the time of your inception. It will cease when life in your body is terminated. In India the same name is used for both time and death: *kala*. Time is the sense of movement. You are not always conscious of the movement of your mentation. It is obscure when you are sleeping or inattentive. You do not see light traveling; it becomes evident only when it illuminates an object. Similarly, the awareness of the mind is unaware of itself until it has an object matter or subject matter of awareness. The object matter of awareness comprises things, persons, and the activity and relation between them. The subject matter of awareness comprises I-consciousness, the sense of time, judgment, volition, and feelings.

Awareness becomes intense and vivid when consciousness concenters in a certain space or meaning uninterruptedly for a long time. Your mind has the power to maneuver. You can direct the course of awareness and shift it from one interest to another. In other words, your mind:

– is in constant motion

– is at times obscured

– shifts from one item to another

– can be restricted

– and it concenters

Take some time and watch all these aspects of your mind. This is a good way to befriend it.

Exercise

1. *Watch time passing and also watch the mind flow exactly as time passes. There is no reversibility in the flow of time or the flow of the mind.*

2. *Try to say without break AUM, AUM; try to have no intervening thoughts. You will find that some stray thought will get in. That comes through the loophole of a moment of obscuration in your awareness.*

3. *Think of one subject and then make a radical shift to another subject.*

4. *Think of whom you love most. Each time the mind moves away from your mental vision of the dear one, bring it back to the same*

subject by recalling a loveable incident.

5. *Allow the beauty and serenity of your joyous inside to sit with you as your greatest friend, your truly beloved.*

Letter Two

After reading the previous letter and quietly watching the flowing stream of your consciousness, you must have observed the five characteristics to which I drew your attention:

– the continuous flow *(kṣipta)*

– occasional obscuration or blindfolding of awareness *(mudha)*

– the discontinuity of interest in one subject and the shifting to another subject *(vikṣipta)*

– your maneuvering power to keep distracting interests in abeyance *(nirodha)*

– total absorption in one interest that occupies the mind at a certain time *(ekāgra)*

Of these five states, the last one has qualities that are universally appreciated. It is not a state that you want to avoid, such as pain or boredom. In a state of absorption you hardly think of yourself. There is no vivid separation of the consciousness of "I" from what is other than "I." You transcend the consciousness of time, space, and the multiplicity of the elements that constitute such an experience. It is not a state of agitation or excitement.

After reading this much, keep your body and mind still, close your eyes and try to get a glimpse of such a state. This will give you a vague idea with which to fix a goal toward which you will be slowly advancing. After sitting quietly for about ten minutes, continue reading.

Perhaps now your mind is serene and you have a clarity to understand everything I say and ask you to do. Also you can recall to your mind several brilliant moments of the past when you have enjoyed a penetrating vision and the wholesomeness of a feeling that you thoroughly enjoyed. Such a state can be called one of transparency or truthfulness.

Now imagine you are standing before a mirror. There is a bright light falling on your face and the mirror is spotless. The result is a very clear image or reflection. This is what happens in what we have called the state of transparency. In this analogy there are three component parts: the light, the face or object, and the mirror. Fortunately, there comes the quality of the image also. In a state of transparency, the light is the spirit of pure consciousness that can be called God or Self or *purusa* or truth. The naming of it varies from culture to culture. The face is the interest that is registered at a given time in your cognitive and sensory complex. The mirror is one of the three modalities of nature after which that state is named. The state of which we have been speaking, transparency, is called *sattva* in Sanskrit.

I want to give you a little trouble at this stage to restructure our analogy because there is a difference between an objective apprehension and a subjective phenomenon. Instead of the analogy of looking into the mirror, think of a slide or film that is projected on a screen. Now the light is coming from behind and it is seeping through the object it is meant to illuminate. To a person who is seeing the image, both the source of the light and the placement of the film are not known. The viewer is only allowed to see the net result. Similarly, you have no direct access to the light that is illuminating your sensory cognitive complex. Also you do not have an immediate awareness of the input and the special structuring of an incidence of interest that has taken full possession of your subjective apparatus. Your consciousness is only of the projection that comes from it. As this projection has for its framework both time and space—which are also intrinsic parts of the same projection—the experience can give you a total conviction of the reality of a four-dimensional depth.

Now we pass on to another mystery: the stream of consciousness is always moving. The momentum of its flow is accelerated, slowed, or stilled by a certain dynamic that is somewhat predetermined by the quality of individuation that has gone into the making of each living organism as a separate psychophysical entity. A person's hormonal flow, glandular secretions, irritability of receptors, synaptic resistance, latent urges, and preprogrammed pursuits are only a few of the known participants that go into the general flow of consciousness. These psycho-biological factors can cause various kinds of eddies, whirlpools, turbulences, and tidal waves. This accounts for another state of consciousness: an interference with the mirroring, which is far from the serene, transparent, clear image that you had been seeing. Now you experience translucency instead of transparency, exaggeration instead of truth, agitation instead of serenity, urgency instead of peace. You cannot run away from it because this is a revelation of another aspect of your nature called *rajas*.

The first kind of mirroring and the second kind of mirroring are part of a continuous process of becoming. There is an inevitable third aspect that has the capacity to freeze an experience so that it can become a replica that can be stored away in memory. What is needed here is not light but a prevention of it so that one unit can be segregated from another. This is a state of inertia, which brings opacity instead of transparency. When it prevails for a considerably long time it is experienced as depression, emptiness, meaninglessness, and a negation of your own self. It is known as *tamas* in Sanskrit.

Learn to accept the altering phases of these triple cases of your nature modalities mirroring the phenomenality of your interest. In the next letter I shall show you the combinations and permutations of the three modalities *(guṇas).*

Letter Three

In this letter I want to call your attention to your psychic dynamics. In Sanskrit this is called *cittam.* It has three aspects. They are knowing *(prakhyā),* doing *(pravṛtti),* and existing or stabilizing *(sthiti).* These three aspects work in conjunction. In a general sense they also correspond to the transparency of vision, the urgency to act, and the objectification and stabilization of that aspect to make it an inseparable part of your life forever. If you look into the life that you have lived so far, you can see that every bit of it came to you in a certain way and thereafter you have held it in your mind as the memory of a reality of your past.

The consciousness in an individual is not mere passive knowledge. It is a knowledge that is always giving directions to seek ways and means by which the individuated consciousness can assert its power over objects of interest and can manipulate the tools available to it to perpetuate and precipitate ever so many possibilities, filling the consciousness with a sense of contentment and self-sufficiency.

In other words, what we have termed in the second letter as sattva is taking advantage of the kinetic energy of rajas to be self-assertive. The coming together of these two aspects of nature bristles with many problems. If the prakhyā or sattva (clear knowledge) is not extremely brilliant, the translucency of the kinetic energy of rajas can dampen its clarity and the supremacy of the lead may even become shifted from sattva to rajas. When such a thing happens, the horizon of your personal interest shrinks from being altruistic to the sorrowful state of naiveté, conceit, and self-centeredness. You might have noticed the highly aggressive and conceited nature of very intelligent people who are incorrigibly egoistic. This is the case of sattva losing its game when bracketed with rajas. The only way to keep the superiority of the leadership of sattva is by making it intimately loyal to the pure light of the Absolute.

In the case of a Buddhist, this is done by taking refuge in the Buddha (the Awakened One), the *dharma* (his teachings), and in the *sangha* (the congregates who are following the doctrine). A good Christian preserves the superiority of his sattva by intensely loving Jesus Christ and guiding every step with the word of Jesus. A disciple preserves the supremacy of *sattva* by establishing an irrevocable bipolarity with his or her true Guru and by constantly looking upon his or her teacher as the most reliable living model.

In the science of union, the supreme teacher, God, and the word *AUM* are looked upon as complementary aspects of the same reality. In the example of guru and disciple, there are a few loose ends that are to be tied together. By teacher we should understand the wisdom that comes in the form of words, deeds, and silence from a wise person who has no intention to make use of his or her disciple for any private or vested interest. A true teacher is compassionate without any special reason. A true guru never advertises his or her glory. Such a person is sometimes compared to a burning ember lying buried in ashes. The visible aspect of a teacher is incidental and sometimes can even be misleading.

A guru should necessarily be faultless in erudition and impartial in judgment. Both his introspection and insight will be matchless. His generosity can be easily sensed from his interpersonal relationships. His intelligence is sharp. He shows no preference of an unjust nature. While being peaceful he will also be dignified. His dignity is not that of social pretense but out of the depth of his ideas. He has absolute control over his passions. He is the master of his senses and mind. All his actions are for the good of others. He is the refuge of the poor and the helpless. He articulates to illuminate, preserve, and defend truth. He sets a norm for social behavior. He accomplishes things with great perfection in the minimum amount of time. He neither neglects nor postpones anything that is to be done. These can be some of your guidelines for recognizing your guru. All these characteristics are of no use to you, however, if you cannot find in your heart a golden link with the light with which you want to become united.

Īśvara (which is often translated as God) is not used in this context in the sense of the creator of the world or the moral dispenser of justice on a doomsday. It is to be understood as the supreme and irrefutable law that operates from within as the functional rhythm of everything and everyone. You advance in perfection when this functional law is clearly understood and adhered to. The triple norms of this universal principle are the uniformity of recurrence of truth, the universal harmony and benevolence that spells goodness, and the coherence and cogency that is expressive of universal beauty.

The word *AUM* is a symbolic key. Its importance will become evident to you as you learn to use an overall scheme of correlation to interrelate the actual with the ideal and the potential with the real.

Apart from sattva and rajas there can be two other kinds of pairing. Your sense of urgency and passion for pleasures, which arise from rajas, can find their associate in tamas. Here you become shut off from the wisdom of sattva. This is a very dangerous situation where you lose the discretion to be virtuous. The hard-heartedness and cruelty of people with criminal tendencies come from the unhealthy combination of rajas and tamas. An even worse situation arises when the negativity of tamas becomes the ruling power of the mind. In such a state you feel like you are sinking into a great depth of total opacity or bleakness. You see nothing but hostility around and are filled with a sense of wretchedness and helplessness. The third possible pairing is between sattva and tamas. Such cases are diagnosed by modern psychiatrists as schizophrenia. There are moments of cheerfulness and love and creative ideas, which are immediately followed by a state of frenzy or catatonia.

You are now sufficiently briefed to enter into the discipline of the science of union.

Letter Four

Sit alone in a comfortable posture where you can sit steadily for a long time without being interrupted or distracted by anything or anyone. Think of your truest being as a flame, like the light of a candle. This flame has three essential qualities:

– It radiates and thus causes the idea of space. Space is that which provides for the possibility of existence, because everything exists in space.

– It illuminates. Illumination creates the awareness of specific forms and names that connote meanings or values.

– It goes on continuously revealing as a process and thus creates a time sense.

In this suggestive pondering you should be careful not to put the imagery before your mind and see it as an objective visualization. Instead you should become this light and experience the ever-expanding space originating from the center of your own beingness in all directions, like the ever-expanding dimension of a sphere. To make yourself familiar with the imagery, allow your consciousness to expand to a conceivably large dimension and then bring it back to the center. By repeatedly doing this the pulsation of consciousness will get into a rhythmic pattern of expansion and contraction.

This is not your mind. It is designated as *puruṣa*, the spirit, the Self, soul, truth, and pure consciousness.

Nature abhors a vacuum. Therefore it enters and fills the space generated by your pure consciousness. Consequently, your experience is as if you are placed in space. As your previous memory is already cluttered with forms of objects that occupy space, you see nothing but the familiar space that you call the external world and the ideas that correspond to the objects in it.

Your time sense is also occupied by events and motions of all kinds that are looked upon in terms of before and after. The beautiful experience with which you began is now completely replaced by your mundane or generative self. The center of pure consciousness has given away its place to your ego. Consciousness has become fragments of awareness, one piled over the other. The discerning power of your consciousness has changed into an efficient tool for reasoning.

The relation between your self-luminous being and illuminated being is very much like that of the unmoved mover and the moving agent of which Aristotle spoke. This analogy is taken from the context of love. The beloved does not do anything. She (or he) only provides for an opportunity to be loved by her (or his) sheer presence. That very presence becomes dynamic. Like a great power of attraction it haunts the lover. The lover has no power to resist the tremendous attraction that is coming to him (or her). The lover becomes filled with thoughts and all kinds of imaginations, which are sometimes blissful, sometimes frightful, sometimes invigorating, sometimes confusing, and sometimes frustrating, depending on the quality of the spell that is experienced. From time to time the lover restlessly engages in all kinds of activities with the full conviction that what he or she is doing is most appropriate and is in reciprocation.

This strange thing happens to everyone, to some in a

beautiful way, and to others in a very weird and drastic way. The true science of union is to find ways by which the duality between the usual beloved and the strangely behaving lover can be effaced so that the duality will cease and the pure aloneness of the Absolute will shine forth. This does not happen by any partial method. This is a search that demands total attention and total commitment.

First of all, make yourself familiar with the lower forms of your mind. The largest area of your mind is your forgetful mind. In Western psychology this is called the unconscious. The unconscious is not always passive. It has a functional purposiveness in veiling or even locking up memories, urges, potentials, talents, and so on. We will have occasion to make a deep probe into this aspect, but for the time being simply make a note of the existence of such a big chunk of consciousness lying below the threshold of awareness.

Very close to your forgetful mind is your fretful mind. This part of you is like a baby wanting to cling to the mother's apron. It is often surrounded by a sense of strangeness and is bewildered by its loneliness. This is one of the tendermost parts of the psyche, which becomes easily annoyed, bruised, and broken. When it is adversely affected it generates inhibitions and withdrawal.

Then you have your obsessive mind. Like Janus, this has two faces. One is attuned to the expectation of pleasure and the other to a will to destroy. This has a close resemblance to the dual principles of *Eros* and *Thanatos* of which Freud spoke.

Above that you have the best and most loveable part of your mind, which is your searching mind. This is your handle with which to steer clear of all anomalies so as to find your way into your deepest truth.

Finally you have your wandering mind, which is like the materials used for packing fragile things. It fills in all the gaps with any garbage or fantasy that you pick up from the big marketplace of irrational transactions.

There are seers who are like the Sun, for whom there is total transparency of time and space and its contents. You cannot attribute any qualities to them. There are also seers who are like bees maddened by the sweetness of the honey they sip, remaining in the lotus petals, oblivious to the fact that the petals sometimes close in and sometimes open up. There are seers who are like a mass of consciousness with no trace of ego, totally alienated from both the objective and the subjective experiences of the mind.

The present science of union is given as an instruction to one who aspires to become a fully developed contemplative while leading a normal and natural life on Earth, both as a person and as a seer.

Letter Five

You are a person with legs to walk, hands to work, senses to perceive, a mouth to speak, a mind to feel, and reason or intellect to judge. You also experience a core of your being that becomes bright with love and happiness, heavy with sadness and the need to be loved, and a general uncertainty that envelops your awareness. You are placed in a world of facts, figures, and fictions, which are either ludicrous or appalling. Part of daily life is the interaction with other people who agree or disagree with you. It is a natural instinct of each of us to evolve into a better being. The highly evolved state is considered saintly by Christians, faithful by Muslims, awakened by Buddhists, emancipated by Vedāntins, and well-attuned or united by yogis. Although there are many models of perfection, the central theme is the same.

You cannot become anything other than what you are. If there is imperfection in you, it has to be either structural or functional. It goes without saying that a structural defect can cause a functional defect. This is not an occasion for going into a thoroughgoing examination of the structural details of your total being or to mark its malfunctioning. To get a general idea of the normalcy of your functioning, you can match your state with a few normative notions.

One norm of the well-attuned is the capacity for regaining tranquility and perfect balance after every incident of disturbance. Life is a flux and therefore there will be a repeated knocking around and tossing caused by the randomness of several things pulled or pushed by circumstances. In your personal case, objects of interest make impact on your senses. Your sense of duty dictates that you do the chores of life and also meet several contingent states. You are exposed to heat and cold and to pain and pleasure. The people with whom you associate are not always thoughtful or cooperative. This can cause strains. Thus, innumerable are the occasions for you to lose the poise of your body and mind. Each gives you an opportunity to apply the norms of sameness in your life. One test is how easily you can regain your tranquility when assailed by pairs of opposites.

We are all familiar with the main theme of learning that is considered most important by the behaviorists. What I mean is the method of trial and error, and the conditioning that is effected positively by an award of pleasure or negatively by an infliction of pain. One who is vigilant about an oncoming shock can either avoid it or meet it squarely with a sense of preparedness. This is the second test: how alert you are not to lose your composure.

The third test is a positive norm. You have many talents and many capabilities that are not fully tapped or exploited. The ultimate attunement is to establish a maximum coordination between your knowledge and your volition, so that your total unfoldment can be effected with perfect poise and efficiency.

In the light of these norms you can set the tasks that are to be done. Like a soiled machine that is blocked with dirt or with foreign matter that has gone into it, you are not always yourself. Parasites in your body bring disease. These are easily diagnosed and corrected with ease or difficulty, but there are psychogenic parasites and dirt which handicap the functioning of your mind. These come to you in the form of false beliefs, wrong programming, and false identities. Then there are congenital defects that are a limitation; there is not always a remedy for them. In this case, you have to accept such limitations.

The fourth norm is the need for nourishment and learning. This can be attended to with the aid of a master who knows how to coach you. The fifth and last test is the most important. It is to know the very source from which your life flows and your intelligence radiates. In fact, you are that. Everything else is an aggregate of transforming incidents that are happening in the mere presence of this numinous center. It is not necessary to name it. Know it to be your truth. The final attunement is with this truth, as in "I am That." Your journey is to arrive at that adorable, precious truth that makes everything truthful, good, and beautiful.

Letter Six

You have a center and a periphery. Instead of visualizing that aspect as a dot in a circle, think of yourself as a centralized consciousness functioning at the core of a sphere. This sphere of consciousness is not static. It is dynamic in so many ways. You have radiation; there is a continuous outflow of energy that assumes different characteristics at different levels. To a large extent this energy circulates and returns to the core like the functioning of a fountain in which the same water is used again and again for a continuous flow. In this general process the magnitude of the energy, the pacing of the quantums of its release, and the stamina that is available at a given point of time of day or night are all limited and regularized by the constitution of each person.

Make a pause. Read the preceding paragraph again and become familiar with that aspect of your self. After visualizing it, then proceed.

The above-mentioned consciousness is basically structureless and therefore of no specific function. At the same time, it evolves a structure to produce a function and that in turn causes the formulation of a continuing structure to effect ever-new functions to facilitate both needs and the appeasement of those needs. To make this clear let us take an example. The first state can be compared to the state of inertia in which the mind of an unborn baby remains functionless. As soon as the baby leaves the mother's body the biologic need to breathe causes the impulse to scream. This releases the motor energy that can affect various muscles of the body and, as a result, the baby screams. Although the rudiments of the structure were there, those physiological parts assumed their structural role only when a demand was placed on them to function in a certain way. In this manner, a person evolves both physical and mental coordinations of several structures, each having a relevant function.

An adult has gone very far from the primal scream of the child to the seeking and fulfilling of thousands of needs. These needs range from basic requirements such as the intake of food and the release of the bowels to subtle levels of gratification such as indulgence of fantasy. This being the case, the radiating, spiraling, and circulating primeval energy of life and consciousness has now become a network of functions, of which some are stagnated, some are colored with various kinds of memories, and some have assumed tensions of varying magnitude. In this biological and psychological growth of the individual, the consciousness that was once meant to be the core of the person has now surfaced. Literally, it has become ex-centric. In this way, you have become somewhat an alien to yourself, caught between the strange world within you and the strange world outside of you. Outside there are other persons like you who are also ex-centered and alienated from the "Kingdom of God" within.

Although you are a reservoir of enormous energy and capabilities, this alienation humiliates you every time you try to make a reentry into your own center. The surface consciousness of your ego-identity finds some consolation in the company of similarly structured persons whose egos are also bewildered in the same manner. When your surface ego establishes its harmonious company with a large number of people such as those who belong to a common religious creed, political ideology, or aesthetic appreciation, the feeling of alienation is substituted with a sense of wholeness. To many people this is very assuring, and they feel strong and excited as long as they can keep their relationship harmonious with fellow members of their creed. This is hard because every now and then you will bump into the personal need of some individual of the creed who is out of tune with the rest. This can cause disruption in your relationship with the entire creed.

Another way to find your feet again is to go deeper and deeper into your own structured whole by patiently programming your own restructuring and re-functioning. Your mind, however complicated it is, has one great virtue: it always cooperates to find a solution for a problem, a supply for a demand, a gratification for a desire, and an escape from a snare. Instead of allowing your life to drift and aimlessly float, you should feed it with a noble purpose. Every day, every hour, every moment, commit yourself to attend to what you consider the most beautiful thing to achieve at that moment. It may not immediately match with the vision of a Buddha or a

Jesus, a Dante or a Michelangelo, but you have plenty of time and there are many moments to live, so there is no need to be dispirited.

Right away start your business of glorifying the approaching moment and infusing it with all the beauty of yourself so that it will become a permanent treasure of your past and the continuous joy of all around you. This may make you somewhat narcissistic but it is not unhealthy. The best model I can recommend to you is of a cheerful and confident baby or child who is continuously enthralling herself and all around her with her cheerful creativity, which in substance is not creating anything except her beaming, sunny nature. Wish you good luck.

Letter Seven

One of the greatest paradoxes that confronts us at every moment is the forgetfulness of the whole with the recall of the part. Partial memory is a snare that can only produce the dual states of pain and pleasure. This seeming recognition of any particular experience is to be understood as a veil woven out of the threads of time and space.

Dynamics implies the dual forces of inertia and kinetics. These are complementary and reciprocal both in structure and function. If you put on a piece of paper ten rows of dots lengthwise and breadthwise to form a square, this will give you a pattern that has the magical power of altering your vision. You can see in it several squares made up of vertically and horizontally arranged dots, or you can see diagonal patterns. Any one way of looking at it automatically blinds you from seeing the other way. Here the object presented does not change and the optical instrument of vision is the same. Now you may ask, "What causes the alteration from the vertical/horizontal to the diagonal?"

You can also see the mystery of a veiling principle that is even more transparent than a transparency. Here the quality of observation is very subtle. No one can tell you how to discern for yourself the obscuring principle of inertia and the projective principle of kinetics. But on the strength of the above analogy, by repeatedly witnessing the veiling and projecting complementarity operating in a given situation, you can enter into deeper and deeper realms, which are always there as a substratum of all forms of consciousness.

This is a meditation in which the meditator does not meddle with the seemingly ludicrous game that is going on as a surface play of the mind. In this peaceful watching, inferential thinking and all argumentative reasoning can be laid to rest for a while. There is no need to worry about how you can sink into the depth of your being without making positive attempts to attain your release. Just as individual units of the projective universe have their constituents (dharma), which necessarily unfold their characteristic functions, the universal substratum also has its own intrinsic nature. It is not projective. Its function is analogically equivalent to the reemergence of the individual existence, which loses its identity in universal existence.

Modulated consciousness becomes unmodulated. The quest for happiness becomes irrelevant to one who has crossed over the dual states of pain and pleasure. The yogis refer to this with poetic imagery such as the fragrance in the wind that attracts bees to flowers and the cloud of virtues that conducts a yogi's mind to its primeval state of aloneness. This is a meditation in which the aspirant is not required to do anything other than witnessing and being intensively vigilant.

Letter Eight

If you want to meditate, that is programming. That

means you want to shift your attention from one theme to another. What you belong to now is the world of objects. You contrast yourself with that as the subject. Before moving away from the world of objects, try to answer this question: "What is an object?" A spontaneous answer is: "That which is specific, something with name and form that confronts the subject. It is a configuration in space."

Let us examine this configuration further. A figure is a study in light and shade. The contrast between light and shade has a backdrop. It can be a sky, a wall, a canvas, a paper, an abstraction, even time and space. In such a situation, the configuration is not of a single item but of juxtaposing and overlapping figures. When one artist sketches and paints an object, another may sketch intervening spaces, in which case space becomes the object and the thing the backdrop. That means we have not grasped the actual field within which the configuration of the object happens. The dichotomy in consciousness is between what is known and what is not known. The human mind is not omniscient. Its physical span of attention is limited to the capacity of our senses and the temporal span of our interest aroused from time to time. Thus what is happening is the evocation of an interest, which is identical with the configuration of an object. This happens against the backdrop of a vast range of what is unknown and what we are not conscious of.

"Ignorance is bliss" is not only an old proverb; it is also a fully operational natural device. Every day, we are relieved of the vast load of our cognizance by the reduction of consciousness to a minimal level in our deep sleep. Nothing is more peaceful than that state. The troubled consciousness of the wakeful or dream experience is like a ripple on the silent ocean of the undisturbed peace of time-transcending ignorance. That state can be designated as the passive. Confrontation with an object is like being aroused from the peace of our psyche's inconscient slumber.

It is interesting to note from where the arousal is generated. One popular account is the kicking off of nervous impulses attributed to physical stimuli. Those who hold this view consider pain and pleasure and the conscious phenomena of sensory appreciation as an epiphenomenon, a by-product of our cerebral function. Certain idealists hold the opposite view of a pre-conditioned psyche projecting a certain gestaltation, which results in the objectification at a physical level. In each case, these alternative theories are leaning on one or two fundamentals that are essentially required to experience an object. Actually, there is no need to take sides. However much one desires an object, it is not found where it is not. No matter how much one may want an apple, if none is there, it cannot be had; while even a cartload of apples will not impress its existence on a mind that is fully occupied with another intensive gestaltation. Thus, physical existence and psychic appreciation are complementary functions that formulate a unitary experience of a thing endowed with qualities.

Although the arousal from the peaceful state of passiveness has in it an element of disturbance, there is a certain evocative element in the psyche that goes into the texture of the disturbance and fashions out of it a plethora of moods and tastes by which everything, from the harsh to the sublime, becomes systematized in the value appreciation of an object. The arousal of interest that is imperative in the objectivization of consciousness has sensory data on the one hand and the creative urge of individuation on the other. These two come together like the sculptor and the marble. The interaction between the medium and the creator is instantaneous. If the sense data is not there, the creative agent goes into dysfunction. You know this instinctively. That is why you assume an attitude of passivity whenever you want to contemplate; consequently you withdraw your senses from all objects.

Now you are shifting your interest from the object to the subject. Paying attention to an object is experienced in the form of an out-going flow of mental energy, which makes an eddy around the nucleus of that object of interest. The shift of interest to the idea of the personal "I" is also experienced as the concentration of mental energy to an area that most people experience in and around their heart. This may be because of the raising of the heartbeat in relation to intensive affectivity. Although for the convenience of distinguishing external objects from this internal experience we use the terms "object" and "subject" respectively, paying attention to the ego or personal self is as much an objectivization as that provoked by objects.

Now let us put one more question: "What is consciousness?" In all the above descriptions, whether of the subject or the object, we have taken for granted the existence of some stuff that has the quality of awareness and also has within it an implied agency that wills it to act in one way or the other. When we look at our volition in the process of willing, it is no longer a simple act. Its origin is obscure. Its function is dynamic. There is an intense personification and identification, which stands out as "I am," "I want," and so on, from which state the consciousness is distinct. Also, there is a movement of the volitional consciousness from an obscure origin to an unknown goal. In that movement the entire passage becomes illuminated with the light of volitional consciousness. As it passes a series of sequential ideas, an overall clarity increases until the whole consciousness becomes established in certitude. The certitude again has in it both a judgment and a resolve.

Now the question is: "Who or what is that which judges? Who or what is that which resolves? Who was inquisitive to know?" When we look for an answer we cannot but postulate the nucleus of a person. This nucleus is what is recognized as the puruṣa, the self-luminous principle in all. The volitional principle, the judging faculty, the affective ego, and the matrix of consciousness, subject to varying transmutations that reflect images of sense data, are all emanations of this central nucleus of the nucleic person. These emanations are recognized as intellect. The relationship between the nucleic person, puruṣa, and its intellect is analogous to the Sun and its radiation. Although the beams of the Sun are qualitatively the same as the Sun itself, they are seen only as the objects they illuminate. Similarly, the intellect becomes identified with what it illuminates such as a question, a location, a proposition, a conjunction, an exclamation, a predication, and a series of affectivity ranging from discontentment to satisfaction. Thus, intellect is the most active link between the nucleic person and the objective world.

In the present meditation we have one final question: "What will happen if this emanation is withdrawn or disconnected from both the sensory function and memory feedback?" What we suggest now is as hard and almost as impossible as the stopping of respiration or the inhibiting of the heartbeat. At this stage we can only hypothetically presume that state. Until we arrive at it, we can hypothetically visualize this final state of restraint as what Patañjali calls the cessation of all modulations that are being engendered from the repository of the past registration of memories.

Letter Nine

Watching your own consciousness is a game of staying with your beingness and going along with the process of becoming. Being is not a state that is either known or recognized. Experiencing knowledge is none other than experiencing the act of discrimination and affirming that which is discriminated. This is a continuous operation. However keen we are in our observation, the act of discrimination does not remain for one moment without becoming fully identified with the ongoing impact of an affective dynamics. If you listen to music with intermittent pauses, every change of note and the variation in pitches and frequencies are faithfully responded to with the identification of consciousness without leaving the slightest trace of a dichotomy between the identifying consciousness and the identified impact.

By constant training and a cultivated discipline of dispassion, the presence of a witnessing consciousness of the process of mental modulation will become more and more felt. Even this witnessing consciousness needs the help of discrimination to distinguish this role of witnessing the modulations of the mainstream of consciousness. If you can stay on with the witnessing consciousness you can further notice its neutral quality. It can be present with a painful experience, and yet that part of consciousness remains detached from the pain that is affecting the organism or causing agitating modulations in your immediate experience. Thus there is a dual registering of your experience, one of pain-pleasure affectivity and the other of neutral witnessing of your being pleased or pained.

An overall tendency of one who watches the subjective modulation of consciousness is to minimize the physical origin of the objective impact and become preoccupied entirely with the changing modes and the very many associations that are hooked on to the sequential development of an ongoing program. Here there is participation between two systems that seem to interpenetrate each other so that the quality of the objective world can be interpreted in terms of the language of consciousness. At the same time the fact remains that the consciousness and the thing are two exclusive entities that do not physically or chemically enter into each other. The coexistence of the two as two separate realities eludes our comprehension because we are not familiar with the concept of juxtaposition, which is neither of spatially understood objects nor temporally simultaneous events.

In this higher form of meditation the long and sustained association we have with the spatio-temporal and nominal-formal ways of discerning things comes as a major block that prevents us from seeing the exact mechanism or method by which the pure consciousness in us (Being) remains detached and also allows a full sway of being drenched with the entire process of becoming.

For all practical purposes it is as if our Being is a myth and we are always in the continuous movement of a figure-of-eight, which is being generated by the ceaseless movement of a single luminous spark. But if you continuously involve yourself in the careful scrutiny of changing consciousness, you will soon come to appreciate the feedback of a memory, which can give you the idea of a past that is regenerated again and again as the immediate present and the only experience that you ever have. The intuitive understanding of the myth of the past can cause a dent in the opaque screen of becoming through which you can visualize your Being.

As we have described in Letter Eight, here also there is an alternation in the function of consciousness. Usually you stay with the uninterrupted process of becoming. Witnessing the witness and witnessing the witnessing witness lowers the intensity of the affective dynamics and you come to stay with the uneventful "periods" of timelessness. This is the first glimpse that you can have of your true Being that is liberated for a split second, as it were, from the programmer of your consciousness.

Letter Ten

Your promptings are to know and to do. Your performances are knowing and doing. Your partial dysfunctions are doubting and hesitating. Your failures are your incapacity to know and your incapacity to do. The polemics between your knowing and doing results in your suppression. Where do the promptings to know come from? The promptings to know presuppose familiarity with a certain field of promise. The promise is of an information that can illuminate a potential happiness or a probable threat. Or it can be the desire to return to an unfulfilled experience of pain or pleasure.

In the ceaseless flow of the life urge, the disposition to know is a punctuation that is identified with the modulating consciousness. The incentive to modulate arises from the provocation of a cause. The provocation can be one of maturation, reaction to the incidence of a stimulus, cyclic, or a functional experience to readjust the system. Every modulation generates or revises a fresh creative incentive, which has then to remain latent as a potential until its turn comes to be actualized through another modulation. The prompting to do is thus a binary function coupled with the prompting to know.

Nothing is more spontaneous than knowing. Knowing is more known by the act of predication than by what causes the act of predication. The Sun shines, the wind blows, it is pleasantly cool—these are predications. Each predication circumlimits a field that is known. The paradox in knowledge is that the act of knowing is presumed from the resultant knowledge. Thus, in a sense, the anterior is recognized only after the posterior. Being effortless, the act of knowing has no action in it except for a metaphorical assertion of an agency and action given to it for semantic purposes. Despite the sequential quality of the series of illuminations, knowing is essentially like being. In fact, it is the revelation of the self-luminosity of being. For this reason, a knowledge modulation is called akliṣṭa (effortless). The source of consciousness in such an instance is the rationale: the puruṣa or person. The carrier of consciousness is the discerning intelligence, buddhi.

The prompting to do comes from the incidental illumination of a field that belongs to any one of the several potentials that are mature to unfold. Or it can influence the person with its propensities because of a cyclic maturation and a biologic need to actualize the potential. Basic needs such as hunger, thirst, and sexual urges originate from the procreative matrix and effect their relationship with the rationale, whereas matters of simple illumination originate solely from the rationale. Doing is more than a simple reflex. It implies various kinds of coordinations and alignments and the direction of energies that excite the system to different degrees of agitation that are recognized as pain or pleasure. After the incidence of an action you are no longer the same person. Something has perished, something has been created; something has been de-structured, something has been structured.

The re-creation of the system thus effected is called samskāra. Knowledge that prevails in the field of action instantaneously recognizes the pain/pleasure value complex of an experience. Like the pairing of the chromosomes of the sperm and the ovum, the model prompted by action and the illumination of the model that comes from the discerning intellect are paired and become a complex whole to be posited again into the memory threshold, which afterward can either be recalled as a memory or can spontaneously present itself as a fresh actualization of a samskāra.

The partial dysfunction of the discerning intellect that results in doubt is caused by the non-apprehension of the distinguishing mark, *lakṣana*. The fragmentation of the field can be caused by external as well as internal reasons. Although knowing is instantaneous, scanning or observation is temporal. When there is not enough time to perceive, the field can become fragmentary. Also there is the likelihood of missing the main characteristics. Internal fragmentation comes from the failure to stimulate a potential samskāra that can effectively connect with the incident of external provocation. Serious doubts such as age-old philosophical problems are not to be confused with the doubt that we refer to here. Serialization of structured reasoning is an entirely different subject. What we are trying to tackle now is the binary function of re-structuring of memory-filled packages of potential value urges called samskāras and the instantaneous modulation called vṛtti.

Samskāras are also called action incentives. Just as doubt inhibits the full illumination of knowing, hesitation inhibits actualization. Hesitation primarily shows the meagerness of the energy that is released to surface as an incentive. The quantum of pleasure or pain with which the potential is related can be one deciding factor for weak-mindedness or feeble-heartedness to do a certain action. Action is not a localized function except when it is a body reflex or a purely autonomous bodily function. Most action cannot be linearly interpreted. The prompting from within should have one or many counterpoints in the external world to elicit from the organism the full stamina of an action thrust. Thus, on the whole, the stream of consciousness is not like the free flow of water, but it is like the circular motion of a chain of functions in which the samskāra produces the modulation and in turn, the modulation recreates the samskāra.

The discerning intellect that links the rationale and the procreative has the ability to oppose the program of the triple modalities of nature when it magnifies the powers of sattva to the pure state of knowledge and happiness that eternally belongs to the rationale. But when the alignment between the discerning intellect and the rationale is feeble, the intellect becomes confused, partly because of the highly potent energy that is being discharged from a surfacing samskāra. Consequently we live with the ambivalence of identifying with the rationale at one time and then shifting the identity to the procreative at another. Yoga is attained only by extricating the discerning intelligence from the continuous drama of recurring modulations and their incentives.

Letter Eleven

Open your eyes and consider your world of immediate perception. You see several objects, each with a distinctive shape, color, size, and name. They are all placed in space. Their topological placement in the field of vision groups these objects into a general gestalt. The first impression is that this is a case of immediate perception. Yet seeing is not merely the photographic registry of the one-to-one correspondence between objects that are outside and the images that are perceived; there are also cases of recognition and gestaltation.

Recognition is an act of orientation, which is achieved by comparing and contrasting an object with a class to which it generally belongs. For instance, the room where I am sitting contains objects like icons, painted vases, lamps, and books. An icon or a book is not an object of pure perception. The book could be the *Gita* or the *Upaniṣads* or the *Qur'an.* The icon could be Nataraja, Narayana Guru, the Buddha, Sarasvati, or Kuan Yin. Each individual book or icon suggests a different set of religious, mystical, psychic, and aesthetic contexts. In other words there are preexisting strings of memory that are evoked by every single act of perception. In the act of perception two images come from opposite sides and are synchronized into a unified imagery.

For instance, when I look at the black icon, its geometrical form and color come from the external object to my visual organ. My preconceived notion of the Buddha, the history behind his name, his biographical impressions, and his spiritual relevancy all come from my memory threshold and coalesce with whatever impulse has stimulated the vision of the icon. Thus there is no simple perception of an individuated object without the impression becoming a confection of both the specific and the generic.

The finality of every perception comes when it is appropriately named. When a perception is named or labeled, that particular image gains the status of a currency in the circulatory system of world communication. Thus conceptualization and nominalization are the general contribution that the individual makes. This contribution enriches and enhances the semantic world to which the individual mind organically belongs. Because of the mind's constant recourse to the words of the language with which it thinks, the individual cannot stand in alienation from the society in which every person is mutually linked through the web of language.

An organized society has its set of patterns of ethical norms and standards to distinguish right from wrong, truth from falsehood, good from evil and beauty from ugliness. Just as a single perception becomes instantly transformed into a confection with your collective memory, your judgment is affected by the nature of your personal allegiance to the society in which you are placed. Because of the mobility of people in a modern society, your grass root adherence is constantly challenged by the systems that belong to different societies in which you are temporarily placed. The heterogeneity of norms is thus constantly creating chaos; as an individual in a modern society, you find it hard to stabilize your footing on a reliable ground even when you can have an objective scrutiny of the environment in which you are placed.

We have now cited two instances of alchemic functions to which every person is exposed. One is the alchemy that happens to every act of direct perception. The other is the social alchemy in which an individual is placed. In the first instance it is hard to discern the bare objective facts of perception; in the second instance it is equally difficult to discern how much truly belongs to an individual.

Perception is to be contrasted with fanciful imagination or even an overpowering hallucination. In such a case of hysteria or epilepsy the objective element can sometimes be traced to a functional disorder of the psychophysical organism but the general content of the entire experience is born out of pre-established memory. The compulsions that are implied in such cases are beyond the power of the individual either to recognize or restrain. But these instances are not so personal or unique as they can be mistaken to be. They conform to general patterns so that a psychoanalyst can see the transformation of archetypal symbols implied in such subjective fancies. Thus even in pathological cases there is a coming together of the personal and the collective.

The exact polemic of perception is an overpowering sleep that annuls all traces of awareness. It is as if the person is melting into nothingness. In all these cases of individual experiences, we can see a power that seems to interfere with every act of a person's consciousness so that the consciousness is colored, transformed, or even obscured. The only voluntary function seems to be that of shifting one's gaze from one object to another or intensifying one's effort in applying certain norms to making judgments in a single sphere of consciousness in the wakeful state. Yoga is the difficult task of disciplining this individuated aspect of the conscious self so as to give it a transparency to the overwhelmingly large area of altering consciousness in which an unconscious and collective compulsion is perennially active. This is the enormity of the problem before the aspirant.

Letter Twelve

We cognize and recognize. Member parts have given data to a meaningful ensemble, and we again re-member the dissipated parts to relive that experience. When we are passive we fantasize. When we are active we actualize. Our main goal orientation is to realize. In all these three pursuits, re-envisioning a previous experience is necessary. The re-envisioning implies mimicking or dramatizing. This is nature's device to etch the impression as deep as possible and to provide it with a dynamic that can instantly put into operation any number of cyclic repetitions. This process is called memory and recall.

The Sanskrit terms that correspond to memory and recall are *citta* and *anusmaraṇa*. The word *citta* is derived from *cit*. To understand the full connotation of citta we should know the principle of horizontalization that is present in all living beings when the element of pure consciousness in them is subjected to transformation. Cit or pure consciousness corresponds to *logos*, or a primeval intelligence, which can be causally attributed to all basic structures and functions. If we begin with an analysis of the prime components of matter, such as the very many known and unknown subatomic particles, it is clear that their behavior is governed by consistent laws, which give them predictable characteristics when they collectively function. This can be taken as one extreme point where the pure principle of *logos*, or primeval intelligence, becomes a potentate to evolve. At that point cit is transformed into caitanya.

An end product of the same caitanya can be seen in the power of the philosopher's or poet's mind to generate abstractions of universal validity. In that vast field of animation the unconscious sphere is called *cetana* and the conscious sphere, caitanya. Every monad of this vast aggregate of conscious/unconscious animation that goes on is a self-activating, miniature theatre in which the essence of a previous impression is spontaneously redramatized because of a direct or indirect relevancy caused by the sequential eventualities to which a living organism is continuously exposed. These monads are called cittam. Patañjali speaks of *citta vṛtti nirodhaḥ* as Yoga. *Vṛtti* means "modulation or operation." What operates is the monad of memory and its modulation is the reenactment of a previous pain/pleasure situation.

Another Sanskrit word that will throw more light on the functional efficiency of recall is *anusmaraṇa. Smaraṇa* is both etymologically and operationally connected with the word *smara,* eros. At the very inception of life, eros prevails as the main incentive for the union of the male and female. Life commences from the interlocking of the genitals and the positing of the male sperm in the female ovum. Thus the generative or creative dynamic is essentially erotic. Erotics is a pain/pleasure principle that can cause both ecstatic spells and the darkest forms of depression. It has in it both the pleasure principle and the death instinct. The entire life process is one of chasing pleasure and avoiding pain. By a repetitive process, several of our pains can be transformed into cultivated pleasures. The twofold functions of acceptance and avoidance are done with the exercising of the recall of previous memories and the use of them as the nuclei for molding a new experience with the given data of sensory stimuli and the emotional impact that arises out of a total reaction of the whole person in each instance. In his *Ātmopadeśa Śatakam* Narayana Guru compares a living organism to a chariot of the libido, yoked to the five senses; the reins are controlled by the mind on behalf of the representative Self identified with the individual.

As human consciousness is subjected to alternation, two main phases prevail whenever a person is not in a deep sleep. One is of dream and the other is of wakeful activity. In a state of dream the monitoring agency is suspended and the place of the doer is temporarily assigned to the seer. The role of the enjoyer is a constant, which has its adherence to both the agencies of doing and knowing. There is a set of monads in memory that mirror the replicas of things and events that were once real. They take the form of name-form aggregates in the time-space continuum in which they were arranged in the sequence of cause and effect. That group of memory monads is called dhāraṇā; their recall comes under the special category of *pratyabhijñā* (recognition).

There is another set of memory monads that are of a composite nature. This is the area of the mind where fantasy is generated. In the actualization of programs pratyabhijñā is restructured to produce the end result of generating a new theme of life, which can present a unique coming together of the triple aspects of existence, subsistence, and value.

While a diseased mind indulges in fantasy, a person of average normalcy engages himself in the pursuit of actualization. A yogi is careful to avoid both these realms, that of fantasizing and that of actualizing. The yogi's goal is to realize. In a negative sense, realization is the avoidance of the unreal that is perpetuated through the composition and retention of various imageries that cannot be validated as real. Hence the yogi terminates associations of ideas whenever an unprofitable memory is seeking a chance to reenter the focus of consciousness. Here the witnessing element assumes the role of the grand discriminator. The incentive for this grand discriminator is nothing other than to visualize one's own true form. This motive is again and again sabotaged by the seeping in of memories, either from the threshold of factual retentions or from the threshold of the phantom-weaving mind. The experiential essence of realization is Being.

Letter Thirteen

Your seat is concrete. It is the given, as is your body. The Sun is shining, the wind blows, and there are people around who are engaged in various actions. These are also given. However, experiencing your seat and your body are not similar. The body is constantly reporting sensations: painful, pleasurable, or indifferent. Like sensations coming through an act of contact with or pressure from the external concrete bodies, the consciousness of impressions passes from one set of ideas to another. They fill the consciousness with all kinds of din and hue and pain/pleasure reactions.

All experiences are shared between the concrete and the ideal, with the focal point of consciousness shifting from the most concrete to the subtle. The concrete support on which you sit, although detached from the ground, has for its foundation a concrete universe whose extension cannot be precisely determined. For brevity's sake it is presumed to be stretching to infinity.

A follow up of the matrix of consciousness that is being woven from any focal point also continues like a stream in which specific awareness glides like waves and there is no definitive boundary where consciousness can be seen to come to a close. Because of our biological peculiarity and the alternation of consciousness, which we share with other living beings, there periodically comes all-obliviating sleep. Thus, you have two extreme points in the range of your consciousness. One is marked by your definite and clear apperception of objects and the other is where your consciousness dissipates into sleep. Where an object is presented to the senses with certitude you have pramāna, or valid appreciation of objects of which you have full certitude.

Take a pause. Allow a couple of minutes to pass. Close your eyes. Recapitulate what has been said so far. You have a world bracketed with both the physical and the ideal; both interlaced with the other.

Now watch this process. See how objectivization takes place. Open your eyes. You see bodies and you recognize each one. This is the pratyabhijñā that was spoken of in the previous lesson. In the recognition of an object, impressions are coming from the outside and memory is coming from inside, but perceptions do not allow you to draw any line between what is presumed to be the external stimulus and what can be deduced as the concept prefabricated by one or several recollections of the past.

Here you are not only seeing objects but are forming the phenomenon of the changing world as a participant creator. The creator, the act of creation, and the created are all inseparable and integral parts of the same process. This is an ongoing process in which there is no detached and stable seat where the witness can alienate itself and look at the process as a separate entity. In the spontaneous separation of the binary function of becoming both the subject and object of an ever-flowing universe, the regularities of physical laws and the reaction of mental expediency operate as counterpoints. The result is the intermixing of the actual and the imagined. Imagination, on the one hand, is something equivalent to the recording of images as in photography. On the other, it is a creative caricaturing monitored by the dictates of impulses that are conditioned by your case history, both genetic and psychological.

The result is getting caught again and again in situations that spell contradiction and drawing conclusions that are absolutely baseless. Contradictions are called viparya̅ and unsubstantiated imagination is called vikalpa. The role that memory plays in concept formation, in the recognition of objects, and in phantom images that cause paranoia or hysterical ecstasy, is an uncharted universe that can accommodate all of the Jungian concepts of the collective and personal unconscious and what Freud postulates as the libidinal depth from which all instincts arise.

In spite of the vast dimension of the subjective realm involved, the happenings of the external world are not to be overlooked and minimized; becoming overly preoccupied with the interiorization of the whole phenomenon is likely to alienate you from the ongoing process of the perennial flow of life in which your greater reality lies. Each confrontation with contrariety spells pain, physical or mental, and the obscuration caused by the negativity of consciousness that you experience as sleep accounts for several shades of confusion called *moha.* Thus there are three major forms of affectivity—pleasure, pain, and confusion (*sukha, duḥkha,* and *moha*).

Pleasure can be passive or agitational. Agitational pleasures are excitements followed by contradictions or fantasies. They also cause confusion. The element of happiness that permeates both a situation and its witness sometimes becomes manifested as a time-transcending presence that has the quality of a beatitude or non-eventuality. Take for example, the situation where you are surrounded by a beautiful panorama and your eyes are focused on the changing colors of the setting Sun. The pale blue sky, blushing clouds, gentle breeze, your rhythmic breath, and unidentified thoughts that gently pass in your head are all one with your inner state of peace. Although technically there are modulations of consciousness, they are like the alpha waves of a relaxed brain. Hence, that can be qualified as a natural cessation of citta vṛtti (mental modulation).

A regular form of citta vṛtti is punctuated with questions

and recalls of memory, resolves and marked forms of ego affectivity. Further, one unit of citta vṛtti stands in contrast with another. In the case of the natural manifestation of equilibrium, the transcendence of time can be attributed to the homogenizing that spontaneously happens in consciousness. As a result the free flow of consciousness goes on like an unbroken streak of oil. Whenever this happens it's a case of *sahaja samādhi (sahaja* - natural and spontaneous; *samādhi* - the equipoise of consciousness).

Let us return to the experience of becoming enveloped by the beauty of the sunset. In that experience there may occur the incidental moving of the eyes from the golden edges of the cloud to the still figure of the Sun and from the Sun to a cluster of flowers that are bathed by its golden rays. In spite of going into the several details of the beautiful phenomena, the total effect of the inner calm is not disturbed and hence the samādhi is one of qualitative manifoldness. In such a case it can be recognized as *savikalpa samādhi.* The unifying and stabilizing effect of sleep assumes here a very distinctive feature. Instead of veiling the pure consciousness from the cognitive self, it veils names and forms and thus gives rise to the non-qualitative form of samādhi that is free of all differentiation of subject-object dualities; hence, that becomes a state of nirvikalpa.

All people, sometime or another, get into such states of consciousness, which may not last for more than a few seconds or minutes. Through constant discipline these states can become our own continuous experience. From here on we have to make ourselves familiar with disciplines that can ensure such a blessed state.

Letter Fourteen

Vyāsa says, "Yoga cannot be achieved without burning

away the dross and cultivating the finest intuitive ability to see and function with precision and harmony." According to him, we stink with the prejudices and unwholesome habits that have been formed during our exposure to unexamined environments and recourse to blind reactions. Endless negative conditionings of *karma* have taken their deep-rooted seats in the series of interests that rise in our minds. To release the mind from them, cleansing is required. *Tapas* cleanses.

Ice does not melt unless it is heated. Steam is not generated unless water is boiled. Lethargy prevails until energy flows. Listlessness and disorientation hold the mind back until enthusiasm wells up. Enthusiasm comes only when initiative is taken. So you should buck up and get ready. You cannot spring to your feet when you are weak and feeble. All crutches and hang-ups should be thrown away and the old tarnished system should be given a good flushing. Let the day begin with a new resolve to live a clean life. Ask the incentives and urges to lay bare their cards before you. Pick up the healthy ones and tidy your habits.

Letter Fifteen

Myths and legends speak of bodiless beings, such as gods and spirits, which are called *videhas*. Materialists describe this world as a continuous process of matter becoming organized into endless patterns according to the compulsive logic of physical laws. In such a world nothing can remain alienated from the rest of the physical world. Those who identify their stream of life as an integral part of the eternal flux of elements are called *prakṛtilayas*. In our individual life we experience a personal consciousness, which resembles the mythical spirit that can detach itself from physical consciousness, even to that extent of imagining the body to be only a dwelling place of the spirit.

After the advent of modern psychology, especially of Freud and Jung, the acceptance of one's own myth has become recognized as necessary to know one's total being. When depth psychology upholds the claims of the mythical powers of the unconscious, other formidable schools such as psychobiology, behaviorist psychology, and genetics continue making probes into the biochemistry and physical chemistry of living organisms and producing evidence that each person is an accomplished fact of the historical organization of nature. For all practical purposes we have to recognize that both these aspects are within us. It is as if they are so closely interwoven that we cannot say which behavior of ours is an expression of our free choice and which is a result of biochemical reaction or genetic mutation.

Make a critical observation of your personal behavior. Most of us have some compulsive behavior in matters of sex, physical appetites, or inquisitiveness. These are problems to us only because we are capable of critically evaluating our behavior in terms of moral or ethical norms. Lower animals, like monkeys, for instance, hardly give a second thought to aggressive behavior in their sexual pursuit or to behavior induced by curiosity. If you aspire to live the disciplined life of a yogi you should have a clear picture of the alternation of your personal consciousness back and forth between the compulsive behavior of an animal and the detached, repressive withdrawal of a conscientious person. Both of these aspects are symptoms of having no control over your life and remaining as a slave to the forces of circumstance.

What is expected of a yogi is to become the master of the situation under all circumstances. Between your myth and your physicality there is a neutral zone where your witnessing consciousness is seated. When the witnessing consciousness also assumes the responsibility to will, the volition becomes more and more freed from irrational forces. Instead of leaving the act of restraint to the whims of your neurotic fears, all intentions can be carried out in the floodlight of your fully operating awareness.

It is not difficult to cultivate an awareness that is both critical and sympathetic. The prevalence of such an awareness slows down the pace at which instincts unfold. This will give more living space between the eruption of desire and its promotion into action because the choice of a commendable wish from a plethora of urges makes constant reference to the ethical criterion of your behavior. Such an attitude is to be understood as the first phase of detachment (vairāgya).

We are not alone in this world. Norms of right and wrong and good and evil are handed down to us by the great ones who have gone before us. People are impressed by the example of those whom they hold in veneration. If a preceptor is an enlightened person, fully established in the understanding of the Absolute, the very bi-polarity with such a person creates a continuous state of osmotic exchange and the student derives strength from the personal example of the preceptor. Although there may be some sentiments developed between the pair, their relationship is essentially based on the constant prevalence of a high form of intelligence. The core of this intelligence is the power to discriminate between what is essential and nonessential and between what has perennial value or only transitory allurement. Without raising your intelligence from its ordinary power of cognition and reasoning to a higher state of alertness and intuitive sensibility, you cannot fully appreciate the teaching of a master.

The compulsions of the myth and physicality of an ordinary person of undisciplined life are in a horizontal range. These aspects become verticalized in the life of an aspirant with a structural hierarchy that is very helpful in transforming the entire psyche. Then your biologic and anthropomorphic basis becomes structured as the alpha. Your myth ascends and assumes the form of the goal that is perennially sought. The voice of the preceptor is placed above. Your mythical goal is the omega that is ever showering grace from above. You experience the quality of revelation in the word of your master. What were previously experienced as physical or biological urges now become transformed into a continuous flow of libidinal energy that is exposed to the light of corrective purification that comes from your master's teaching.

When this happens the quality of life changes. You have within yourself the feeling of having found your true way. This wholesome transformation is very often recognized as a spiritual conversion. This is the second and superior phase of the highest kind of detachment. It goes without saying that there should be great yearning and zeal on the part of the aspirant to achieve spiritual conversion.

Notes

Introduction

1. Guru Nitya Chaitanya Yati, *The Psychology of Darśanamālā* (New Delhi: D.K. Printworld, 2004), 418.
2. Alain Danielou, *A Brief History of India,* (Rochester, Vt.: Inner Traditions, 2003), 27.
3. *Ibid.* 15, 20.
4. Nataraja Guru, *The Word of the Guru,* (New Delhi: D.K. Printworld, 2003), 96-97.
5. Barbara Stoler Miller, *Yoga, Discipline of Freedom* (Berkeley: University of California Press, 1996), 1.
6. "Yoga in America Market Study," *Yoga Journal,* yogajournal.com, February 26, 2008.
7. *Gurukulam,* English Language Edition (Bainbridge Island, Washington: Narayana Gurukula and East-West University of Unitive Sciences, 1986-1999).

Chapter I: Samādhi Pāda

1. Nataraja Guru, trans., *Bhagavad Gita* (New Delhi: D.K. Printworld, 2008), 227.

Chapter II: Sādhana Pāda

1. Nataraja Guru, trans., *Bhagavad Gita* (New Delhi: D.K. Printworld, 2008), 166.
2. *Ibid*. 168-169.
3. Paul Reps, *Zen Flesh, Zen Bones* (New York: Anchor Books, n.d.), 33.
4. Nataraja Guru, trans., *Bhagavad Gita* (New Delhi: D.K. Printworld, 2008), 238-239.

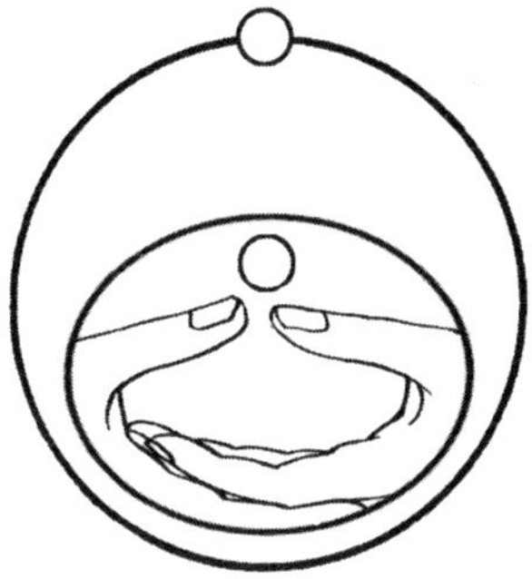

Sanskrit Glossary

abhyāsa: repetitive practice, application

ahamkāra: ego, I-consciousness, affectivity, affective core of *antaḥkaraṇa*, the inner organ (psychic dynamism)

ahimsā: nonviolence, non-hurting

akliṣṭa: spontaneous, not painful, unobstructed, not afflicted

ānanda: bliss, ecstasy, value, normative notion

antaḥkaraṇa: the inner organ (psychic dynamism) composed of *manas*, *citta*, *buddhi*, and *ahamkāra*

anubhava: experience

anubhūti: imperience

apāna: the descending flow of vital energy or breath

aparigraha: non-acquisitiveness, non-possessiveness

asamprajñāta: unconditioned, pure

asamprajñāta samādhi: unconditioned, pure, absorption or equipoise in consciousness

āsana: posture, seat, steady position, foundation (one of the eight limbs of Yoga)

asmitā: identification with the center of one's consciousness, ego identity, sense of individuality, I-consciousness

aṣṭāṅga: eightfold, eight-limbed

asteya: non-misappropriativeness, non-stealing, honesty
āvaraṇa: covering, veiling principle
avidyā: nescience, ignorance

bhāna vṛtti: oscillation of consciousness (between seer and seen)
brahmacarya: adhering to uprightness in life, walking in the path of the Absolute (*brahman*)
buddhi: intellect, intelligence, faculty of judgment, an aspect of *antaḥkaraṇa*, the inner organ (psychic dynamism)

cit: self-radiant knowledge, pure consciousness
citiśakti: pure consciousness, psychic or spiritual energy, transforming medium of consciousness
citta: mental, mind, mind-stuff, faculty of memory and recall, an aspect of *antaḥkaraṇa*, the inner organ (psychic dynamism), main body of consciousness
citta vṛtti: modulations of *citta*, mental modifications

darśana: vision, view
dhāraṇā: holding the focus of the mind, the consistent focusing of consciousness, retaining or sustaining an idea or principle (one of the eight limbs of Yoga)
dharmamegha: elevating catalyst; literally "a cloud of showering virtues;" virtues that come like a rain cloud to favor the aspirant
dhyāna: pure contemplation, even and harmonious flow of consciousness (one of the eight limbs of Yoga)
duḥkha: pain, misery, distress, sorrow, suffering

ekāgra: concentered consciousness, one-pointed attention
ekendriya: single sensory stimulus

guṇa: the three qualities, triple modalities, or primary

constituents of nature *(sattva, rajas, tamas)*

īśvara: spirit par excellence, supreme spirit, noumenon, higher Self, designated by *praṇava, AUM*
īśvara praṇidhāna: continuous contemplation on *īśvara*

kaivalya: aloneness, liberation, ultimate goal of Yoga
karmāśaya: the reservoir of the conditioned or processed impressions of action, permanent features engraved on the mind
karuṇā: compassion
kleśa: afflictions, obstacles
kliṣṭa: labored, painful, obstructed, afflicted
kriyā yoga: practical or active Yoga
kṣipta: motion or change in consciousness, stream of consciousness, volatile central core

maitrī: friendliness
manana: contemplation, vertical absorption
manas: mind, interrogative aspect of *antaḥkaraṇa,* the inner organ (psychic dynamism)
mūḍha: forgetfulness, veiling, obscuration, stupor
muditā: gladness

nidrā: deep sleep, dreamless sleep state
nirbīja: non-seeded
nirodha: restraint, inhibition, intercepting or inhibiting agent in consciousness
nirvicāra: the undisturbed flow of consciousness, consciousness devoid of conceptual configuration or cognitive function
nirvicāra samādhi: absorption without thoughts
nirvikalpa: unconditioned, undeluded
nirvikalpa samādhi: absorption without confused cognitions,

non-qualitative absorption

nirvitarka: unobstructed or unmodified consciousness, without perceptual confrontation

nirvitarka samadhi: absorption without perceptual confrontation

niyama: observances, carrying out of positive programs of injunctions (one of the eight limbs of Yoga), consisting of *śauca, santoṣa, tapas, svādhyāya, īśvara praṇidhāna*

prajñā: unmodulated consciousness, wisdom, discernment, higher consciousness

prakhyā: clear or distinctive cognition of the specific, a comprehensive vision of an object or idea presented to the mind

prakṛti: nature, procreative energy, somatic aspect of the psyche, literally, "that which replicates through its natural power of propagation"

pramāṇa: real cognition, right or valid knowledge

prāṇa: vital energy or breath, the ascending flow of vital energy or breath

prāṇāyāma: regulation of the vital forces, regulation of the breath (one of the eight limbs of Yoga)

prasaṅkhyāna: discrimination of Self from non-Self

pratyāhāra: withdrawal from distraction, withdrawal from the instrumentality of the mind and senses (one of the eight limbs of Yoga)

pratyaya: cognition, content, consciousness

pravṛtti: excitement of psychic energy leading to action or reaction, modification with an emphasis on action, instrumental consciousness

puruṣa: spirit, the pure Self, pure effulgence of awareness, self-conscious principle, both the individuated consciousness of the finite being and the transcendent spirit

rāga: attachment, affectivity, attraction
rajas: colored-passionate modality of nature, kinetic, operational dynamics

sabīja: seeded
sādhana: practice, discipline, means for attainment
samādhi: absorption, equipoise in consciousness (one of the eight limbs of Yoga)
samāpatti: stabilization of consciousness
samprajñāta: cognitive or conditioned
samprajñāta samādhi: cognitive absorption, conditioned absorption
saṁskāra: registered and preserved impressions or conditionings, registration and preservation of impressions, formation of incipient memories, culture
saṁyam: repetitive practice, *dhāraṇā*, *dhyāna*, and *samādhi* taken together
sānanda samādhi: absorption in bliss, ecstasy; absorption in value or normative notion
saṅkalpa: creative cognition
santoṣa: contentment
sasmitā samādhi: absorption in the center of one's consciousness
sat: being
sattva: clear-pure modality of nature, sublime, identifiable factuality
satya: truthfulness, truth
śauca: inward and outward cleanliness or purity
savicāra: conceptual configuration of consciousness
savicāra samādhi: absorption in an idea or a concept
savitarka: in an object of perception, a perceptual configuration or confrontation
savitarka samādhi: absorption in a perception; total identification of the experiencer with the experienced
siddhi: perfection, accomplishment, attainment

smṛti: memory

sphoṭa: burst or flash of meaning

sthiti: stability, inertial steady state, preservation of an impression

sukha(m): good, happiness, comfortable

sūtra: aphorism, statement of intense condensed meaning, a work composed of such aphorisms

svādhyāya: self-study

svarūpa: own essential nature, own form

tamas: dark-inertial modality of nature, obscuring, stabilizing fixations

tanmātra: thing in itself

tapas: self-purification, austerity, the general term meaning both *abhyāsa* (practice) and *vairāgya* (detachment)

vairāgya: detachment, non-attachment, dispassion, desirelessness, restraint

vāsanā: latent impressions, consolidated memory, established inner conviction, incipient memories

vicāra: presentation of an idea or concept, ideation

vidyā: knowledge

vikalpa: confused cognition, imaginary cognition, verbal delusion

vikṣepa: distraction, projecting principle, depositing one's interest in an external object

vikṣipta: flickering, flitting or shifting of consciousness from one specific occurrence or provocation to another, distraction

viparyaya: unreal or false cognition

vitarka: perceptual confrontation or configuration, object of perception, conflict

viveka: discriminative knowledge, unitive discrimination, discrimination between Self and non-Self *viveka khyāti:* discriminative light, discriminative function

vṛtti: modifications, modulations, oscillations, functions, operation in time-space that structures the ensembles of the present

yama: restraints, self-control (one of the eight limbs of Yoga), consisting of *ahimsā, satya, asteya, aparigraha, brahmacarya*

yoga: contemplative union in harmony, *samādhi* (equipoise in consciousness), restraint of mental modifications

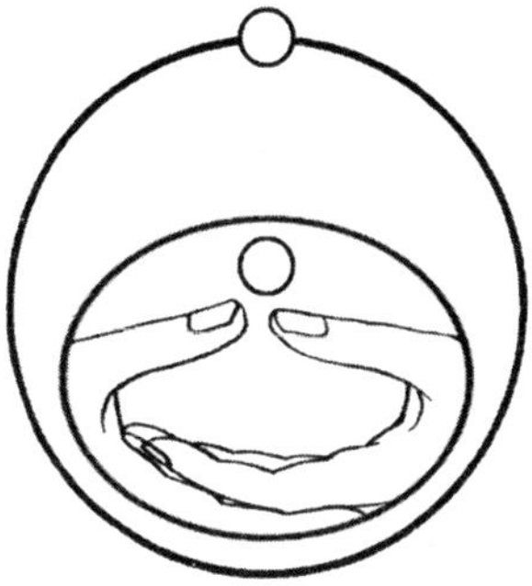

Index